Leaving Certificate
Higher and Ordinary Level

Agricultural Science

Carol Cronin & Sandra Tiernan

The Educational Company of Ireland

Edco

Published 2015

The Educational Company of Ireland

Ballymount Road

Walkinstown

Dublin 12

www.edco.ie

A member of the Smurfit Kappa Group plc

ISBN: 978-1-84536-565-3

Book design: Liz White Designs

Cover design: Identikit

Layout: Carole Lynch

Editor: Dog's-ear

Illustrations: Daghda

Proofreader: Dog's-ear

The paper used in this book comes from Managed Forests in Northern Europe For every tree felled, at least one new tree is planted

CONTENTS

Introduction

This revision book covers all areas of the Agricultural Science syllabus for your Leaving Cert exam in Agricultural Science at Higher and Ordinary Levels.

What you have to study

The course covers the following topics:

- Plant physiology
- Microbiology
- Animal physiology
- Genetics
- Soil science
- Grassland
- Crops
- Animal production
- Plant and animal identification
- Scientific explanations.

Questions appear each year on soil, genetics and a range of experiments throughout the course. The remaining topics are examined but may not appear as a complete question, especially at Higher Level. Since there is no specific list of experiments on the syllabus, it is advisable for students to have studied a number of experiments. In particular, students should be familiar with experiments for each of the following areas: plant physiology, animal physiology, genetics, soil science, microbiology and ecology, since these are examinable in the practical assessment.

How this book can help you

- The language used in this book is straightforward and to the point. Key words and terms are highlighted in bold throughout the book.
- Exam questions and references to exam questions are included for each topic.

- Tables, graphs, diagrams and bullet points facilitate effective revision.
- Learning objectives at the start of each chapter and Key-points at the end help to reinforce learning.
- Experiments relevant to topics in the chapter are included. Experiments are outlined in a concise manner and include experiment results.
- Top Tips and Points to note further highlight important information.

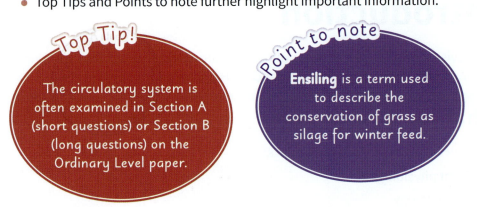

Top Tip!

The circulatory system is often examined in Section A (short questions) or Section B (long questions) on the Ordinary Level paper.

Point to note

Ensiling is a term used to describe the conservation of grass as silage for winter feed.

Before starting your revision, read the Exam Section (p. vii). It contains advice on:

- The format of the paper
- The format of the practical assessment
- How to approach your exam
- How to gain full marks when answering questions.

The Study Guide on p.303 will help you to plan your revision.

Exam Section

How is Agricultural Science assessed?

- Written examination = 75% (June, Sixth Year)
- Practical assessment = 25% (May, Sixth Year)

Structure of paper: Higher and Ordinary Levels (300 marks)

- Before the exam, study previous exam papers to familiarise yourself with the layout of the paper.
- On the day of the exam, spend 10 minutes reading the exam paper and deciding on questions.
- Before you answer a question, write down key points to help you plan your answer.

Higher Level

- There are nine questions on the paper. Students must complete six questions.
- There are 60 marks allocated to Question 1. All other questions are allocated 48 marks each.
- Question 1 is not compulsory, but it is strongly recommended that you attempt this question, since the total marks for the paper are calculated by including this question as one of the six questions.

Question	Type of question	Number of parts	Marks per question	Time allocation
1	Short	6 out of 10 short questions to be attempted	10 marks per part, 60 marks in total	35 minutes
2 (Soil)	Long	Question normally subdivided into 3 or 4 parts; all parts to be attempted	48 marks in total	20 minutes

Question	Type of question	Number of parts	Marks per question	Time allocation
3	Long	Option 1 or Option 2. Attempt either; both options cannot be counted in your 6 questions	48 marks in total	20 minutes
4 (Experiments)	Long	2 out of 4 experiments to be completed	24 marks each, 48 in total	20 minutes
5	Long	Question normally subdivided into 3 or 4 parts; all parts to be attempted	48 marks in total	20 minutes
6	Long	Question normally subdivided into 3 or 4 parts; all parts to be attempted	48 marks in total	20 minutes
7 (Genetics)	Long	Question normally subdivided into 3 or 4 parts; all parts to be attempted	48 marks in total	20 minutes
8	Long	2 out of 3 parts to be attempted; there may be an internal choice within 1 of the parts	24 marks each, 48 in total	20 minutes
9 (Scientific explanations)	Long	4 out of 5 parts to be attempted	12 marks each, 48 in total	20 minutes

Ordinary Level

Section	Type of question	Number of parts	Marks per question	Time allocation
A	Short questions to be answered on exam paper	7 questions; 6 must be attempted	120 in total, 20 marks for each part	45 minutes
B	Long questions to be answered in answer booklet	6 questions; 3 must be attempted	180 in total, 60 marks per question	90 minutes

Exam guidelines

Read the questions carefully and highlight the important words.

- Both Higher and Ordinary Level papers are 2.5 hours long.
- Leave 5 minutes at the end to read over your paper and ensure you have answered all parts of your chosen questions.
- Remember: marks are only given for information relevant to the question asked.
- Address all parts of the question. For example, if feeding and management of livestock is asked for, subdivide your answer into the two areas; otherwise you could lose marks for not referring to one of the specified areas.
- Answer in point form and answer each new question on a new page. Label each question and each part clearly.
- Try to stick to your allocated time; otherwise you may have to rush at the end of the exam.
- Think before you answer the questions. For example, if a question asks for a graph or a labelled diagram, marks may be lost if one is not provided in your answer.
- Label all diagrams clearly.
- Do not leave until the exam is finished.

Understanding terms

- **Characteristics:** List the qualities.
- **Classify:** Group the items into categories.
- **Compare:** Describe the similarities and/or differences between two terms, e.g. paddock grazing and strip grazing.
- **Define:** Write down the precise definition or meaning of a word or phrase.
- **Describe:** Give a written description in point form. Use a diagram to back up your answer, if possible.
- **Discuss:** Requires a detailed description of what is being asked. A question like this requires a number of points in your answer, e.g. Discuss the role of hay in Irish agriculture.
- **Distinguish between**, **differentiate between:** Identify the differences between two similar terms, e.g. zoonose and zoospore.
- **Give a scientific explanation:** Apply a scientific reason to a principle or practice in agriculture, i.e. *why* the practice is carried out, not a definition of the practice.

- **Give advantages/disadvantages:** Clearly identify which of your answers are advantages and which are disadvantages when answering this type of question, e.g. give three advantages of using a mixed-grazing system.
- **Explain:** Give a detailed account. Back up your answer with specific examples or a diagram, if applicable.
- **Identify**, **name**, **give an example:** State the answer in one or two words; there is no need for detail, e.g. identifying a picture of a plant/animal and the family it comes from.
- **Illustrate:** Make something clear by the use of concrete examples (diagrams) to explain or clarify a point.
- **List**, **state:** List the points, no elaboration necessary.
- **Outline**, **write a brief note:** Give a brief description.
- **Principle:** Give a reason for or a description of a working method, e.g. the principles involved in the management of lowland sheep production.
- **Properties:** The features of a substance, e.g. the properties of a sandy soil.

Answering questions

In order to gain full marks:

- Read the questions carefully.
- Highlight the important terms and note the specific requirements of each question.
- Where a question does not state how many points are required in the answer, it is advisable to provide a minimum of four points.

How marks will be awarded

In order to attain full marks in a question, ensure you have addressed all parts of the question and that the information you have provided is accurate and relevant to the question asked.

Example: An A-grade answer

Explain the difference between flushing and steaming up in sheep production.

Flushing:

- Flushing is carried out prior to mating.
- Sheep are moved from a low plane of nutrition to a high plane of nutrition.
- This increases the number of eggs released at ovulation.
- There is also better attachment of embryos to the uterine wall.
- This increases litter size and results in more regular heat periods.

Steaming up:

- This is carried out 6–8 weeks prior to lambing.
- The ewes are placed on a high plane of nutrition by increasing the amount of concentrates in their diet.
- 75% of the growth of the foetus occurs at this stage.
- Steaming up prevents twin lamb disease and ensures the development of a healthy lamb.
- It also ensures good milk production by the ewe.

Remember

The explanation is relevant, detailed and accurate, with a description of both terms provided.

Practical exam

The practical coursework for Agricultural Science is worth 25% (100 marks). The total for the paper and the practical coursework combined is 400 marks.

The practical coursework is divided into the following sections:

- Plant and plant family identification (10 marks)
- Animal identification (four food-producing animals and six others related to agriculture) (10 marks)
- Livestock production project (10 marks)
- Two crop projects (15 marks)
- Farm plan (10 marks)
- Experiments (total 45 marks)
  - Soil
  - Ecology
  - Animal physiology
  - Plant physiology
  - Genetics
  - Microbiology.

The project work in Agricultural Science **must** be supervised by an Agricultural Science teacher.

Exam Paper Analysis Chart: Higher Level

	2014	2013	2012	2011	2010	2009	2008	2007	2006	2005	2004
Q1	Short questions	Short questions	Short questions	Short questions	Short questions	Short questions	Short questions	Short questions	Short questions	Short questions	Short questions
Q2	Soil	Soil	Soil	Soil	Soil	Soil	Soil	Soil	Soil	Soil	Soil
Q3 Option 1	Hay making Silage conservation	Weed control Oats Insect metamorphosis	Milk composition and processing	Beef, dairy, food conversion ratio	Dairy	Dairy Replacement heifers	Crop rotation Certified seed Plant diseases	Animal nutrition Sheep production	Animal phyla Soil minerals Grassland	Tillage Crop production Certified seed	Fertilisers Microbiology
Q3 Option 2	Animal physiology – liver Liver fluke	Sheep husbandry Animal health Lamb production	Sheep breeding and production	Silage Colostrum Grazing systems	Plant minerals Pests and diseases Crop establishment	Animal health Sheep management Grassland	Grassland Grazing systems Silage production	Root crop Cereal crop Catch crop	Plant diseases Animal diseases	Ruminant digestion Animal nutrition	Animal health Milk quality
Q4	Experiments	Experiments	Experiments	Experiments	Experiments	Experiments	Experiments	Experiments	Experiments	Experiments	Experiments
Q5	Plant structure and function Soil	Bull beef production Dairy management Milk hygiene	Cereal crops Potatoes	Circulatory system Animal diseases	Sheep production Grassland management Silage	Cereals/root crop Fertilisers Potatoes	Milk Dairy production Suckler production	Grass Silage/hay	Grassland Cereals Animal nutrition Fodder crops	Silage	Ecology Grassland
Q6	Dairy herd management Digestive system	Silage production Crop rotation Plant structure	Beef production Dairy production	Cereals	Blight Tillage crops Soil Cereals	Animal phyla Dental formula Ruminant digestion	Animal nutrition Dairy Sheep production	Dairy herd Suckler beef Body condition score	Grassland Dairy Animal nutrition	Grazing systems Sheep/pig production Dairy	Grazing systems Suckler beef Animal production
Q7	Genetics	Genetics	Genetics	Genetics	Genetics	Genetics	Genetics	Genetics	Genetics	Genetics	Genetics
Q8	Pig management Cereal crop production Scientific definitions	Weeds, pests and diseases Carbon cycle Scientific definition	Nitrogen cycle Hay making Scientific definitions	Pigs Pollution Scientific definitions	Sheep production Plant physiology Scientific definitions	Carbon cycle Manures Scientific definitions	Tillage Plant physiology Scientific definitions	Ruminant digestion Plant nutrition Manures	Animal production Sheep production Crops	Animal production Soil Fertilisers	Ruminant digestion Animal nutrition Root crops Plant diseases
Q9	Scientific explanations	Scientific explanations	Scientific explanations	Scientific explanations	Scientific explanations	Scientific explanations	Scientific explanations	Scientific explanations	Scientific explanations	Scientific explanations	Scientific explanations

Revise Wise • Agricultural Science

Exam Paper Analysis Chart: Ordinary Level

	2004	2005	2006	2007	2008	2009	2010	2011	2012	2013	2014
Q1	Tooth	Earthworm	Dairy	Pigs	Plant and animal pests	Liverfluke	Soil	Plant physiology	Bacteria and clover	Animal diseases	Livestock breeds
Q2	Milk hygiene	Animal production	Soil	Plant minerals	Plant physiology	Soil	Machinery	Fertilisers and manures	Animal phyla	Agricultural Machinery	Machinery
Q3	Soil	Animal physiology	Animal housing and nutrition	Animal hormones	Fertilisers	Ecology	Dairy	Animal physiology	True or false	Potatoes	Animal diseases
Q4	Animal phyla	Grassland	Grassland	Animal phyla	Machinery	Milk hygiene	Notifiable diseases	Animal phyla	Scientific explanations	True or false	Insect life cycles
Q5	Potatoes	Animal and plant physiology	Animal diseases	Environment	Animal phyla	Plant and animal Minerals	Plant identification	Animal definitions	Animal physiology	Farm tools/equipment	True or false
Q6	Soil	Scientific explanations	Animal physiology	Beef	Plant physiology	Soil	Plant physiology	Scientific explanations	Plant physiology	Dairy	Animal dentition
Q7	Sheep	Machinery	Grassland	Scientific explanations	Soil	Pigs	True or false	Microbiology	Pig management	Scientific explanations	Scientific explanations
Q8	Silage and hay	Manures and fertilisers	Crop pests and diseases	Soil	Dairy	Dairy Grazing systems	Grazing systems	Sheep, Animal husbandry	Sheep breeding and management	Barley	Calf management Ruminant stomach
Q9	Fertilisers Microbiology	Pollution Beef Heart Soil	Beef Animal health Condition scoring	Grazing systems Milk Animal production	Cereals	Crop production Plant diseases	Soil	Grass	Potatoes	Pig production and management	Grassland Grazing methods Fertilisers
Q10	Forestry Genetics Cereals Pigs	Plant physiology	Plant physiology	Heart Digestion Tooth	Scientific definitions Crop production	Sheep Ruminant digestion	Heart Reproduction	Soil	Cattle breeding and management Dairy and milk production	Beef production and management	Sheep production Liver fluke
Q11	Plant physiology Microbiology	Animal nutrition Sheep	Genetics	Genetics	Animal nutrition Sheep	Cereals	Beef Sheep	Parasites Animal phyla Cereal or root crop	Grass species and grazing systems Hay and silage production	Earthworms Soil	Soil
Q12	Beef Animal physiology Sheep production	Cereal/root crop	Soil	Catch crops Root crops Experiments	Genetics	Silage Beef Plant physiology Scientific explanations	Ecology Pig production Environment	Animal digestion Scientific explanation Composition of milk Environment	Beef production Soil texture and structure Ruminant digestion Scientific explanations	Genetics	Genetics
Q13	Genetics	Genetics	Cereal or root crop	Sheep	Digestion	Genetics	Genetics	Genetics	Genetics	Forestry Grass Sheep production Respiratory system	Silage production Germination in plants Earthworms Animal feeds

Cell Structure and Physiology

1

Learning objectives

In this chapter you will learn about:

1 Plant and animal cells

2 Experiment: To examine a plant cell

3 Aerobic respiration

4 Experiment: To investigate if heat is released from germinating seeds

5 Movement of substances across cell membranes

6 Experiment: To investigate osmosis across a semipermeable membrane

Plant and animal cells

Under a light microscope, plant and animal cells have many features in common, including cell **membrane**, **cytoplasm** and **nucleus**. In addition, plant cells have a **cell wall**, **large vacuole** and **chloroplasts**.

Plant and animal cells are classified as **eukaryotic cells**.

> **Remember**
>
> A eukaryotic cell is a cell containing a membrane-bound nucleus and membrane-bound organelles (mitochondria and chloroplasts).

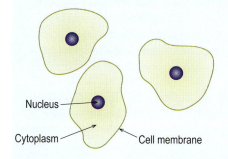

Fig 1.1 *Animal cell*

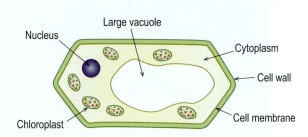

Fig 1.2 *Plant cell*

Experiment

To examine a plant cell

1. Remove a thin piece of **epidermal tissue** from the inside of an onion leaf.

2. Using a **forceps**, transfer this piece of epidermal tissue onto a **microscope slide**.

3. Place a drop of **water** onto the tissue to prevent it from drying out.

4. Add **iodine** to stain the tissue.

5. Using a mounted needle, place a **cover slip at an angle** over the tissue. This eliminates air bubbles.

6. Remove any **excess stain using filter paper**.

7. Using a **microscope**, view the slide first under **low power** and then high power.

Table 1.1 Cell structure and function		
Cell structure	**Cell type**	**Function**
Cell wall	Plant cells only	Composed of the carbohydrate **cellulose**. Its function is to strengthen and protect the cell. The cell wall prevents the overexpansion of plant cells when water enters the cell by osmosis.
Cell membrane	Plant and animal	Holds the cell's contents in shape and gives support. Selectively permeable, controlling the passage of substances into and out of the cell.
Cytoplasm	Plant and animal	A watery fluid called the cytosol with the cell organelles suspended in it.

Cell structure	Cell type	Function
Nucleus	Plant and animal	The control centre of the cell. Composed of chromatin (mixture of DNA and protein). During cell division, chromatin forms **chromosomes**. Chromosomes carry genetic instructions.
Mitochondria	Plant and animal	Release energy from glucose during **aerobic respiration**.
Chloroplasts	Plant cells only	Contain the pigment **chlorophyll**, which is essential for **photosynthesis**.
Large vacuole	Plant cells only	Provides extra support to the cell. Can be used for the storage of salt and sugars.

Aerobic respiration

Aerobic respiration involves the release of energy from glucose in the presence of oxygen. Aerobic respiration occurs in two stages. The first stage, **glycolysis**, occurs in the cytosol. Glucose is broken down into two molecules of **pyruvic acid**. The second stage occurs in the **mitochondria**. Pyruvic acid passes into the mitochondria, where it is further broken down in a series of chemical reactions known as the **Krebs cycle** and the **hydrogen carrier system** to produce carbon dioxide and water. Aerobic respiration produces large amounts of energy in the form of ATP. The overall equation for the reaction is:

$$\text{Glucose} + \text{Oxygen} \rightarrow \text{Carbon dioxide} + \text{Water} + \text{Energy}$$
$$C_6H_{12}O_6 + 6O_2 \rightarrow 6CO_2 + 6H_2O$$

Experiment

To investigate if heat is released from germinating seeds

1 **Soak peas** overnight in a beaker of water.

2 Divide peas into two equal groups, A and B. Group A is used as a **control** and is **boiled for 5 to 10 minutes to kill the peas**.

3 **Sterilise** both groups of peas by soaking them in a dilute solution of **Milton** or another suitable **disinfectant**.

Remember

Always include a control whenever possible in your experiments, as it provides a comparison.

4. Place both groups of peas into two clean, sterile **thermos flasks**.

5. Place a **thermometer** into each flask and seal both flasks with some cotton wool.

6. **Record the initial temperature** in both flasks.

7. Record the **temperature change** daily in each flask for a week.

Result

The temperature of flask B (the live peas) increases. This is due to the germinating peas producing heat energy by **aerobic respiration**. There is no change in the temperature of flask A, as the dead peas are not respiring.

Movement of substances across cell membranes

Movement of substances across cell membranes occurs by diffusion, osmosis and active transport.

Top Tip!

It's important to be able to distinguish between diffusion, osmosis and active transport and give examples of each.

Diffusion

Key definition

Diffusion is the movement of a substance from an area of high concentration to an area of low concentration along a concentration gradient.

Diffusion is the random movement of particles and requires no energy. In animal cells, oxygen diffuses across cell membranes from the blood into the cell and carbon dioxide diffuses from the cell into the blood.

Osmosis

Key definition

Osmosis is the movement of water across a semipermeable membrane from an area of high water concentration to an area of low water concentration.

Osmosis is a passive process and does not require energy.

To investigate osmosis across a semipermeable membrane

1   Cut two pieces of **dialysis tubing** (Visking tubing) the same length. Dialysis tubing is a **semipermeable membrane**.

2   The **dialysis tubing is softened by placing it under a stream of running water**.

3   A knot is tied in one end of the tubing.

4   One dialysis tubing bag is half filled with sucrose solution and the other is half filled with **deionised water.** The dialysis tubing with the deionised water will act as a **control**.

5   The air is squeezed out of both tubings and a knot is tied in the other end.

6   Each bag is then dried off and their **mass is recorded**.

7   Each bag is placed into **a beaker containing deionised water and left for an hour**.

8   The bags are then removed, dried and reweighed.

Result

The **dialysis tubing containing the sucrose will have increased in mass.** The contents of this tube will also have increased due to water moving from the beaker into the dialysis tubing by osmosis. There will be no change in the control.

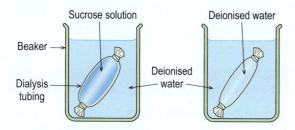

Fig 1.3 *Movement of water by osmosis*

Osmosis in plant cells

Water is always moving into plant cells by osmosis, causing the cytoplasm of plant cells to swell and push against the cell wall. This causes a pressure to build up, known as **turgor pressure**. When water supply is scarce, plants will start to wilt due to a loss in turgor pressure in the plant cells.

If plant cells are placed in a concentrated salt solution, water will move out of the plant cell by osmosis. This causes the cytoplasm and the cell membrane to shrink away from the cell wall. This is known as **plasmolysis**.

Active transport

> ### Key definition
>
> **Active transport** is the movement of a substance from an area of low concentration to an area of high concentration against a concentration gradient.

Active transport requires energy. Plant roots absorb nitrates and phosphates from the soil solution by active transport.

Questions

1 (a) Draw a diagram of a plant cell. Label the cell wall, nucleus and cytoplasm.
   (b) What is the name of the green pigment found in the chloroplasts?
   (c) What is the function of the green pigment?

2 (a) Explain the term *aerobic respiration*.
   (b) Aerobic respiration occurs in two stages. Where in the cells do these stages occur?
   (c) Write a chemical equation for aerobic respiration.

3 Explain the function of each of the following in a plant cell:
   (a) cell wall   (b) nucleus   (c) large vacuole.

4 Compare diffusion and osmosis.

5 Describe an experiment to demonstrate osmosis.

Exam question

1 Describe a laboratory experiment to prepare a sample of plant cells for examination under a microscope.   (HL 2012)

Key-points!

- Plant and animal cells are classified as eukaryotic cells. A eukaryotic cell is a cell containing a membrane-bound nucleus and membrane-bound organelles (mitochondria and chloroplasts).

- Plant and animal cells have the following cell organelles in common: cell membrane, nucleus, cytoplasm and mitochondria. Plant cells also contain a cell wall, chloroplasts and a large vacuole.

- Aerobic respiration involves the release of energy from glucose in the presence of oxygen. Aerobic respiration occurs in two stages (glycolysis and the Krebs cycle). Glycolysis occurs in the cytosol and the Krebs cycle occurs in the mitochondria.

- The balanced chemical equation for aerobic respiration is:
  $C_6H_{12}O_6 + 6O_2 \rightarrow 6CO_2 + 6H_2O$.

- Diffusion is the movement of a substance from an area of high concentration to an area of low concentration along a concentration gradient. Diffusion does not require energy.

- Osmosis is the movement of water across a semipermeable membrane from an area of high water concentration to an area of low water concentration. Osmosis is a passive process and does not require energy.

- Active transport is the movement of a substance from an area of low concentration to an area of high concentration against a concentration gradient. Active transport requires energy.

2 Structure of a Flowering Plant and Photosynthesis

Learning objectives

In this chapter you will learn about:

1 The structure of a flowering plant

2 Classification of plant tissues

3 Structure and function of vascular tissue in plants

4 Classification of plants into monocotyledons and dicotyledons

5 Structure of a dicot root and monocot and dicot stems

6 Experiment: To prepare a slide of a dicot stem and examine it under a light microscope

7 Photosynthesis and the structure of a leaf

8 Experiment: To extract and separate the pigments in a sample of grass

9 Experiment: Investigation to show that light is necessary for photosynthesis and to test a leaf for starch

10 Experiment: To demonstrate that carbon dioxide (CO_2) is necessary for photosynthesis

11 Experiment: To demonstrate the effect of light intensity on the rate of photosynthesis and to show that oxygen (O_2) is produced during photosynthesis

The structure of a flowering plant

The flowering plant can be broken up into two parts: the shoot system and the root system.

The shoot system

The shoot system consists of the stem, leaves and flowers.

Functions of the shoot system:

- Leaves carry out **photosynthesis**
- Flowers are necessary for **reproduction**
- Stem is responsible for the **transport** of **water**, **minerals** and **food**.

The root system

Functions of the root system:

- **Anchors** the plant into the ground
- **Absorbs** water and minerals
- **Stores** food.

Classification of plant tissues

- **Dermal tissue:** Outer layer of tissue on a plant. Its function is protection.
- **Ground tissue:** Function depends on location. Some of these functions include photosynthesis, storage of food and support.
- **Vascular tissue:** Transport tissue. It is composed of **phloem** and **xylem**. Phloem transports sugars and xylem transports water and minerals. Xylem and phloem tissue are found together in **vascular bundles** in the leaves and stems of plants.

Structure and function of vascular tissue in plants

Xylem

- Xylem is composed of **xylem vessels** and **tracheids**.
- Xylem tissue is **dead tissue**.
- The cell walls of xylem tissue are reinforced with **lignin**.
- Xylem vessels are larger than tracheids.
- **Pits** in the walls of xylem vessels allow for lateral movement of water.
- Xylem vessels allow water to travel in a continuous route from the roots to the leaves.

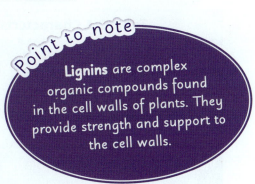

Point to note

Lignins are complex organic compounds found in the cell walls of plants. They provide strength and support to the cell walls.

Phloem

- Phloem is composed of a **sieve tube** and **companion cell**.
- Phloem tissue is **living tissue**.
- The companion cell controls and maintains the sieve tube.
- Sieve tubes have perforated end walls, known as sieve plates.
- Movement of sugars in the sieve tube can occur up or down the tissue.

Classification of plants into monocotyledons and dicotyledons

Flowering plants are divided into two groups:

1. **Monocotyledons** (or monocots) have one cotyledon in the seed or one seed leaf. Examples of monocots include grasses and cereals.

2. **Dicotyledons** (or dicots) have two cotyledons in the seed or two seed leaves. Examples include daisies, dandelions and most other flowering plants.

Top Tip!

The classification of seeds as monocots or dicots, their characteristics and examples of each can appear on both the Ordinary Level and the Higher Level Leaving Cert papers.

Point to note

The cotyledons provide energy for the germinating seed until the true leaves have formed and can photosynthesise. In some cases the cotyledons may become the first leaves of the germinated seedling; hence, the cotyledons are often referred to as seed leaves.

Table 2.1 Characteristics of monocots and dicots

Monocot	Dicot
One cotyledon in the seed	Two cotyledons in the seed
Fibrous root, no main root	One large root known as a tap root
Narrow leaf with parallel veins	Broad leaf with netted veins
Vascular bundles are scattered in the stem	Vascular bundles are arranged in a ring in the stem
The flower parts are arranged in threes or multiples of three	Flower parts are arranged in multiples of four or five

Structure of a dicot root, and monocot and dicot stems

Dicot root

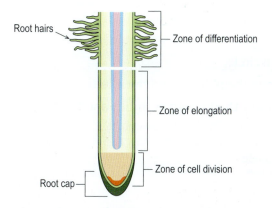

Root hairs

Zone of differentiation

Zone of elongation

Zone of cell division

Root cap

Fig 2.1 A longitudinal section of a dicot root

A dicot tap root can be broken up into four main parts:

- **Root cap:** Protective layer over the **meristematic** tissue behind it.
- **Zone of cell division:** Composed of **meristematic tissue**, the cells in this are constantly dividing by mitosis to produce new cells for the root cap and the zone of elongation.

- **Zone of elongation:** Cells here grow and become larger.
- **Zone of differentiation:** Identified by the presence of root hairs. In this region, cells become specialised.

In the transverse section of a root, the xylem tissue appears in the centre in the shape of a cross. The phloem tissue occurs between the arms of the xylem.

Monocot and dicot stems

Monocot stems

- Vascular bundles are scattered.

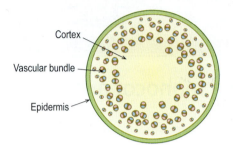

Point to note

Secondary thickening is a process that takes place in dicot plants and can result in the formation of wood.

Fig 2.2 *A monocot stem*

Dicot stems

- Vascular bundles are arranged in a circle.
- **Cambium tissue** is present between the phloem and the xylem.
- Cambium tissue allows for **secondary thickening** in shrubs and trees.

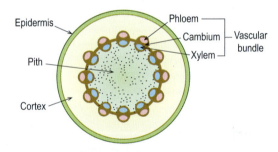

Fig 2.3 *A dicot stem*

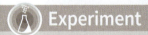 Experiment

To prepare a slide of a dicot stem and examine it under a light microscope

1. Cut a section of stem between two nodes.

2. Using a wet blade, **cut very thin sections of the stem**. Thin sections are required, as this allows light to travel through the tissues when viewed under a microscope.

3. Place the cut sections into a **petri dish with some water to prevent them from drying out**.

4. Transfer a thin section of the stem to a **microscope slide**.

5   Place the **cover slip at an angle over the stem** and lower onto the slide.

6   View the slide under the microscope using low power and then using high power.

7   Draw and label a diagram of the result.

Photosynthesis and the structure of a leaf

Plants are **autotrophic**, as they can produce their own food.

Plants use **chlorophyll** to trap light energy from the sun. This energy is then used to combine hydrogen from water and carbon dioxide to make glucose and oxygen.

$$\text{Carbon dioxide + Water} \xrightarrow[\text{Sunlight}]{\text{Chlorophyll}} \text{Glucose + Oxygen}$$

$$6CO_2 + 6H_2O \xrightarrow[\text{Sunlight}]{\text{Chlorophyll}} C_6H_{12}O_6 + 6O_2$$

Oxygen produced by photosynthesis can be excreted by the plant through the **stomata** or used for respiration. Plants store excess glucose as starch.

Adaptations of the leaf for photosynthesis

- Leaves are flat, which maximises the surface area for photosynthesis.
- **Waxy cuticle** on the upper epidermis prevents water loss.
- Tightly packed **palisade** cells contain large numbers of chloroplasts (the majority of photosynthesis is carried out by these cells).
- **Spongy mesophyll layer**, with its many air spaces, allows the rapid diffusion of carbon dioxide to the palisade cells and oxygen from the palisade cells.
- **Vascular tissue** facilitates transport. Xylem supplies water and minerals and phloem removes sugars (products of photosynthesis).
- **Stomata** allow gaseous exchange (carbon dioxide into the leaf and water vapour and oxygen out of the leaf).

To extract and separate the pigments in a sample of grass

1 Place some grass in a **mortar and pestle** with some sand and **ethanol**.

2 **Grind the grass leaves**. The extraction of the chlorophyll pigments can be improved by boiling the grass for several minutes in the ethanol. *Note: Ethanol is flammable. Avoid using a naked flame.*

3 **Pour solvent (equal parts of petroleum ether and acetone) into a covered gas jar**.

4 Draw a pencil line roughly 2 cm from the end of some chromatography paper.

5 **Transfer a drop of extract onto the pencil line on the chromatography paper**.

6 Allow the drop to dry and repeat this procedure several times until a **concentrated spot** of chlorophyll extract has been formed.

7 Place the chromatography paper into the gas jar, ensuring that the level of the solvent is below the pencil line.

Result

The solvent **separated the pigments** in the chlorophyll. The order in which they appear from the bottom is **chlorophyll b**, **chlorophyll a**, **xanthophylls**, **phaeophytin** and **carotene**.

Top Tip!

Experiments on photosynthesis have appeared on both Higher Level and Ordinary Level papers. There are a number of different experiments on photosynthesis, looking at different variables (light intensity, presence of CO_2, etc.). Make sure you do not get them mixed up.

🧪 **Experiment**

Investigation to show that light is necessary for photosynthesis and to test a leaf for starch

1 Place a **geranium** in a cupboard for 48 hours to destarch it.

2 **Cover a leaf or part of a leaf** with some aluminium foil. This leaf will act as a **control**.

3   **Leave the plant in light** for several hours.

4   **Test a leaf and the control leaf for starch**.

5   Remove the leaves and dip them into a beaker of **boiling water** to kill both leaves.

6   Place the leaves into separate test tubes containing **methylated spirits**. Place both test tubes into a beaker containing hot water. **The warm methylated spirits removes the chlorophyll** from the leaves, making a colour change easier to see. *Note: Do not use a flame around the methylated spirits, as it is flammable.*

7   Remove the leaves from the methylated spirits and dip them into the beaker of hot water. This softens the leaves.

8   Spread the leaves out on a white tile and add **iodine** solution to both leaves.

Result

The iodine solution added to the leaf that was exposed to sunlight **turns blue-black**, indicating that starch is present in this leaf. The iodine solution added to the control leaf remains **brown**, indicating that starch is absent.

 **Experiment**

To demonstrate that carbon dioxide (CO_2) is necessary for photosynthesis

1   Place **two identical geranium plants** in a cupboard for 48 hours to **destarch** them.

2   Label the plants **A** and **B**.

3   Place a small container of **soda lime (sodium hydroxide)** under plant A. The soda lime **absorbs carbon dioxide**.

4   Place a small container of **sodium bicarbonate (sodium hydrogen carbonate)** under plant B. The sodium bicarbonate **supplies carbon dioxide** to plant B. Plant B acts as a **control**.

5   Cover both plants with a clear plastic bag and leave in front of a light source for 4 to 5 hours.

6   Take a leaf from plants A and B and test both leaves for **starch**.

Result

When tested with iodine, the leaf from plant A remains brown, indicating that there is no starch present. The leaf from plant B turns blue-black, indicating that starch is present. Carbon dioxide is essential for photosynthesis.

To demonstrate the effect of light intensity on the rate of photosynthesis and to show that oxygen (O_2) is produced during photosynthesis

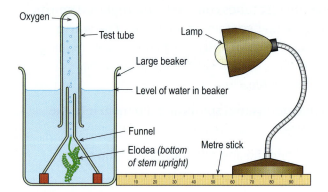

Fig 2.4 *Effect of light intensity on photosynthesis*

1   Fill a large beaker with some water and add a small amount of sodium hydrogen carbonate to the water. The sodium hydrogen carbonate (also known as bicarbonate of soda) ensures that there will be plenty of carbon dioxide available for photosynthesis.

2   **Cut the stem of an elodea**. Remove a few leaves from the cut part of the stem.

3   **Place the elodea in the beaker of water and place a funnel over the plant**.

4   **Fill a test tube with water. Invert the test tube underwater** and place on top of the funnel.

5   Set a **lamp** 100 cm away from the apparatus and leave for a few minutes to allow the plant to adjust.

6   **Record the number of bubbles of oxygen that are produced in 1 minute**.

7   Repeat this procedure by moving the lamp closer to the apparatus. Record both the distance and the number of oxygen bubbles produced.

Result

As the lamp is moved closer to the apparatus (light intensity increases), the rate of photosynthesis increases up to a point. An increase in the rate of photosynthesis is evident if there is an increase in the number of oxygen bubbles produced.

To prove that the gas produced during photosynthesis is oxygen, place a **glowing splint** into the test tube of gas collected and the splint **relights**.

Questions

1 Draw a labelled diagram of a longitudinal section of a root. On your diagram, clearly indicate where each of the following occurs:
   (a) The zone where cells become specialised as phloem and xylem
   (b) Where cell division occurs
   (c) Where cells grow in size.

2 List **four** adaptations of leaves for photosynthesis.

3 (a) Name **two** types of vascular tissue found in plants. Give a function for each of the plant tissues you have named.
   (b) Draw a labelled diagram for **one** of the tissues you have named in part (a).
   (c) Identify **two differences** between the two types of tissue you have identified in part (a).

4 Explain the following terms:
   (a) Dermal tissue
   (b) Cambium
   (c) Lignin.

Exam questions

1 (a) Name **one** monocot plant and **one** dicot plant.
   (b) List **two** differences between monocot plants and dicot plants.
   (HL 2012)

2 State the function of **each** of the following plant tissues:
   (a) Xylem
   (b) Meristem
   (c) Palisade. *(HL 2012)*

3 Describe a laboratory experiment to show that carbon dioxide is necessary for photosynthesis. *(HL 2012)*

4 Draw a labelled diagram of a transverse section of a monocot stem.
   (HL 2009)

5 Write a short note on the following: monocotyledons and dicotyledons.
   (HL 2009)

Key-points!

- Plant tissue can be classified as:
  - Dermal tissue: Outer layer of tissue on a plant. Its function is protection.
  - Ground tissue: Functions include photosynthesis, storage of food and support.
  - Vascular tissue: Transport tissue. It is composed of phloem and xylem. Phloem transports sugars and xylem transports water and minerals. Xylem and phloem tissue are found together in vascular bundles in the leaves and stems of plants.

- Xylem is composed of xylem vessels and tracheids. Xylem tissue is dead tissue. The cell walls of xylem tissue are reinforced with lignin.

- Phloem tissue is composed of sieve tubes and companion cells. Phloem tissue is living tissue. Companion cells control and maintain sieve tubes.

- Monocotyledons (or monocots) have one cotyledon in the seed or one seed leaf. Examples of monocots include grasses and cereals.

- Dicotyledons (or dicots) have two cotyledons in the seed or two seed leaves. Examples include daisies, dandelions and most other flowering plants.

- The longitudinal section of a root is composed of the following sections: root cap (protection), zone of cell division (meristematic tissue), zone of elongation (cells increase in size) and zone of differentiation (cells become specialised).

- Monocot stems have scattered vascular bundles. Dicot stems have their vascular bundles arranged in a circle.

- Cambium tissue is present in the vascular bundles between the phloem and the xylem in dicot stems. Cambium tissue allows for secondary thickening in shrubs and trees.

- Plants are autotrophic, as they can produce their own food. Chlorophyll traps light energy from the sun. This energy is then used to combine hydrogen from water and carbon dioxide to make glucose and oxygen.

$$\text{Carbon dioxide + Water} \xrightarrow[\text{Sunlight}]{\text{Chlorophyll}} \text{Glucose + Oxygen}$$

$$6CO_2 + 6H_2O \xrightarrow[\text{Sunlight}]{\text{Chlorophyll}} C_6H_{12}O_6 + 6O_2$$

- The leaves of plants have many adaptations for photosynthesis, including:
  - The leaf is flat, maximising the surface area for photosynthesis.
  - The palisade cells are packed with chloroplasts to maximise photosynthesis.
  - The spongy mesophyll layer allows for the diffusion of carbon dioxide to the palisade layer.
  - Stomata allow for gaseous exchange and vascular tissue facilitates transport (xylem provides water and phloem removes sugars produced by photosynthesis).

3 Transport in Plants

Transpiration stream

Water and minerals are carried by the xylem tissue. A combination of four forces – **root pressure**, **cohesion**, **adhesion** and **transpiration** – ensures that water moves as a continuous column from the roots to the leaves. The movement of water from the roots of the plants up to the leaves is known as the **transpiration stream**.

1 **Root pressure:** Water continuously moves by osmosis from the soil into the root hairs. This causes a pressure known as root pressure, which forces water upwards into the xylem vessels and tracheids. However, root pressure on its own is not sufficient to push water to the leaves of large plants. *Note: Minerals enter the root hairs by **active transport***.

2 **Cohesion:** Water molecules are attracted to each other and stick together, forming a continuous column.

3 **Adhesion:** Water molecules are attracted to the cellulose walls of the xylem vessels and this draws water along the xylem vessels.

4 **Transpiration:** Water is continuously lost through the **stomata** of plant leaves by transpiration. Water is pulled from the xylem vessels to replace this lost water.

Key definition

Transpiration is the loss of water by evaporation from the leaves.

Factors that affect the rate of transpiration

The rate of transpiration is not constant and is influenced by a number of factors.

Factor	Effect
Table 3.1 Factors that affect the rate of transpiration	
Temperature	Evaporation of water from the leaves of plants helps to keep them cool. On hot days, the rate of transpiration increases. The rate of transpiration decreases on cold days.
Wind	On calm days, a layer of water vapour builds up around the stomata, increasing the humidity and decreasing the rate of transpiration. On windy days, the rate of transpiration increases, as air movement across the stomata prevents the build-up of humid air.
Soil water	If plants experience a water shortage, as in the case of droughts, the stomata of the leaves close to reduce transpiration in an effort to conserve water. When soil water is plentiful, plants respire at a higher rate.
Light	Light stimulates the opening of the stomata, increasing the rate of transpiration. Stomata are normally closed at night, reducing the rate of transpiration.
Humidity	If the air is dry and low in water vapour, the rate of transpiration increases. If there is rain or the air is high in water vapour, the rate of transpiration decreases, as the air becomes saturated with water vapour and can hold no more water.

Key definition

Humidity is a measure of the amount of water vapour (moisture) in the air.

To measure the rate of transpiration

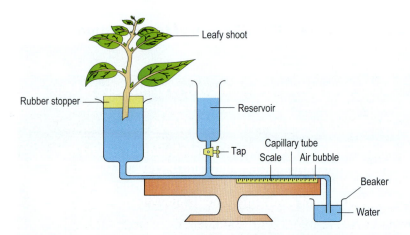

Fig 3.1 *Using a potometer to measure the rate of transpiration*

1   Cut a **leafy shoot**. Use a plant that has a thin, waxy cuticle, e.g. beech or lilac.

2   Cut the shoot at an angle underwater.

3   Immerse a **potometer** underwater. *Note: If air gets into the xylem vessels, it can form an air lock and interfere with transpiration.*

4   Place the leafy shoot into the potometer.

5   **Seal all the joints where the shoot is placed with Vaseline** to prevent air from entering.

6   Place the potometer in front of a **light**.

7   Remove the capillary tube from the beaker of water and allow an **air bubble** to enter the capillary tube.

8   Re-immerse the capillary tube in the beaker of water.

9   Using a scale, **note the start position of the bubble**.

10   **Leave** the potometer for 2 hours.

11   **Measure the position of the bubble** after 2 hours.

12   Measure the distance travelled by the air bubble.

13   The rate of transpiration is **calculated** by dividing the distance moved by the air bubble by the time taken.

   Note: The experiment can be repeated using a fan or a hair dryer to investigate the effect of wind on the rate of transpiration.

Result

Water was lost due to transpiration. A potometer can be used to measure the rate of transpiration, as the plant removes water from the potometer to replace that lost by evaporation from the leaves.

Translocation

> ## Key definition
>
> **Translocation** is the movement of sugars produced in the leaves (sources, sites of photosynthesis) to other parts of plants (sinks, sites of storage).

- Phloem tissue is responsible for the movement of sugars.
- Sugars move into the phloem tissue by **active transport**.
- The movement of sugars can occur up and down the phloem tissue.
- The mechanism by which phloem sap (mixture of sugars and water) moves is described by the **pressure-flow hypothesis**.

Questions

1   Outline the function of each of the following in the movement of water by transpiration:
    (a) Root pressure
    (b) Cohesion
    (c) Adhesion
    (d) Transpiration.

2   Describe **three** factors that affect the rate of transpiration in plants.

3   Briefly describe the movement of phloem sap in plants.

Exam questions

1   Describe a laboratory experiment to determine the rate of transpiration of a plant.   *(HL 2010)*

2   Distinguish between the following: transpiration and translocation.   *(HL 2007)*

3   Agricultural Science students study the general structure and function of plants.
    (a) Describe the functions of the xylem tissue **and** phloem tissue.
    (b) Explain the difference between transpiration and translocation.
    (c) Describe an experiment to show water movement in a plant stem.   *(OL 2009)*

Key-points!

- The movement of water from the roots of the plants up to the leaves is known as the transpiration stream. Water and minerals are carried by the xylem tissue. A combination of four forces – root pressure, cohesion, adhesion and transpiration – ensures that water moves as a continuous column from the roots to the leaves.

- Root pressure is caused by the continuous movement of water by osmosis from the soil into the root hairs.

- Adhesion is caused by the force of attraction that water molecules have for each other.

- Cohesion is caused by the attraction that water molecules have for the cellulose walls of the xylem vessels.

- Transpiration is the continuous loss of water through the stomata of plant leaves.

- Factors that affect the rate of transpiration include temperature, wind, soil water, light and humidity.

- Translocation is the movement of sugars produced in the leaves (sources, sites of photosynthesis) to other parts of plants (sinks, sites of storage).

- Phloem tissue is responsible for the movement of sugars. Sugars move into the phloem tissue by active transport. The movement of sugars can occur up and down the phloem tissue.

Plant Reproduction

4

Reproduction in plants

- Many plants have the ability to reproduce sexually and asexually. **Asexual reproduction** requires one parent, and the offspring are genetically identical to the parent plant. **Sexual reproduction** requires the fusion of a male and a female gamete, or two parents.

- The reproductive organ of a flowering plant is the flower.

- Normally, both male and female reproductive parts occur together in the flower. However, there are exceptions to this. For example, in maize the female part (the silk) and the male part (the tassel) are separate.

- The male reproductive part is the **stamen**. It consists of the **anther** and the **filament**.

- The female reproductive part is the **carpel**. It consists of the **stigma**, the **style** and the **ovary**.

Table 4.1 The parts of the flower and their function

Structure	Function
Receptacle	Base of the flower
Anther	Produces **pollen** (male gamete)
Pollen	**Male gamete**
Filament	Supports the anther
Stigma	Pollen lands on the stigma during pollination
Style	Found between the stigma and the ovary; the pollen tube travels down through this
Ovary	Contains one or more ovules; the ovary becomes the fruit after fertilisation
Ovules	Located inside the ovary and contain the **egg cell (female gamete)**
Petals	In insect-pollinated plants, the petals are brightly coloured to attract insects for pollination
Sepals	Protect the flower when it is a bud

Top Tip!

It is important to be able to draw and label both an insect-pollinated and a wind-pollinated flower. In addition, students need to be able to identify how a flower is pollinated based on the structure of the flower. To help you do this, always look to see where the anthers and stigma are in the flower. If they are inside, the flower is pollinated by insects. If they are outside, the flower is pollinated by wind.

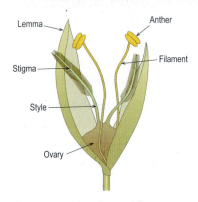

Fig 4.1 *A wind-pollinated flower*

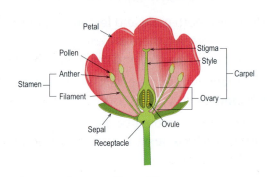

Fig 4.2 *An insect-pollinated flower*

The importance of pollination

- It allows plants to reproduce sexually.
- Cross-pollination between flowers brings about genetic variation.
- Pollination is required for seed and fruit formation.
- Seeds and fruits are important food sources for wildlife.

Key definition

Pollination: The transfer of pollen from the anther of one flower to the stigma of another flower of the same species.

Adaptations of wind-pollinated and insect-pollinated flowers

Table 4.2 Adaptations of wind-pollinated and insect-pollinated flowers		
Structure	**Wind-pollinated**	**Insect-pollinated**
Petals	Small, green, no scent, no nectaries	Large and brightly coloured, scented and nectaries
Stamens	Hang outside the plant	Lie inside the plant
Stigma	Large and feathery, hang outside the plant	Small, sticky and inside the plant
Pollen	Large amounts and very light	Small amounts, sticky or with spines

Examples of wind-pollinated flowers include grasses and cereals (wheat, barley, oats, maize, etc.).

Examples of insect-pollinated flowers include dandelions, daisies, buttercups, etc.

Fertilisation and seed formation

- The pollen grain contains two male gametes and a tube nucleus.
- Once pollination has occurred, the tube nucleus forms the **pollen tube**.
- The pollen tube allows the male gametes to travel from the stigma down into the ovary.
- Once the tube nucleus reaches the entrance into the embryo sac, it disintegrates.

- One of the male gametes fuses with the egg cell to form a **zygote**. This is known as **fertilisation**.
- The other male gamete fuses with a pair of cells called the polar nuclei cells to form the **endosperm**.
- The zygote becomes the **seed**.
- The walls of the ovule become the seed coat (**testa**).
- The endosperm is sometimes used as a food reserve as the zygote grows into an embryo.
- The ovary of many flowers develops into a **fruit**.

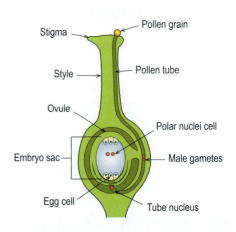

Fig 4.3 A pollen tube containing male gametes en route to the embryo sac

Monocot and dicot seeds

Monocot seeds have only **one cotyledon**. In monocots, the endosperm remains present. Upon germination, the cotyledon makes the energy in the endosperm available to the embryo.

The embryo consists of the **radicle** (future root of the plant), the **plumule** (future shoot of the plant) and the **cotyledons** (seed leaves).

The seeds of grasses and cereals are monocots.

Dicot seeds have **two cotyledons**. In most dicots, the cotyledons grow and absorb the endosperm completely. As a result, they are referred to as non-endospermic seeds.

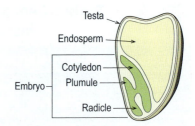

Fig 4.4 A monocot seed (sunflower seed and cereal grain)

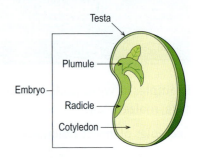

Fig 4.5 A dicot seed (broad bean)

Seed dispersal

Seed dispersal is vital in order to prevent competition with the parent plant for light, water, minerals and space to grow. It also allows plants to colonise new areas.

Table 4.3 Mechanisms for seed dispersal

Mechanism	Description	Examples
Wind	Seeds are extremely light and are attached to a parachute or have wings, or have fine hairs that open to form a ball.	Dandelion and ragwort (parachute) Sycamore and ash (wings) Thistle (fine hairs)
Animals	Edible fruits contain seeds that pass through the animal's digestive system unharmed. Dry fruits with hooks on them attach themselves to the coats of animals. Animals often bury seeds for periods of food shortages but forget about them.	Blackberries and strawberries Burdock and goose grass Squirrels bury acorns
Self-dispersal	Members of the leguminosae family (pea family) have a pod that contains the seeds. The pod dries out and splits, firing the seeds out.	Gorse, peas and beans
Water	Produces light seeds that are buoyant and can float.	Water lilies

Top Tip!

A common mistake students make in exams is mixing up pollination with seed dispersal. Remember: pollination occurs by either wind or insects (not animals), whereas seed dispersal can occur by animal, wind, water or self.

Germination

Seeds require three conditions for germination:

Key definition

Germination is the growth of a seed into a new plant.

1. Water: Is a solvent and is required for many enzyme reactions.
2. Oxygen: Enables aerobic respiration.
3. Suitable temperature: Enzyme activity is temperature dependent.

Germination is classified as **hypogeal** or **epigeal** depending on whether or not the cotyledons come above the ground and photosynthesise.

Hypogeal germination

The radicle emerges first and grows downwards, followed by the plumule. The cotyledons remain below the ground and supply energy to the growing plumule and radicle.

Epigeal germination

The radicle emerges from the seed and grows downwards. The region between the radicle and the cotyledons – the hypocotyl – starts to grow. This pushes the cotyledons above the ground. The old seed coat falls off and the cotyledons emerge and start to photosynthesise.

 **Experiment**

To investigate factors required for germination

1. Place four test tubes into a rack with a small amount of cotton wool in each.

2. Add an equal number of **cress seeds** to each test tube.

3. Add water to the first test tube. This is the **control**.

4. Fill the next test tube two-thirds full with **cooled, boiled water**. The water has been boiled to remove the oxygen. **Pour a layer of oil onto the water** to prevent any oxygen from entering the water.

5. **Leave the cotton wool of the third test tube dry.**

6. Moisten the cotton wool of the fourth test tube and place this test tube in the **fridge**.

7. Place the three remaining test tubes in a warm location.

Result

Only the seeds in the first test tube will germinate, as these seeds have water, oxygen and a suitable temperature for germination to occur.

Modified organs and vegetative reproduction

Many plants have modified organs for food storage, while others use their modifications for asexual reproduction (**vegetative reproduction**).

The majority of modifications in plants are for food storage and are associated with the lifespan of the plant.

- **Annuals** complete their life cycle in one year.
- **Biennials** complete their life cycle in two years.
- **Perennials** flower and produce seeds many times over the course of their life.

> ### Point to note
>
> **Vegetative reproduction** is a form of asexual reproduction in plants, where new individual plants (offspring) are produced without the parent plant forming seeds. All the offspring are genetically identical to the parent plant.

Modified stems

- **Stolons** are horizontal stems that grow above the ground from the base of a plant and produce a new plant from buds at its tips. Stolons are often called **runners**. Strawberries and creeping buttercup reproduce vegetatively by producing stolons.
- **Rhizomes** are horizontal underground stems that can send out both shoots and roots. If rhizomes are broken into pieces, each piece can produce a new plant. Scutch grass reproduces asexually by rhizomes.
- **Tubers** produced by potatoes can produce new shoots from lateral buds known as eyes. In addition, the tuber also stores food in the form of starch.
- **Corms** are modified stems that grow vertically. The crocus is an example of a plant with a corm.

Modified roots

- **Tap root** is the central root, which is modified to store food in carrots, parsnips and sugar beet.
- **Root tubers** are modified lateral roots for food storage. An example of this is dahlias.

Modified leaves

A **bulb** is an example of modified leaves used for food storage. Plants that have bulbs are monocots. Examples are onions and tulips.

Plant tropisms

Growth responses in plants are under the control of plant hormones.

Experiment

The growth response of a plant shoot to light (phototropism)

1 Cut a window in the side of a shoebox. At the other end of the shoebox, cut a window in the roof.

2 Place some moist cotton wool in two petri dishes and add equal numbers of cress seeds to each dish.

3 Place the petri dishes inside the shoebox. The petri dish with the **light** entering from the roof of the box is the **control**.

4 **Leave the shoebox in a sunny spot for over a week.**

5 **Inspect the seeds regularly.**

Result

The cress seeds with the window on the roof of the shoebox have grown straight up, while the cress seeds with the window on the side of the box have grown towards the window, as the shoots are growing towards the light. This response is known as **phototropism**.

Artificial vegetative propagation

Humans have developed methods for reproducing desirable plants asexually. Many of the following are common practices used in horticulture and in agriculture to allow the rapid multiplication of desirable plant species.

Table 4.4 Methods of artificial vegetative propagation	
Method	How it works
Cuttings	Remove a healthy stem from the desired plant. Cut the stem at an angle and apply rooting powder (which contains plant hormones, auxins). This promotes the growth of roots.

Method	How it works
Grafting	Remove the shoot of a desired plant (the scion) and cut at an angle to fit into the root stock of another similar plant. The vascular tissue of the scion and the rootstock must be aligned and the graft is then secured with grafting tape. Grafting is common practice in the production of apple trees.
Layering	An incision is made into a healthy aerial stem and rooting powder is placed into the damaged stem. While still attached to the parent plant, the stem is then pegged into the soil where the stem has the incision. Roots grow where the incision is made and eventually the stem will become strong enough to be detached from the parent plant.
Micropropagation	This is also known as tissue culture propagation and is commonly used in the production of potatoes. Sprouts are removed from a disease-free parent plant. These are grown in a sterile medium containing sucrose and plant hormones. The tissue cultures are incubated under low light conditions at 25°C. The shoots can be removed from the culture, divided into sections and re-inoculated onto fresh medium. This process can be repeated several times to produce thousands of clones, all genetically identical to each other and to the parent plant.

Questions

1 (a) What is the function of the endosperm in a monocot seed?
   (b) What is meant by the germination of a seed?
   (c) Identify **three** factors necessary for the germination of a seed.

2 (a) Distinguish between hypogeal and epigeal germination in seeds.
   (b) Plants disperse their seeds to avoid competing with their own offspring. State **two** ways in which plants disperse their seeds.
   (c) Identify **two** resources for which plants compete.

3 From your study of plant families, you learned that the flower is the reproductive shoot of the plant.
   (a) Draw a labelled diagram of a wind-pollinated plant.
   (b) What is the function of the anther?
   (c) State **two** ways in which a flower developed for insect pollination differs from wind-pollinated flowers.

Exam questions

1 Match **each** plant structure from the following list with a description in the table. The first one has been completed as an example.

root hairs   xylem   ~~phloem~~
carpels   stomata   stamens

Plant structure	Description
Phloem	Carries products of photosynthesis
	Male parts of flower
	Carries water from the roots
	Allows gas exchange in leaves
	Absorbs water from soil
	Female parts of the flower

(OL 2012)

2 Give a scientific explanation for the importance of pollination in plants.
(HL 2012)

3 (a) Mention **two** methods by which weed seeds are dispersed.
   (b) For **each** method, name a common weed that uses this method of dispersal. *(HL 2012)*

4 Distinguish between a stolon (runner) and a rhizome and give **one** example of each from agriculture. *(HL 2011)*

5 Highlight the main differences between the members of the following pair: annual and biennial plants. *(HL 2011)*

6 In the case of each of the following, name the part of the plant that is modified and give an example of a plant with this modification.
   (a) Bulb
   (b) Tuber. *(HL 2008)*

7 Give **one** example, in each case, of a plant that reproduces using one of the following:
   (a) Runners
   (b) Rhizomes
   (c) Tubers
   (d) Bulbs *(HL 2006)*

8 Draw a labelled diagram to show the main structures of a cereal grain in longitudinal section. *(HL 2011)*

9 Outline an experiment to show the conditions necessary for germination. *(OL 2010)*

10 Describe **one** natural method of vegetative reproduction in plants. *(HL 2012)*

Key-points!

- Asexual reproduction requires one parent, and the offspring are genetically identical to the parent plant. Sexual reproduction requires the fusion of a male and a female gamete, or two parents.

- The male reproductive part of the flower is the stamen and consists of the anther and the filament.

- The female reproductive part is the carpel and consists of the stigma, the style and the ovary.

- Pollination is the transfer of pollen from the anther of one flower to the stigma of another flower of the same species. Pollination can occur by wind or by insect.

- Wind-pollinated flowers have reduced petals. Their stigma is large and feathery and it hangs outside the flower. The stamens of wind-pollinated flowers hang outside the flower and produce large amounts of light pollen.

- Insect-pollinated flowers have large colourful petals to attract insects. Their stigma and stamens lie inside the flower. They produce a small amount of sticky pollen and they often have nectaries and are scented.

- Pollination is important for sexual reproduction in plants in order to bring about genetic variation and to produce seeds and fruits.

- Fertilisation and seed formation: The pollen grain contains two male gametes and a tube nucleus. The tube nucleus forms the pollen tube. The male gametes travel from the stigma down into the ovary. One of the male gametes fertilises the egg cell to form a zygote. The other male gamete fuses with a pair of cells called the polar nuclei cells to form the endosperm. The zygote becomes the seed.

- In monocots, the endosperm remains present and upon germination the cotyledon makes the energy in the endosperm available to the embryo. The embryo consists of the radicle, the plumule and the cotyledons.

- In most dicots, the cotyledons grow and absorb the endosperm completely. As a result, they are referred to as non-endospermic seeds.

- Seed dispersal is vital in order to prevent competition with the parent plant for light, water, minerals and space to grow. It also allows plants to colonise new areas. Seeds can be dispersed by animals (carried on their coats or eaten), wind, water or self (where the parent plant fires the seeds away from it).

- Seeds require three conditions for germination: water, oxygen and a suitable temperature.

- Germination is classified as hypogeal or epigeal. In hypogeal germination, the cotyledons of the germinating seed remain below the ground. In epigeal germination, the cotyledons of the germinating seed emerge above the surface of the ground.

- Annuals complete their life cycle in one year. Biennials complete their life cycle in two years. Perennials flower and produce seeds many times over the course of their life.

- Vegetative reproduction is a form of asexual reproduction in plants, where new individual plants are produced without the parent plant forming seeds. All the offspring are genetically identical to the parent plant.

- Stolons, rhizomes, tubers and corms are all examples of modified stems. Their main function is for vegetative reproduction, but tubers and corms can also be used for food storage.

- Tap roots and root tubers are modified roots used for food storage. Root tubers are used for vegetative reproduction.

- A bulb is an example of modified leaves. Its main function is food storage.

- A tropism is a plant's growth response to an external stimulus. Phototropism is a plant's growth response to light. Geotropism is a plant's growth response to gravity. Growth responses in plants are under the control of plant hormones.

- Artificial vegetative propagation involves methods developed by humans for reproducing desirable plants asexually.

- Cuttings, grafting, layering and micropropagation are all examples of artificial vegetative propagation.

Ecology 5

Common ecological terms

- **Ecology:** Study of the interactions between organisms and their environment.
- **Ecosystem:** Interaction between organisms and the environment in which they live. Examples of ecosystems in agriculture include grassland, tillage, hedgerows, bogland, forestry and freshwater.
- **Biodiversity:** The variety of life in a particular habitat or ecosystem.
- **Niche:** The position in an ecosystem that a species occupies.
- **Habitat:** The place where a plant or animal lives.
- **Abiotic:** Non-living factors in the environment, e.g. aspect, light intensity and temperature.
- **Edaphic:** Factors that relate to the soil, e.g. pH, drainage, soil temperature.
- **Biotic:** The living factors in the environment, e.g. plants, animals and microorganisms.

Top Tip!

Ecology is an important component of the practical exam. It is a good idea to have a small ecology study completed as part of your ecology practical work.

- **Producer:** An organism that can make its own food, e.g. plants photo-synthesise.
- **Consumer:** Organisms that eat another organism for food.
- **Decomposer:** An organism that breaks down dead organic matter.
- **Predator:** An organism that hunts, kills and eats other animals.

 Experiment

Measuring abiotic and edaphic factors in an ecosystem

1 **Aspect:** Does something face north or south? Use a compass to find north. Plants grow better with a south-facing aspect.

2 **Light intensity:** Can be measured using a light meter. The light meter is held close to the ground and pointed in the direction the light is coming from.

3 **Soil temperature:** Is important for plant growth and seed germination. Soil temperature is measured using a soil thermometer or a thermometer with a layer of wax on it. Place the thermometer in the ground. Ensure the thermometer is not in bright sunlight. Give the thermometer time to adjust to the soil temperature.

4 **Soil pH:** pH determines the types of plants growing in a habitat. Place a sample of soil in a test tube and add a pinch of barium sulfate (flocculating agent). Add a small volume of universal indicator. Stopper and shake the test tube. Allow the contents to settle and match the colour of the indicator to the pH colour chart.

 Experiment

Measuring biotic factors in an ecosystem

Experiment: Collecting animals using a beating tray and a pooter

1 Place a **beating tray** under a tree or bush.

2 Shake or hit the tree.

3 The insects will fall on the beating tray.

4 Use a **pooter** to collect the insects.

5 Use an **invertebrate key** to identify the animals.

Tullgren funnel

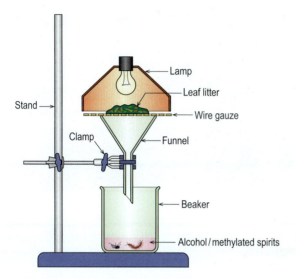

Fig 5.1 *A Tullgren funnel*

A Tullgren funnel is used to **extract** small invertebrates from the soil and the leaf litter.

1　Place a sample of soil on a sieve.

2　Leave overnight under a **lamp**.

3　Invertebrates present in the soil or leaf litter will move away from the light source. They pass through the sieve and fall into the **alcohol**, where they are preserved.

4　Remove any floating invertebrates from the surface of the alcohol and place under a **microscope**. Observe under low power.

5　Inspect large invertebrates using a magnifying glass.

6　Use an **animal key** to identify the invertebrates.

Point to note

A pitfall trap could also be used to collect invertebrates. A sample of alcohol can be placed in the bottom of the pitfall trap to preserve any invertebrates that fall into it. The animals collected can be identified using a key.

Experiment

Determination of the botanical composition of permanent grassland

1   **Throw a pen randomly** over your shoulder.

2   Place a **quadrat** where the pen lands.

3   Using a plant key, **identify the species** inside the quadrat.

4   **Repeat** this 10 times.

5   **Record** the varieties of plants found in each of the 10 quadrats.

6   Calculate the **percentage frequency**.

Top Tip!

The term botanical *composition* refers to the percentage of different types of plants that are growing in a grassland habitat. Quadrat studies (to measure frequency) or the use of a line transect are common field investigations carried out to determine botanical composition.

Top Tip!

To determine the effect of grazing on the botanic composition of grassland, the experiment above could be modified so that an area of a field is closed off using a cage or fenced off to prevent animals grazing the vegetation in that section. Then the remainder of the field should be grazed as normal. The field, both grazed and ungrazed, should be observed over a period of time (six months to a year or more). The botanical composition of the grazed and ungrazed areas should be regularly sampled using the quadrat experiment above. Weeds will start to dominate the ungrazed area of the field.

Experiment

To examine the change in vegetation from a hedgerow into a field

1   Select an area that is representative of the habitat.

2   Stretch a **line transect** with **intervals of 1 m marked on it**.

3   Record the plants that **touch the line at each interval**.

4   The vegetation changes as you move from the shade of the hedgerow to the openness of the field. There is more shade-loving vegetation close to the hedgerow.

Questions

1. (a) Name two pieces of equipment that could be used to sample the variety of plants in a habitat.
   (b) Describe how you would use **one** of the pieces of equipment named in part (a).
   (c) State **two** characteristics that help to identify a grass when carrying out a habitat study.

2. Define the following terms used in ecology:
   (a) Niche
   (b) Habitat
   (c) Abiotic factor
   (d) Decomposer.

3. Describe a laboratory investigation to determine the invertebrates present in a soil sample or a leaf litter sample.

4. Identify what factor you would measure with **each** of the following pieces of equipment **and** explain how the piece of equipment is used:
   (a) Quadrat
   (b) Light meter
   (c) Soil thermometer
   (d) Line transect
   (e) Compass.

Exam questions

1. Describe a field experiment to determine the effect of grazing on the botanical composition of grassland. *(HL 2011)*

2. Describe a field experiment to determine the botanical composition of an old pasture. *(HL 2007)*

3. Give a scientific explanation why farm hedges are trimmed only after the first of September. *(OL 2014)*

4. A line transect is used in ecology. True or false? *(OL 2014)*

Key-points!

- Abiotic: Non-living factors in the environment, e.g. aspect, light intensity and temperature.

- Edaphic: Factors that relate to the soil, e.g. pH, drainage, soil temperature.

- Biotic: The living factors in the environment, e.g. plants, animals and microorganisms. Biotic factors can be measured by using either a pooter and beating tray or a Tullgren funnel.

- Quadrat studies and line transects are used to determine the botanical composition of habitats. A quadrat study will determine the frequency of certain plants in a habitat, while a line transect will determine the change in vegetation as you move from a shaded area (hedgerow) into an open field.

- The procedure for using a quadrat is to throw a pen over your shoulder (random selection). Place the quadrat down where the pen lands. Use a key to identify the plants present. Record the result. Repeat the procedure 10 times. Calculate frequency.

Microbiology

6

Learning objectives

In this chapter you will learn about:

1 Bacteria

2 Fungi

3 Viruses

4 Notifiable diseases

5 Experiment: To demonstrate the presence of microorganisms in soil, in air and in an animal feed

6 Experiment: To determine the hygiene quality of milk

7 Experiment: To show the presence of bacteria in the root nodules of clover

Bacteria

- Bacteria belong to the **Kingdom Monera**.
- Bacteria are **prokaryote**, as their genetic material is not bound within a membrane.
- Bacteria are classified according to their shape: spherical (cocci), spiral or rod shaped.

Bacteria are either **autotrophic** (can make their own food) or **heterotrophic** (organism that relies on food made by other organisms).

The heterotrophic bacteria important to agriculture fall into three categories and are summarised in Table 6.1.

Table 6.1 Important bacteria in agriculture	
Decomposers	Bacteria present in the soil help to break down dead and decaying organic matter. These bacteria play important roles in the Carbon and Nitrogen Cycles. In the production of silage, *Lactobacillus* bacteria break down sugars in the grass into lactic acid.

Symbiotic bacteria	Clover has a symbiotic relationship with the bacteria *Rhizobium*, which lives in the root nodules of clover. The bacteria fix atmospheric nitrogen into nitrates for the clover and the bacteria get sugars from the clover. Bacteria that live in ruminant animals produce enzymes to help digest the cellulose in grass.
Pathogenic bacteria	Pathogenic bacteria cause disease. In agriculture, bacteria are responsible for diseases such as bovine tuberculosis, brucellosis, mastitis and blackleg. Pathogenic bacteria can also be classified as parasites, as they cause damage to the host animal. Some bacteria are zoonoses.

Top Tip!

Students are often asked to define terms or to distinguish between two different terms, e.g. pathogen and parasite. It is important to know the meaning of, and understand, common terms used in agricultural science.

Key definitions

Pathogen: A microorganism that causes a disease.

Zoonose: A disease that can pass from animals to humans.

Parasite: When two organisms live in close association with each other and only one organism (the parasite) benefits and causes the other organism (the host) harm.

Symbiotic relationship: When two organisms of different species live in a close relationship that benefits both organisms.

Point to note

In biology, symbiotic relationships where both organisms benefit from the relationship are referred to as **mutualism**.

Structure of bacteria

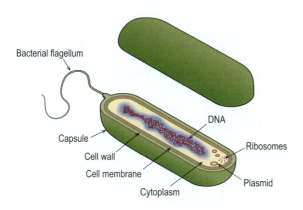

Fig 6.1 *The basic structure of a bacterium*

Table 6.2 Bacterial cell structure and function

Structure	Function
Flagellum	The flagellum helps bacteria to move; locomotion.
Capsule	The capsule enhances bacteria's ability to cause a disease, as it prevents white blood cells in an animal's body from engulfing the bacterial cell (phagocytosis). The capsule can also help prevent the bacterial cell from drying out.
Cell wall	This prevents the cell from bursting as a result of water moving into the cell by osmosis. The cell wall also provides shape to the bacteria.
Cell membrane	The cell membrane controls what enters and exits the cell.
DNA	DNA controls the activities of the cell and is replicated when the bacteria reproduce.
Ribosomes	Ribosomes are responsible for protein synthesis.
Plasmid	Plasmid are circular pieces of DNA. In some bacteria, these additional pieces of DNA can code for antibiotic resistance.

Respiration in bacteria

Some bacteria, such as *Mycobacterium bovis* (responsible for bovine tuberculosis), carry out aerobic respiration. They release energy from sugars in the presence of oxygen.

Lactobacillus species of bacteria carry out **anaerobic respiration** (also known as **fermentation**), where they release energy from sugars in the absence of oxygen. In the production of silage, *Lactobacillus* bacteria under anaerobic conditions convert sugars in grass to lactic acid. This decreases the pH of the grass, thus preserving it as silage.

Reproduction

Under favourable conditions, bacteria reproduce asexually by a process known as **binary fission**. If environmental conditions for the bacteria become unfavourable, some bacteria have the ability to survive by producing an **endospore**. Endospores are highly resistant structures and allow bacteria to survive heat, freezing, drying and chemicals.

Fungi

- Fungi belong to the **Kingdom Fungi**.
- Fungi can be microscopic in size (e.g. yeasts) or very large (e.g. mushrooms).
- They lack chlorophyll, so they cannot carry out photosynthesis.
- Fungi are either **saphrophytic decomposers** (break down dead organic matter) or **parasitic**.
- Fungi are important decomposers in the Carbon and Nitrogen Cycles.
- Parasitic fungi cause ringworm in cattle and blight in potatoes.

Structure of fungi

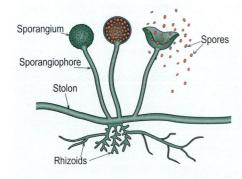

Fig 6.2 *Rhizopus*

Table 6.3 Fungi structure and function	
Structure	**Function**
Hyphae	Long filaments
Mycelium	Entire mass of hyphae
Rhizoids	Anchor the fungi to its substrate and absorb nutrients from the substrate

Structure	Function
Stolon	Horizontally growing hyphae
Sporangiophore	A hyphae that grows upwards and has a sporangium on top
Sporangium	Produces spores

Reproduction in fungi

Fungi can reproduce asexually by producing **spores** or sexually by producing a **zygospore**.

Potato blight

- Potato blight is caused by an airborne fungus, *Phytophthora infestans*.
- It is a parasitic fungus.
- Blight zoospores germinate to produce hyphae, which invade the cells of the potato leaves.
- Hyphae exit through the stomata of the leaves, where they develop into sporangia.
- In warm, humid weather, **zoospores** develop inside the sporangia.
- The zoospores infect other leaves, stems and tubers of the potato plant.
- Blight appears as brown spots on the leaves of the plant. Infected tubers have black patches on them.
- Spraying the potato crop with a **fungicide** can prevent blight when the Meteorological Service issues **blight warnings**.

> **Key definition**
>
> **Zoospore:** A mobile spore. Each spore has two flagella that help it move. Potato blight reproduces by producing zoospores.

Viruses

- Extremely small (range in size from 0.01 to 0.03 micrometres).
- All viruses are **obligate parasites** (viruses can only replicate themselves inside other living organisms).
- Viruses have a very simple structure.
- As viruses lack any cellular structure, **antibiotics** are ineffective at treating viral diseases.
- Some viral diseases can be vaccinated against.
- Viruses are responsible for BVD (bovine viral diarrhoea) in cattle and leaf roll and tomato mosaic virus in potatoes.

BVD (bovine viral diarrhoea) is a disease in cattle caused by a virus. Symptoms of this disease include infertility, miscarriages and ill-thriving calves. The virus also suppresses the immune system of the infected animal, making it more susceptible to respiratory infections. Calves born with the virus are known as PI (persistently infected) and these animals shed large quantities of the virus over their lifetime. A national eradication programme was set up in 2012 and farmers were encouraged to participate in this programme on a voluntary basis. This eradication programme became compulsory in 2013.

Notifiable diseases

A notifiable disease is a disease that must be immediately reported to the district veterinary office. These diseases are notifiable because they are normally infectious and highly contagious.

Notifiable diseases are a serious agricultural threat, as they can:

- Cause significant economic loss
- Decrease productivity
- Result in both affected and unaffected animals being destroyed to prevent the spread of the disease
- Pose a threat to human health (some notifiable diseases are zoonoses).

Examples of notifiable diseases include avian influenza, bovine spongiform encephalopathy (BSE), foot and mouth disease and Newcastle disease.

Microbiology is an important section in the practical coursework. It is also examinable in the written exam paper. The following experiments have appeared on recent exam papers.

Experiment

To demonstrate the presence of microorganisms in soil, in air and in an animal feed

1   Label four **sterile nutrient agar plates** A to D.

2   Agar plate A is the **control** and remains unopened.

3   Expose plate B to air for 15 minutes.

4   Shake 1 g of soil in a small volume of **sterile water**.

5   Heat an **inoculating loop** until it glows red. (This sterilises the loop.)

6   **Inoculate agar plate** C with the soil solution.

7   Reheat the loop and this time streak the loop on some animal feed (silage, hay, concentrates, grass, etc.).

8   **Inoculate agar plate** D with the animal feed.

9   **Incubate the agar plates upside down** in an incubator at 25°C for **four to five days**.

Result

Fungal and bacterial growth occurs on plates B to D. **No growth occurs on the control.** Bacterial colonies are raised, circular and shiny, while fungal growths are furry.

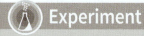
Experiment

To determine the hygiene quality of milk

1   Label four **sterile test tubes**.

2   Add different milk samples to each test tube. (Milk samples could include pasteurised milk, fresh raw unpasteurised milk, sour milk, etc.).

3   Add **resazurin solution** to each test tube.

4 **Stopper and shake**.

5 **Incubate** samples in a water bath **at 37°C for 10 minutes**.

6 **Note colour change**.

Result

The milk samples with the best hygiene quality will remain **blue**. The milk samples with a poorer hygeine quality will be **pink** and the samples with the worst quality will be **white** in colour, indicating that the sample is heavily contaminated with bacteria.

Top Tip!

This can appear as an experiment on the exam papers with the heading **To determine the bacterial quality of a sample of milk**. In addition, this experiment can be done by streaking milk samples onto sterile agar plates, incubating these for a number of days and then checking for the presence of colonies.

 Experiment

To show the presence of bacteria in the root nodules of clover

1 **Cut off the root of a clover plant and wash to remove soil.**

2 **Sterilise the surface of the root nodules with some mild disinfectant.**

3 Rinse the root nodules with sterile water to remove disinfectant.

4 **Squash the root nodule** with a sterile glass rod in a sterile petri dish.

5 **Sterilise an inoculating loop** in a Bunsen burner flame until it glows red hot.

6 **Streak** contents of root nodule **onto the agar plate** (yeast mannitol agar).

7 **Incubate the agar plate upside down at 25°C for one week.**

8 Use one unopened sterile agar plate as a **control**.

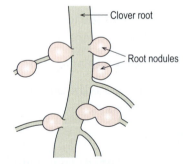

Fig 6.3 *Pink nodules on a clover root*

Result

Small white colonies grow on the agar plates. These are colonies of *Rhizobium*, the bacteria responsible for nitrogen fixation in the roots of clover.

Question

1 Highlight the main differences between the members of **each** of the following pairs:
   (a) Heterotrophic and autotrophic
   (b) Decomposers and pathogens
   (c) Parasitic and symbiotic relationships
   (d) Aerobic respiration and fermentation
   (e) Endospore and zoospore.

Exam questions

1 Highlight the main differences between zoonoses and zoospores. *(HL 2012)*

2 (a) Explain the term *symbosis*.
   (b) Give two examples of symbiosis from agriculture. *(HL 2011)*

3 Describe a laboratory experiment to determine the hygiene of quality of milk. *(HL 2011)*

4 (a) What type of organism is contained in the root nodules of clover plants?
   (b) State **one** function of the organisms referred to in (a).
   (c) **Draw** and **name** the piece of equipment normally used in a laboratory to transfer the organisms referred to in (a) onto an agar plate.
   (d) Give **one** reason for using clover in grass seed mixtures. *(OL 2012)*

5 (a) Name **two** diseases of livestock caused by bacteria.
   (b) Give **two** benefits of bacteria in agriculture.
   (c) Which **type** of organism is the cause of potato blight? *(OL 2011)*

6 Notifiable diseases must, by law, be reported to the authorities. Place a tick (✓) in the correct box in each case to indicate if a disease is notifiable or not. The first one has been done for you.

Name of disease	Notifiable	Not notifiable
Foot and mouth disease	✓	
Mastitis		
Swine fever		
Brucellosis		
Liverfluke		
Tuberculosis		

(OL 2010)

7   Describe a laboratory experiment to show the presence of bacteria in the
     root nodules of clover.   *(HL 2009)*

8   (a) Name **two** viral diseases of potatoes.
     (b) In the case of any **one** disease, state how it is spread.
     (c) Mention **one** method used to prevent the spread of this disease.
     (d) Give **two** examples that show the beneficial effects of bacteria in
         farming.
                                                                  (HL 2006)

Key-points!

- Bacteria belong to the Kingdom Monera. Bacteria are prokaryote, as their
  genetic material is not bound within a membrane. Bacteria are classified
  according to their shape: spherical (cocci), spiral or rod shaped.

- Important bacteria in agricultural science fall into three categories:
  decomposers (bacteria that break down dead and decaying organic matter),
  symbiotic bacteria (**Rhizobium** fixes nitrogen into nitrates in the root nodules of
  clover, therefore benefiting the clover) and pathogenic bacteria (bacteria that
  cause disease).

- Some bacteria can respire aerobically (with oxygen), while other bacteria, such
  as **Lactobacillus**, require anaerobic conditions (without oxygen). Anaerobic
  respiration is also known as fermentation and is an important process in the
  production of silage.

- Bacteria reproduce by binary fission in favourable conditions. If environmental
  conditions become unfavourable, then some bacteria can survive by producing
  an endospore.

- Fungi belong to the Kingdom Fungi. Fungi can be microscopic in size (e.g.
  yeasts) or very large (e.g. mushrooms). They lack chlorophyll, so they cannot
  carry out photosynthesis. Fungi are either saprophytic decomposers (break
  down dead organic matter) or parasitic.

- Fungi can reproduce asexually by producing spores or sexually by producing a
  zygospore.

- Potato blight is caused by an airborne fungus, *Phytophthora infestans*. It is a
  parasitic fungus. Hyphae exit through the stomata of the leaves, where they
  develop into sporangia. In warm, humid weather, zoospores develop inside the
  sporangia. The zoospores infect other leaves, stems and tubers of the potato
  plant. Blight appears as brown spots on the leaves of the plant. Infected tubers

have black patches on them. Spraying the potato crop with a fungicide can prevent blight when the Meteorological Service issues blight warnings.

- Viruses are extremely small. All viruses are obligate parasites (viruses can only replicate themselves inside other living organisms). Viruses have a very simple structure. Viruses are responsible for BVD in cattle and leaf roll and tomato mosaic virus in potatoes.

- A notifiable disease is a disease that must be immediately reported to the district veterinary office. These diseases are notifiable because they are normally infectious and highly contagious.

- Notifiable diseases are a serious agricultural threat, as they can result in significant economic loss and decreased productivity. They can result in both affected and unaffected animals being destroyed to prevent the spread of the disease. They can also pose a threat to human health (some notifiable diseases are zoonoses). Examples of notifiable diseases include avian influenza, bovine spongiform encephalopathy (BSE), foot and mouth disease and Newcastle disease.

7 The Skeletal System

Learning objectives

In this chapter you will learn about:

1 Functions of the skeleton

2 The structure of bone

3 Connective tissue

4 Muscle types

Functions of the skeleton

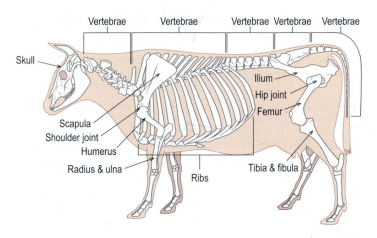

Fig 7.1 *Skeleton of a cow*

The skeleton is the framework that gives the body its shape. Figure 7.1 shows the name and location of the major bones in the animal body. The skeleton has a number of important functions, including:

- **Support:** It gives the body shape and supports the soft tissues of the body, some of which are attached to the skeleton, e.g. muscles, tendons.

- **Protection:** Some skeletal bones provide protection to the internal organs by enclosing them and protecting them from injury, e.g. the ribcage protects the heart and lungs, the skull protects the brain and the vertebrae protect the spinal cord.

- **Movement:** Muscles are attached to bones, so when they contract they cause bones to move.

- **Mineral storage:** Calcium (Ca) and phosphorus (P) are stored in bone. They can be released into the bloodstream when needed.

- **Production of blood cells:** Red blood cells are produced in bone marrow.

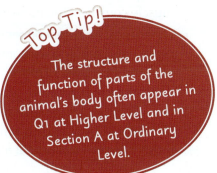

Top Tip!

The structure and function of parts of the animal's body often appear in Q1 at Higher Level and in Section A at Ordinary Level.

The structure of bone

- **Joint:** The place where two or more bones meet.
- **Cartilage:** A layer of tissue that is found on bones in between joints. It is softer than bone and reduces friction where bones meet as joints.
- **Spongy bone:** This occurs in long bones and contains red bone marrow, which is responsible for the production of red blood cells.
- **Medullary cavity:** This is also known as the marrow cavity. It contains yellow marrow, which is responsible for the production of white blood cells.
- **Compact bone:** This is the outer layer of bone. It is white in appearance and is hard.

The composition of bone is both organic and inorganic. One of the main organic components of bone is collagen, a form of protein that is mainly found in connective tissues such as tendons, ligaments and cartilage in addition to bone. It is not found in plants. The inorganic component of bone consists of bone minerals such as calcium (Ca).

Connective tissue

Connective tissue in the animal body has a number of functions. It provides support and protection, stores fat, forms blood cells and binds structures together. There are a number of types of connective tissue in the mammalian body, including loose connective tissue, fibrous connective tissue and muscular tissue.

- **Adipose tissue:** A loose type of connective tissue. Its main function is to **store fat**. It is also used for **insulation**. It is found **beneath the skin and around internal organs** such as the kidneys.

- **Tendons:** Connect muscle to bone. They are inelastic fibres consisting of **collagen**. Due to the attachment of a muscle to a bone via a tendon, when a muscle contracts the bone moves with it.
- **Ligaments:** Another connective tissue consisting of fibres of **collagen**. Ligaments connect two bones together at a joint. They are slightly elastic, allowing the joints to move, while at the same time controlling the range of movement of the joints.
- **Muscle:** Accounts for approximately 40% of the body's total weight. When muscles contract (or shorten), they cause movement in the body. Some muscle, known as skeletal muscle, is attached to bone.

Muscle types

There are three types of muscle in the body: skeletal muscle, smooth muscle and cardiac muscle. Each has its own characteristic composition, location and function.

- **Skeletal muscle:** This type of muscle is attached to the bones of the skeleton. It is also found in the diaphragm and between the ribs. It is a **voluntary muscle** that is under conscious control, i.e. it does not move of its own accord. One of its main functions is for **movement and breathing**. In the mammalian body, skeletal muscle assists the movement of the legs.
- **Smooth muscle:** This type of muscle is found in the internal organs, such as the digestive system, the blood vessels and the reproductive system. It is an **involuntary muscle** that moves independently. Some of its functions include the movement of food through the alimentary canal (oesophagus), which is known as **peristalsis**, and dilation of the cervix during birth.
- **Cardiac muscle:** This type of muscle is only found in the **heart**. It is an involuntary muscle that **does not fatigue** and is responsible for pumping blood around the body in the circulatory system.

Questions

1. Name **two** chemical elements that influence bone formation in animals.
2. Mention **four** functions of bones in the animal body.

Exam question

1. State the precise location of the humerus in the body of a mammal. *(OL 2012)*

Key-points!

- The skeleton's main functions include support, protection, movement, mineral storage and production of blood cells.

- Adipose tissue is a loose connective tissue found beneath the skin and around internal organs. Its main function is the storage of fat.

- There are three types of muscle: smooth, skeletal and cardiac.

- Joint: The place where two or more bones meet.

- Cartilage: A layer of tissue between joints that is softer than bone and reduces friction.

8 The Digestive System

Digestion

The breakdown of food into components that can be used within the body is called digestion. Digestion occurs in two ways: mechanical and chemical.

- Mechanical digestion is the physical breakdown of food into smaller pieces.
- Chemical digestion is the chemical breakdown of food by substances known as enzymes.

Food is first taken into the body through the mouth, where both mechanical and chemical digestion first occur.

The digestive process

1 Ingestion is the intake of food into the mouth, where it is chewed and swallowed.

2 Digestion is the breakdown of food by mechanical and chemical means.

3 Absorption takes place when food that has been digested enters the bloodstream.

4   Assimilation is the use and conversion of absorbed nutrients within the body.

5   Egestion is the removal from the body of undigested material remaining from the digestive process.

The tooth

Teeth are used in the first stages of digestion to break up food into smaller pieces by tearing, crushing and grinding it. There are four types of tooth: incisor, canine, premolar and molar. Each has a different shape and function. The number and type of teeth present in an animal's mouth is related to the diet of the animal.

Key definitions

Incisor: Chisel-like tooth used for cutting and biting.

Canine: Pointed, sharp tooth used for tearing food.

Premolar: Relatively flat tooth used for grinding.

Molar: Flat tooth used for crushing food.

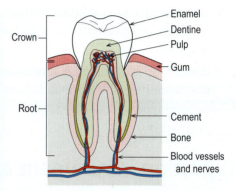

Fig 8.1 *A longitudinal section of a tooth*

- **Herbivores**, which only eat plant material, use their premolars and molars for crushing and grinding material such as grass. Sheep, cattle and horses are all herbivores.
- **Carnivores**, which eat meat, use their canine teeth for tearing flesh.
- **Omnivores** such as pigs, which eat both plant material and meat, do not have a specialised dentition but use all the types of teeth listed to aid the digestion of a variety of foods.

Dental formulas of animals

Dental formulas are written to represent the dentition in the upper and lower jaw of the mouth of the animal. The formulas given show the number of incisors, canines, premolars and molars present on one side of the mouth, as the other side of the mouth is identical.

Top Tip!

Students are often asked to give the dental formula of a pig or ruminant animal.

Dental formula of a pig

$$I: \frac{3}{3} \quad C: \frac{1}{1} \quad P: \frac{4}{4} \quad M: \frac{3}{3}$$

Dental formula of a herbivore
(cow, sheep, goat)

$$I: \frac{0}{3} \quad C: \frac{0}{1} \quad P: \frac{3}{3} \quad M: \frac{3}{3}$$

Chemical digestion in the mouth

- The mouth has three pairs of salivary glands.
- The glands secrete an enzyme called amylase.
- The amylase breaks down starch to maltose.
- Saliva also acts as a lubricant that wets the food and makes it easier to chew and swallow.
- When food is swallowed, it is passed to the oesophagus. It is moved along the oesophagus to the stomach by peristalsis.

> ### Key definition
>
> **Peristalsis:** Food entering the oesophagus is moved along to the stomach by muscular contractions, which have a rhythmic, wave-like motion.

Digestion in ruminant animals

Cattle and sheep are ruminant herbivores. They have a ruminant stomach with four chambers: the rumen, reticulum, omasum and abomasum. This allows them to digest cellulose, which is found in grass, the main constituent of their diet.

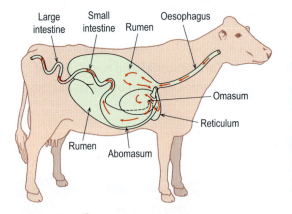

Fig 8.2 *Ruminant digestive system*

> ### Key definition
>
> **Ruminant animal:** Any animal that has a stomach that is modified and adapted for the digestion of cellulose. The stomach has four separate chambers, each with a specialised function.

The rumen

- Food that is swallowed by the ruminant animal is passed down the oesophagus to the rumen.
- The rumen contains microorganisms such as bacteria and protozoans that allow the ruminant animal to consume and digest fibrous plant material such as grass, hay and silage.
- The rumen is an anaerobic environment with a pH in the range of 6.5 to 7.0.
- The microbes break down the cellulose into smaller molecules such as glucose to provide energy for the animal. Other products resulting from the breakdown of cellulose include carbon dioxide and methane gas. The rumen contracts to force these gases out of the rumen.

Key definition

Symbiosis: A relationship where both species benefit. For example, the ruminant animal and the microbes living in the rumen have a symbiotic relationship. The microbes help to break down the cellulose for the animal and the animal provides a suitable living environment and nutrient supply to the microbes.

The reticulum

The reticulum is the second chamber of the ruminant stomach. It resembles a honeycomb in its appearance. It is responsible for regurgitating partially digested material from the rumen back to the mouth for further chewing. This is known as chewing the cud.

The omasum

The omasum is the third chamber of the ruminant stomach. Food that has been regurgitated for further chewing is passed to the omasum when it is swallowed. The omasum has many layers of tissue that squeeze the food and reabsorb water from it.

The abomasum

The abomasum is the fourth chamber in the ruminant stomach. It acts much like the stomach of a monogastric animal (human or pig). Digestive enzymes (protease and gastric lipase) are secreted here to aid the final stage of digestion, which is the digestion of proteins and fats. Because of the similarity between the abomasum and the monogastric stomach, it is often called the 'true stomach'.

The small intestine

The first section of the small intestine is called the duodenum. Bile and pancreatic juices are secreted into the small intestine to aid the breakdown of food and the absorption of nutrients through the thin intestinal wall. Bile is secreted by the liver and stored in the gall bladder. Its role is to emulsify fats and lipids in the duodenum. It also helps to neutralise food that has come from the acidic stomach environment.

Pancreatic juice contains a number of enzymes that aid in the digestion of food.

As the digested food makes its way through the duodenum, about 90% of the nutrients released in digestion are absorbed. Food is moved through the small intestine by peristalsis.

The large intestine

The large intestine consists of the caecum and the colon. Its main function is to absorb water and to pass waste to the rectum for egestion through the anus. Bacteria in the colon manufacture vitamin K, which is also absorbed by the body.

Digestive disorders in ruminant animals

Bloat occurs in cattle that have been put on early grass. Gases build up in the rumen and are unable to escape. The left side of the abdomen becomes swollen. In mild cases this can be relieved by an antacid solution. A tube may also be inserted through the mouth into the rumen to release the gas. In more severe cases the use of a trocar and cannula is necessary to relieve the bloat.

Acidosis occurs in ruminant animals when the pH of the rumen falls below 5.5. The result of this is that the rumen stops moving, which leads to a loss of appetite in the animal. Acid-loving microbes take over, producing even more acid. The acid can be absorbed through the walls of the rumen, which in severe cases can lead to death. Acidosis is brought on by feeding animals a diet of high concentrates/rapidly digestible carbohydrates/low fibre. Excess lactic acid is produced that cannot be used up quickly enough. Signs of acidosis include reduced milk yield, weight loss, loss of condition and reduced appetite.

Digestion in monogastric animals

A monogastric animal has only one stomach, e.g. pigs. They cannot digest cellulose. The digestive system of a monogastric animal works in the exact same way as that of a human. Food is passed from the oesophagus directly to the stomach for digestion. The monogastric stomach is the equivalent of the abomasum in a ruminant animal. Assimilation and absorption of nutrients in the small and large intestines are carried out in the same way as in the ruminant.

The digestive system of a chicken

Digestion in poultry is different from that in ruminant or monogastric animals. Chickens have a short, sharp beak that aids them in eating grains. Food is passed down the oesophagus to the stomach. Unlike other animals, birds possess a **crop**, which allows them to **store food** for later consumption. Food can be passed from the crop to the stomach when it is needed.

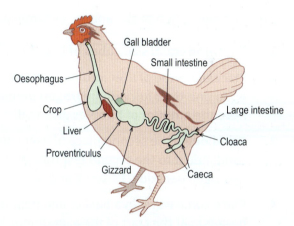

Fig 8.3 A chicken's digestive system

The stomach of a bird consists of two parts:

- **Proventriculus:** Secretes enzymes and digestive juices to aid chemical digestion.
- **Gizzard:** Grit swallowed by poultry is stored in the gizzard and used to grind down food mechanically.

Digested food is then passed to the intestines for assimilation. As birds do not have a separate digestive and urinary tract, urine and faeces are excreted together.

Functions of the liver

- **Production:** The liver secretes bile, which emulsifies fats and lipids in the duodenum. Bile produced by the liver is stored in the gall bladder.
- **Storage:** Glucose in the form of glycogen is stored in the liver, along with minerals such as copper and iron and fat-soluble vitamins A, D, E and K. Stored glycogen can be broken down into glucose for use in the body when blood glucose levels are low.

- **Breakdown of toxic substances:** Ammonia is converted to urea in the liver. Ammonia is one of the substances produced when excess amino acids are broken down.
- **Breakdown of red blood cells:** Red blood cells are broken down in the liver and used as pigments in the production of bile.
- **Temperature regulation:** Heat is produced by the liver and warms the blood as it passes through the organ. This helps to regulate the temperature of the body.

 Experiment

To demonstrate the action of the animal enzyme liver catalase

1 Cut **three equal size cubes of liver** from a **fresh liver sample**.

2 Place one cube of liver into the bottom of a test tube and fill the test tube up to one-third full with **hydrogen peroxide**. Observe the reaction and **note the amount of bubbles** given off.

3 **Grind down** the second piece of liver using **the mortar and pestle and sand**. Add it to the second test tube and fill to the **same depth** with hydrogen peroxide. Observe and note the reaction.

4 Place some water in a beaker and heat to boiling on a hot plate. (This can be set up at the start of the experiment.) Add the third piece of liver to the boiling water to 'cook' it.

5 Remove the **cooked liver** from the boiling water with the forceps. Add it to a third test tube and add hydrogen peroxide as in the previous two test tubes. Keep all three test tubes at a **constant temperature.** Observe any reaction.

Result

Hydrogen peroxide is broken down in the liver by catalase. More oxygen bubbles are produced in the second sample, as the liver has a greater surface area. There is no reaction in sample 3, as the enzymes were denatured when the liver was boiled.

Questions

1 Draw a labelled diagram of the digestive system of a **named** monogastric animal.

2 Describe a laboratory method to determine the action of a named animal enzyme.

3 Using labelled diagrams, where appropriate, compare the digestive system of a named adult ruminant with that of a named non-ruminant animal under the following headings:
   (a) Structure
   (b) Function

4 Give a scientific explanation for a change in the colour of blue litmus on being poured into the dissected stomach of an animal.

5 Give a scientific explanation for a difference in the dental formula in a ruminant and a monogastric animal.

6 Give a scientific explanation for a low water content in food as it passes through the abomasum of a ruminant animal.

Exam questions

1 Describe an experiment to investigate the action of one **named** digestive enzyme.   *(OL 2011)*

2 State the precise location and function of the abomasum in the animal body.
                                                                                (HL 2012)

Key-points!

- Carnivores use their canines to eat meat. Herbivores use their premolars and molars to grind plant material and vegetations. Omnivores eat both plant and animal material.
- Dental formula of a pig: $I: \dfrac{3}{3}$ $C: \dfrac{1}{1}$ $P: \dfrac{4}{4}$ $M: \dfrac{3}{3}$
- Dental formula of a herbivore (cow, sheep, goat): $I: \dfrac{0}{3}$ $C: \dfrac{0}{1}$ $P: \dfrac{3}{3}$ $M: \dfrac{3}{3}$
- The rumen is the first chamber of the ruminant stomach. It contains bacteria and protozoans that aid in the breakdown of fibrous plant material.
- The reticulum is the second chamber in the ruminant stomach. It is responsible for regurgitating partially digested material from the rumen back to the mouth for further chewing.
- The omasum is the third chamber in the ruminant stomach. The omasum has many layers of tissue that squeeze the food and reabsorb water from it.
- The abomasum is the fourth chamber in the ruminant stomach. Digestion of proteins and fats by enzymes takes place here.
- The functions of the liver include the production of bile, the storage of glucose as glycogen, the storage of vitamins and minerals, the breakdown of toxic substances and temperature regulation.

9 The Kidney and the Urinary System

Learning objectives

In this chapter you will learn about:

1 The urinary system

2 Structure and function of the kidney

3 Production of urine

4 Excretion

The main function of the kidney in the body is the production of urine. It is also responsible for the removal of wastes from the blood, such as excess water, salt and urea. The kidneys form an important part of the urinary system.

The urinary system

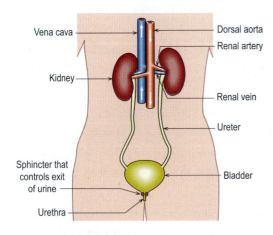

Fig 9.1 *The urinary system*

- **Kidney:** Site where urine is produced.
- **Ureter:** A duct that connects the kidney to the bladder, carrying urine to the bladder for storage.

- **Bladder:** Urine is stored here until it is expelled from the body.
- **Urethra:** A duct through which urine is expelled from the body.
- **Renal artery:** Supplies oxygenated blood to the kidney from the dorsal aorta. This blood also carries wastes to be filtered from the blood.
- **Renal vein:** Carries blood away from the kidney after it has been filtered.

Structure and function of the kidney

The kidney consists of approximately 1 million tubules called nephrons. The function of the nephron is to produce urine.

Production of urine

- Blood enters the glomerulus and is filtered under high pressure.
- Glucose, salts and waste filter from the glomerulus through the walls of the Bowman's capsule. The filtered blood leaves the glomerulus through the arteriole.
- The filtrate moves from the Bowman's capsule to the proximal convoluted tubule for reabsorption. **Selective reabsorption** of nutrients prevents the constant removal of glucose, salts and water from the blood. Nutrients and water are reabsorbed by a combination of active transport and osmosis into the capillaries. Na^+ and Cl^- ions are also reabsorbed. Other toxins accumulated by the body are added to the waste fluid as it passes through the distal convoluted tubule.

> **Key definition**
>
> **Selective reabsorption:** A process where the body reabsorbs certain molecules for use in the body by active transport.

Excretion

Water is also reabsorbed from the collecting duct by osmosis. Reabsorption is controlled by a hormone called anti-diuretic hormone (ADH), which is produced in the pituitary gland. ADH increases the permeability of the collecting duct, allowing water to be absorbed. The more water that is reabsorbed, the smaller the volume of urine that is produced. If the osmotic pressure of the blood falls, ADH is not produced by the pituitary gland. The collecting duct ceases to be permeable and water is not reabsorbed. A greater volume of urine is produced.

Questions

1   Give a scientific explanation for the production of urine in the animal body.

2   Draw a labelled diagram of the urinary system.

Exam question

1   Where in a pig's body would you find the ureter and what is the ureter's function?   *(HL 2002)*

Key-points!

- The main function of the kidney in the body is the production of urine. It is also responsible for the removal of wastes from the blood, such as excess water, salt and urea.

- Selective reabsorption is a process where the body reabsorbs certain molecules for use in the body. This includes glucose, salt and water.

- Anti-diuretic hormone (ADH) is produced by the pituitary gland and controls the reabsorption of water.

The Circulatory System, Blood and the Lymphatic System

10

Learning objectives

In this chapter you will learn about:

1 Arteries, veins and capillaries

2 Blood

3 Regulation of body temperature

4 Environmental consideration and critical temperature

5 The lymphatic system

6 The immune system

Arteries, veins and capillaries

The circulatory system in vertebrates is a closed system and is known as the cardiovascular system. It transports oxygen and nutrients to cells and carries waste away from cells. The heart is central to this system and acts as a pump to keep blood moving around the body. Blood is transported around the body in three types of blood vessels: arteries, veins and capillaries.

Table 10.1 Blood vessels and their structure and function

	Arteries	Veins	Capillaries
Function	Transport blood away from the heart	Transport blood to the heart	Connect arteries to veins

	Arteries	Veins	Capillaries
Structure	Thick elastic walls

No valves

Fast blood flow, has a pulse | Thin walls

Have valves to prevent the backflow of blood

Slow blood flow, no pulse | Walls only one cell thick

No valves

Slow blood flow, no pulse

Semipermeable, allowing gaseous exchange by diffusion |

Blood

Circulation of blood

1   Deoxygenated blood (low in O_2, high in CO_2) is carried to the heart through the vena cava and enters the right atrium (auricle).

2   Blood then passes from the right atrium through the tricuspid valve into the right ventricle.

3   It then leaves the right ventricle through the pulmonary artery, which brings the deoxygenated blood to the lungs, where gaseous exchange takes place.

4   Oxygenated blood leaves the lungs through the pulmonary vein and is brought back to the heart, where it enters the left atrium.

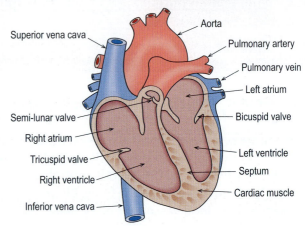

Fig 10.1 The heart

5   It passes through the bicuspid valve into the left ventricle. It exits the left ventricle through the aorta to be pumped around the body.

Constituents of blood

Blood has a number of important functions in the animal body, including transport, providing immunity and temperature regulation. Blood consists of a liquid called plasma and three types of cell that are suspended in the plasma. The cells are red blood cells, white blood cells and platelets.

Table 10.2 Constituents of blood

Constituent	Role
Red blood cells (red blood corpuscle)	Contain the pigment haemoglobin. Haemoglobin contains iron, which binds to oxygen molecules, allowing oxygen to be transported around the body. Low iron levels cause a lack of haemoglobin, which is known as anaemia. Red blood cells are produced in bone marrow.
White blood cells	Immune response. White blood cells move to the site of infection to destroy invading pathogens. Some white blood cells produce antibodies.
Platelets	Fragments of cells produced in bone marrow that help clot the blood.
Plasma	Liquid part of blood. Glucose, proteins, vitamins, minerals and salts are dissolved in plasma and transported around the body. It also contains wastes.

Blood clotting

- Two proteins, fibrinogen and prothrombin, are produced in the liver and deposited in blood plasma.
- When a blood vessel is damaged, platelets form a cluster at the site to partially seal the wound. The damaged tissue and the platelets release an enzyme called thromboplastin.
- This converts the protein prothrombin into a substance called thrombin. Calcium ions need to be present for this reaction to take place.
- Thrombin then converts fibrinogen from its soluble form in the blood plasma into an insoluble form. The insoluble fibrinogen is simply known as fibrin.
- Fibrin forms threads that trap red blood cells, allowing a blood clot to form. This seals the wound, preventing further blood loss and preventing microbes from entering the wound.

Functions of blood: summary

- **Transport:** Nutrients and oxygen, wastes and carbon dioxide are carried in the blood. Hormones are also carried in the blood to their site of action.
- **Immunity:** Defence against disease-causing pathogens through the production of antibodies. Blood clotting by platelets prevents pathogens from entering an open wound.
- **Temperature regulation:** Heat produced in the liver as a result of metabolism is carried around the body in the bloodstream.

Regulation of body temperature

Cattle, sheep and pigs have normal body temperatures in the range of 38°C to 39°C. There can be a slight variation in these temperatures depending on the animal.

Animals can control their body temperature in a number of ways:

- **Keeping the body warm:** Movement (walking, running, shivering), wool, hair, burning energy through respiration.
- **Keeping the body cool:** Lying in a shaded area, sweating, rolling in mud (pigs).

Environmental consideration and critical temperature

The environment an animal is kept in plays an important role in **thermoregulation**. This is particularly the case in pig production. If housing is too cold, the pig must use energy to keep warm; and if it is using energy for warmth, it is not using it to gain weight. The same can be said if housing is too warm and an animal needs to cool down. The point at which pigs must use energy to increase heat production within the body to keep warm is called the lower critical temperature. The point at which they need to cool down is called the upper critical temperature. Pigs should be kept within the upper and lower range for optimum production.

Factors that affect the critical temperature of an animal include age, weight, feed intake, feed type, building type, building insulation and floor type.

The lymphatic system

The lymphatic system transports fluid called lymph around the body. It consists of a network of capillaries, ducts and nodes. It is separate from the circulatory system while at the same time it is closely linked to it.

Functions of the lymphatic system

The lymphatic system has three main functions:

- Collect excess tissue fluid and return it to the bloodstream
- Absorb fats from the intestine and transport them to the bloodstream
- Defend the body against disease.

The immune system

There are two types of immunity: active immunity and passive immunity.

Active immunity

Point to note

Immunity is an organism's ability to resist disease. It can be achieved in three ways: by the production of antibodies and white blood cells in response to exposure to the disease, by inoculation against the disease, or by the transfer of antibodies from a mother to her young.

Active immunity is acquired when the body is infected by bacteria or a virus. The body produces antibodies to fight the infection. These antibodies persist to provide protection against the disease in the future.

Active immunity can also be acquired artificially by a vaccine. Vaccines are viruses and bacteria that have been treated so they no longer cause disease. When a vaccine is administered to an animal, its body produces antibodies in response. If the animal comes in contact with the disease, those antibodies are ready to attack the bacteria or virus and protect the body.

Passive immunity

Passive immunity is short-term immunity due to the fact that the individual did not itself produce the antibodies, but acquired them either through the mother's milk in the days following birth or when antibodies are passed across the placenta from mother to foetus. The young animal acquires the same antibodies present in the mother's body. It is important for young animals to consume the first milk (colostrum) produced by the mother, for this reason.

Exam questions

1   Use a labelled diagram to describe the structure of a sheep's heart.   (HL)

2   (a) Name the disease caused by a lack of iron in the animal diet.

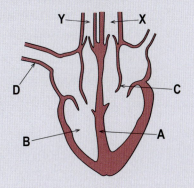

Fig 10.2

   (b) Discuss the role of iron in the blood.

   (c) Mention **one** way of preventing iron deficiency in livestock.

   (d) The diagram shows a dissected mammalian heart. Name the parts labelled A, B, C and D.

   (e) State the destination of the blood flowing in:
     (i) X   (ii) Y

   (f) State the key characteristic of the blood
     (i) X   (ii) Y.   (HL 2011)

3   Explain the difference between active and passive immunity and give an
    example of each from agriculture.   (HL 2011)

4   Give three functions of the lymphatic system in mammals.   (HL 2014)

5   The liver is often referred to as a storage organ.
    (a) Name two substances that are stored in the liver of a farm animal.
    (b) Name two other locations in the animal body where metabolically
        useful substances are stored and indicate the substance stored in
        each case.   (HL 2014)

Key-points!

- Blood is transported around the body by arteries, veins and capillaries. Arteries carry blood away from the heart, veins carry blood to the heart and capillaries connect arteries to veins.

- Blood consists of red blood cells, which carry oxygen, white blood cells, which fight infection, platelets needed for blood clotting and plasma, which is a liquid in which all blood cells are carried and nutrients are dissolved.

- Blood plays a role in transport (nutrients, wastes), immunity and temperature regulation.

- Thermoregulation is the control of temperature within the body.

- Critical temperature is the maximum or minimum temperature the animal body reaches before it needs to cool down or warm up.

- The functions of the lymphatic system are to collect excess tissue fluid and return it to the bloodstream, to absorb fats from the intestine and to defend the body against disease.

- Active immunity is acquired when the body is infected by bacteria or a virus. The body produces antibodies to fight the infection. Active immunity can also be acquired artificially by a vaccine.

- Passive immunity is short-term immunity acquired from antibodies received either through the mother's milk in the days following birth or when antibodies are passed across the placenta from mother to foetus.

The Respiratory System 11

Equation for respiration

Respiration involves the intake of oxygen (inhalation) and the removal of carbon dioxide (exhalation) from the body through the lungs. Oxygen is used in the breakdown of glucose to produce energy. Carbon dioxide and water are waste products of this process.

$$Glucose + Oxygen \rightarrow Carbon\ dioxide + Water + Energy$$

The intake of oxygen and the removal of carbon dioxide by the lungs is known as gaseous exchange.

Parts and function of the respiratory system

- Air is inhaled through the nose and mouth, passing through the pharynx and the glottis, which opens into the larynx. The epiglottis closes over the throat when swallowing food to prevent it from entering the respiratory system.
- The air passes through the larynx to the trachea. The trachea is held open permanently by the rings of cartilage, which give it shape and structure.
- The trachea divides into two bronchi that lead into the left and right lungs, which are protected by the ribs. Movement of the rib cage outwards and upwards during inhalation is assisted by the intercostal muscles. The diaphragm located below the lungs flattens during inhalation to allow the lungs to expand. During exhalation, the diaphragm and ribs return to their normal position, forcing air out of the lungs.
- Inside the lungs, the bronchi split into a number of smaller ducts called bronchioles, which get smaller as they branch. Each bronchiole ends in an

air sac called an alveolus. **Gaseous exchange** takes place in the alveoli.

- The alveoli are thin, elastic tissues that can expand when they inflate with air. Each alveolus is wrapped in blood capillaries. Gaseous exchange occurs by diffusion between the blood capillaries and alveoli.

- Inhaled air contains a high concentration of oxygen. This is higher than the oxygen concentration in the blood capillaries. Therefore, the oxygen diffuses from the

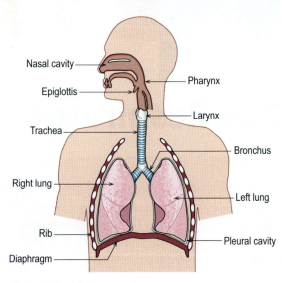

Fig 11.1 *Respiratory anatomy*

alveoli into the capillaries and is transported to where it is needed. The capillaries also have a high concentration of carbon dioxide, which is higher than the concentration in the inhaled air in the alveoli. The carbon dioxide diffuses from the capillaries into the alveoli and from there it is exhaled.

Question

1   Give a scientific explanation for the increase in the rate of breathing of a farm animal following excessive exercise.

Exam questions

1   Draw a labelled diagram to describe the structure of the lung of a farm animal.   *(OL 2000)*

2   State the precise location of the trachea in the body of a mammal.   *(OL 2012)*

3   State the precise location and function of the alveolus in the body of a farm animal.   *(HL 2012)*

Key-points!

- Respiration equation: Glucose + Oxygen $\rightarrow$ Carbon dioxide + Water + Energy
- Gaseous exchange takes place in the alveoli of the lungs and by the process of diffusion.

The Brain, Nervous System and Endocrine System   12

Learning objectives

In this chapter you will learn about:

1 The nervous system

2 Functions of the brain

3 The endocrine system

The nervous system

Animals use their skeleton and muscles, their brain, nerves and hormones to respond to stimuli. The brain, nervous system and hormones (endocrine system) control the behaviour and actions of animals in a rapid response to a stimulus.

The nervous system in vertebrate animals consists of two parts: the central nervous system (CNS) and the peripheral nervous system (PNS).

The central nervous system (CNS):

- Consists of the brain and spinal cord
- Receives sensory information through cranial nerves.

The peripheral nervous system (PNS):

- Consists of sensory nerves and motor nerves.
- The sensory nerves include the cranial nerves, which bring sensory information to the brain and spinal cord from sensory organs such as the ear or skin.
- Other internal organs, such as the lungs, heart and digestive system, are monitored by the automatic nervous system and are not under the conscious control of the animal.

Functions of the brain

The brain has a number of different regions, each with its own function.

- **Cerebral hemispheres:** Used for reasoning, hearing (and the other senses) and memory.
- **Cerebellum:** Regulates balance, movement and muscle coordination.
- **Pituitary gland:** Secretes hormones (see 'The endocrine system' section below).
- **Medulla oblongata:** Controls automatic functions such as breathing and heartbeat.

The endocrine system

Endocrine glands secrete hormones into the bloodstream. Hormones are produced in very small quantities and transported by the circulatory system to specific parts of the body, where they can stimulate or inhibit actions in the target organ or tissue.

Table 12.1 Endocrine glands, hormones and their function

Gland	Location of gland	Hormone secreted	Function of hormone
Pituitary	Brain	Growth hormone	Regulates growth of bone and other tissues
		Prolactin	Production of milk
		ADH	Regulates water retention in the body. Raises blood pressure
		Oxytocin	Contractions during birth. Milk let-down after birth
Thyroid glands	Below larynx in neck	Thyroxine	Regulates metabolism. Responsible for growth
Parathyroid glands	Embedded in the surface of the thyroid glands	Parathyroid hormone (PTH)	Controls the level of calcium in the bones and blood
Pancreas	Above the duodenum	Insulin	Controls blood sugar (glucose) levels
Adrenal glands	Above the kidneys	Adrenalin	Causes the body to respond to a stress

Gland	Location of gland	Hormone secreted	Function of hormone
Testes	Scrotum	Testosterone	Development of male sex characteristics
Ovary	Female reproductive system	Progesterone	Growth of uterus and inhibition of lactation and labour during pregnancy
		Oestrogen	Development of female sex characteristics

Point to note

Freemartin condition: This condition occurs in mixed-sex twin calves (one heifer calf and one bull calf). While in the uterus, hormones from the male twin pass to the female twin. The male hormones masculinise the female and the result is known as a freemartin. The female calf will be infertile and cannot be used for breeding. Her genitals will be reduced in size.

Question

1 Name the hormone-producing organs in the male and female reproductive systems in animals.

Exam questions

1 Explain the term *freemartin condition*.   (HL 2010)

2 State the location of the cerebrum in the animal body.   (OL 2011)

3 State the location of the cerebellum in the animal body.   (OL 2012)

4 Outline the role of any **one** hormone in milk production in a lactating cow.
                                                                     (HL 2012)

Key-points!

- The central nervous system consists of the brain and spinal cord.
- The peripheral nervous system consists of motor neurons and sensory neurons.
- The pituitary gland is responsible for the production of a number of hormones, including growth hormone, prolactin, ADH and oxytocin.
- Freemartin condition occurs in mixed-sex twin calves, where hormones from the male twin pass to the female twin in the womb, causing her to be infertile.

13 Reproduction in Animals

Learning objectives

In this chapter you will learn about:

1 Asexual and sexual reproduction

2 The male reproductive system

3 The female reproductive system

4 Male and female sex hormones

5 Gestation, oestrous and oestrous cycle

6 Birth hormones – the role of oxytocin and prolactin

Asexual and sexual reproduction

Reproduction is the method by which animals pass their genes on to their offspring, ensuring the survival of the species. There are two main patterns of reproduction: asexual and sexual.

Asexual reproduction only involves one parent and the offspring is identical to the parent in terms of its genetic makeup.

Sexual reproduction takes place in vertebrates and involves sex cells known as gametes. Gametes produced by a female are called eggs and those produced by a male are called sperm. When animals reproduce sexually, the offspring produced inherits half of its genes from one parent and half from the other parent. Reproductive organs that produce gametes (sex cells) are known as gonads.

The male reproductive system

- In the male reproductive system, the gonads are the testes, which are paired. The testes are responsible for the production of the male gametes (sperm). The testes are suspended in the scrotum, which hangs outside the body cavity. This is to keep sperm at a lower temperature, allowing it to develop and mature properly.

- Sperm is stored in the epididymis. It is also stored in a duct leading out of the epididymis called the vas deferens.

- As sperm travels along the vas deferens, three fluids are secreted from the seminal vesicle, the prostate gland and Cowper's glands.
- The combination of sperm and fluids is known as semen.
- The sperm has a head, which contains the genetic material, and a tail (flagellum), which enables it to swim.

The female reproductive system

- The gonads in a female are called the ovaries. Ovaries produce eggs (ova).
- Fertilisation of eggs by sperm takes place in the fallopian tubes.
- The fertilised egg, known as a zygote, then makes its way to the uterus (womb), where it implants itself in the uterine wall.
- As the cells divide in the zygote and it starts to develop, it is known as an embryo.
- The narrow opening at the end of the uterus is called the cervix, which dilates during birth. The vagina, which held the penis during copulation, also serves as the birth canal when the young animal is born.

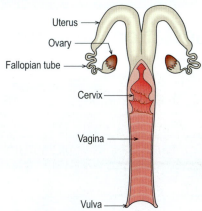

Uterus
Ovary
Fallopian tube
Cervix
Vagina
Vulva

Fig 13.1 *A cow's reproductive organs*

Male and female sex hormones

Table 13.1 Male and female hormones		
Hormone	Function in male	Function in female
FSH	Promotes sperm production	Promotes the development of a follicle that produces oestrogen
LH	Controls the production of testosterone	Stimulates ovulation Promotes the development of the corpus luteum, which secretes progesterone
Testosterone	Development of male sex characteristics and male sex organs	

Hormone	Function in male	Function in female
Oestrogen		Promotes the development of female sex characteristics, including the development and growth of mammary glands
Progesterone		Allows the uterus to grow during gestation Inhibits lactation and labour during pregnancy Inhibits the immune response to the embryo

Gestation, oestrous and oestrous cycle

Top Tips!

Students are often asked to distinguish between the following terms:

Gestation is the term given to pregnancy in mammals. It is the period of time from conception to birth.

Oestrous: The time when a female animal is 'in heat' and releases eggs during a process called ovulation.

Duration of oestrous: The length of time during which an egg has been released from the ovary and is available for fertilisation.

Oestrous cycle: A recurring cycle that is the length of time between consecutive heat periods in an animal.

Table 13.2 Gestation period, oestrous cycle and duration of oestrous of cattle, sheep and pigs

Animal	Gestation	Oestrous cycle	Duration of oestrous
Cow	9.5 months (283 days)	21 days	18–24 hours
Sheep	5 months (149 days)	17 days	36 hours
Pig	3 months, 3 weeks and 3 days (115 days)	21 days	2–3 days

Seasonal breeding is determined by the length of day (photoperiod). Sheep are short-day breeders and breed when the length of daylight shortens (autumn and winter).

Birth hormones – the role of oxytocin and prolactin

- Oxytocin is responsible for contractions in the uterine wall during birth and milk let-down after the birth.
- The production of oxytocin is stimulated by suckling in mammals, when a signal is sent from the udder to the brain.
- The message is relayed to the posterior pituitary gland and oxytocin is secreted.
- This causes the milk ducts to contract and let down the milk to the young mammal.
- Prolactin is responsible for the production of milk in mammals.

Question

1 Name the parts labelled A, B, C and D of the genital tract of a cow, as in the diagram.

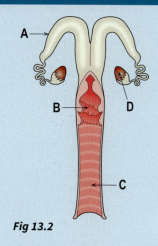

Fig 13.2

1   State the location of the testes in the body of the mammal.   *(OL 2011)*

2   The gestation period in pigs is three months, three weeks and three days. True or false?   *(OL 2012)*

Key-points!

- Testosterone is responsible for the development of male sex characteristics. Oestrogen is responsible for the development of female sex characteristics, such as the mammary glands.

- Oxytocin is responsible for contractions in the uterine wall during birth and milk let-down after the birth.

- Prolactin is responsible for the production of milk in mammals.

- Gestation is the period of time from conception to birth in mammals.

- Oestrous is the time during which a female ovulates, or is 'in heat'. Oestrous cycle is the period of time that elapses between successive ovulations.

- Duration of oestrous is the length of time during which an egg has been released from the ovary and is available for fertilisation.

- Polyoestrous refers to animals that come into heat repeatedly at regular intervals. Seasonally polyoestrous animals come into heat repeatedly but only for a certain period of the year.

UNIT 4

Mitosis and Meiosis

14

Chromosomes

The nucleus of the cell is composed of a material called **chromatin**. Chromatin is a mixture of **DNA** (deoxyribonucleic acid) and protein. Prior to the start of cell division, the chromatin forms structures called **chromosomes**. Sections of DNA on a chromosome code for the production of proteins. These sections are called **genes**. Chromosomes occur in pairs, and a cell with a complete set of chromosomes is known as **diploid**, or **2n. Somatic cells** (body cells other than gametes) are all diploid. A cell with half a set of chromosomes is known as **haploid**, or **n. Gametes** (egg and sperm cells) are haploid.

Significance of mitosis

- Mitosis produces two genetically identical daughter cells.
- Mitosis allows for the growth, repair and replacement of dead and worn-out cells.
- Meristematic tissue (found in the tips of plant roots and shoots) is constantly producing new cells by mitosis.
- In animals, mitosis occurs in the bone marrow to produce new red blood cells.
- Mitosis occurs during metamorphosis in insects.

Interphase

- Cells spend the majority of their time in this phase.
- The cell grows bigger and produces additional organelles.
- The cell **prepares itself for cell division**.
- The nuclear membrane is still present and the chromatin has not yet formed chromosomes.

Stages of mitosis

Mitosis can be divided into four main stages: prophase, metaphase, anaphase and telophase.

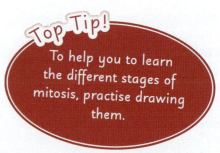

Top Tip!
To help you to learn the different stages of mitosis, practise drawing them.

Table 14.1 Stages of mitosis

Stage of mitosis	Diagram of stage
1 Prophase • **Chromosomes become visible and duplicate themselves** • **Nuclear membrane and the cell organelles disappear** • **Spindle fibres start to form**	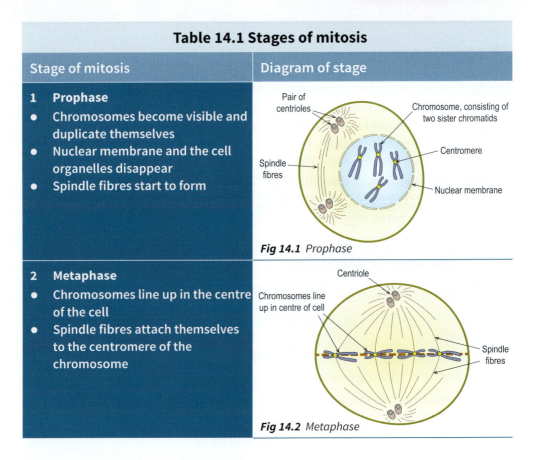 *Fig 14.1* Prophase
2 Metaphase • **Chromosomes line up in the centre of the cell** • **Spindle fibres attach themselves to the centromere of the chromosome**	*Fig 14.2* Metaphase

3 Anaphase • Spindle fibres contract, separating the duplicated chromosome from its copy • Chromosomes are pulled to opposite poles of the cell	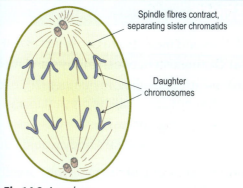 Spindle fibres contract, separating sister chromatids Daughter chromosomes *Fig 14.3* Anaphase
4 Telophase • Final stage of cell division • Cytoplasm divides to form two new cells in animal cells • Chromosomes uncoil to form chromatin • Nuclear membrane reforms • In plant cells, a cell plate grows between the two new cells and a new cell wall develops from this	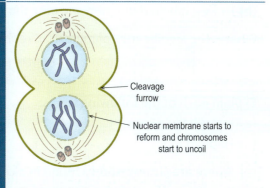 Cleavage furrow Nuclear membrane starts to reform and chromosomes start to uncoil *Fig 14.4* Telophase

Significance of meiosis

- Meiosis reduces the chromosome number by half.
- Meiosis produces gametes (egg and sperm).
- Cells produced by meiosis are haploid, or n (cells have half a set of chromosomes).
- Meiosis occurs in the reproductive organs (testes and ovaries) of animals and the ovaries and pollen of plants.
- **Crossing over** (homologous chromosomes swap genetic information) occurs during meiosis. This brings about **variation in the combination of genes** in the resulting gametes.
- Upon fertilisation, the diploid chromosome number is restored.

Questions

1   Mitosis and meiosis are two types of cell division on your course.
   (a) Distinguish between mitosis and meiosis.
   (b) In cattle, the diploid number (2n) of chromosomes is 60. How many chromosomes will be present in a gamete?
   (c) What are gametes?
   (d) Where in an animal's body would you expect to find gametes?

2   (a) Mitosis is one of the two types of cell division. Name the other type of cell division.
   (b) Draw a labelled diagram showing the metaphase stage of mitosis.

3   What is the significance of meiosis in reproduction?

Exam questions

1   Explain **each** of the following terms:
   (a) Interphase
   (b) Haploid.   *(HL 2011)*

2   (a) Where are chromosomes found in a cell?
   (b) What type of cell division leads to a reduction in chromosome number?
   (c) What term is used to describe the number of chromosomes in a sex cell?
                                                                    (OL 2009)

Key-points!

- Chromosomes occur in pairs. A cell with a complete set of chromosomes is known as diploid, or 2n. Somatic cells (body cells other than gametes) are all diploid.

- A cell with half a set of chromosomes is known as haploid, or n. Gametes (egg and sperm cells) are haploid.

- Mitosis produces two genetically identical daughter cells. Mitosis allows for the growth, repair and replacement of dead and worn-out cells.

- Interphase: Cells spend the majority of their time in this phase. During interphase, the cell prepares itself for cell division.

- Mitosis can be divided into four main stages: prophase, metaphase, anaphase and telophase.

- Meiosis reduces the chromosome number by half. Meiosis produces gametes (egg and sperm). Cells produced by meiosis are haploid, or n (cells have half a set of chromosomes).

Monohybrid and Dihybrid Crosses

15

Learning objectives

In this chapter you will learn about:

1 Genetic terms

2 Gregor Mendel and his laws of inheritance

3 Monohybrid crosses

4 Incomplete dominance

5 Dihybrid crosses

6 Sex determination

7 Sexed semen

8 Sex linkage or X-linkage

Genetic terms

Genetics is the study of inheritance.

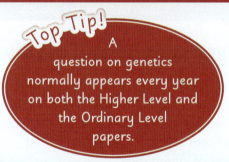

Top Tip! A question on genetics normally appears every year on both the Higher Level and the Ordinary Level papers.

Table 15.1 Summary of genetic terms

Term	Meaning
Gene	Part of a chromosome that contains information to produce a protein.
Alleles	Alternative forms of the same gene, e.g. height in pea plants; Tall (T) and dwarf (t).
Gamete	Sex cell (egg and sperm). Gametes are haploid (n).

Term	Meaning
Genotype	The genes present in the organism whether they are expressed or not, e.g. TT, Tt and tt.
Phenotype	Outward appearance of the organism.
Dominant	Expressed in the phenotype when present in the genotype and normally represented by a capital letter, e.g. T.
Recessive	Expressed only when an individual has no dominant gene present and is usually represented with a lower case letter, e.g. t.
Homozygous	The alleles present in the genotype are the same, e.g. TT (homozygous dominant) or tt (homozygous recessive). True breeding.
Heterozygous	The alleles present in the genotype are not the same, e.g. Tt. This organism has one dominant and one recessive gene. Commonly known as a hybrid.
Incomplete dominance	Neither allele present in the genotype is dominant. This results in a blend of the two alleles in the phenotype, e.g. Shorthorn cattle, red x white = roan.
Multiple alleles	When a characteristic is controlled by two or more alleles, the alleles are known as multiple alleles, e.g. blood groups in humans.
Continuous variation	When a characteristic is controlled by a number of genes interacting with each other to give a range of phenotypes rather than two distinct groups.

Gregor Mendel and his laws of inheritance

Mendel was the first scientist to identify patterns of inheritance. He completed all his genetic studies on pea plants. He identified that the characteristics of the pea plant were controlled by a pair of 'factors'. Today these factors are called genes. From these studies he identified two laws of inheritance.

Mendel's second law only applies to genes that are not linked (linked genes occur on the same chromosome). If genes occur on the same chromosome, it is possible for them to travel together into the gamete.

Top Tip!

It is important to be able to define genetic terms and definitions. Both the Higher Level and the Ordinary Level papers often ask students to explain the meaning of genetic terms.

Why did Mendel use pea plants?

- The traits he chose had easily distinguishable alternatives (round and wrinkled seeds).
- He could concentrate on the inheritance of one characteristic at a time.
- He controlled pollination by crossing the plants by hand.
- Peas are easily grown and produce a large number of seeds.
- The traits he chose were controlled by genes that were not linked, but rather occurred on different chromosomes.

Monohybrid crosses

A monohybrid cross studies the inheritance of one characteristic. In the following examples, there is one allele for the **dominant** characteristic and the other form is **recessive**.

Example 15.1

In guinea pigs, the allele for black coat (B) is dominant over the allele for brown coat (b). A homozygous black coat guinea pig is crossed with a homozygous brown coat guinea pig. Give the genotypes and phenotypes of the F1 produced by this cross.

Answer

Parents' genotypes:	BB	×	bb
Gametes:	Ⓑ		ⓑ

F1	Bb
F1 Genotype:	100% Bb
F1 Phenotype:	100% black

Top Tip!

When describing a cross, it is important to use headings to clearly identify the parents' genotypes, the gametes produced and the genotypes and phenotypes of the offspring. Get into the habit of laying out your crosses with headings when you practise questions, especially at Higher Level. On the Ordinary Level paper, students are normally asked to copy the headings given in the question paper into their answer book.

Example 15.2

In peas, the allele for round seed (R) is dominant over the allele for wrinkled seed (r). Outline the cross between a heterozygous round seeded plant and a wrinkled seeded plant. In your answer show the gametes produced and the genotypes and the phenotypes of the offspring. *(HL 2007)*

Point to note

In the question, the second parent has the wrinkled seed characteristic expressed in its phenotype. As the gene for wrinkled seed is recessive, this parent must have both recessive genes for this characteristic to be expressed. The first parent is heterozygous, meaning this parent has both the dominant and recessive gene present in its genotype.

Answer

Parents' genotype:	Rr	×	rr
Gametes:	Ⓡⓡ		ⓡ

F1 punnett square

Gametes	R	r
r	Rr	rr

F1 Genotypes:	50% Rr and 50% rr
F1 Phenotypes:	50% round and 50% wrinkled
Ratio:	1:1

Example 15.3

In maize, **G** represents green and **g** represents albino. 55 maize seeds are sown and the results show 42 green plants and 13 albino plants. Show by means of a suitable cross how this result might occur with homozygous parents. *(HL 2009)*

Point to note

The final ratio of green to albino plants in this example is roughly 3:1, a typical Mendelian ratio. This ratio occurs when you cross two parents whose genotype is heterozygous for the characteristic.

Answer

Parents:	GG (green)	×	gg (albino)
Gametes:	Ⓖ		ⓖ

F1 Genotype:	Gg
F1 Phenotype:	100% green

F1 × F1:	Gg	×	Gg
Gametes:	Ⓖ and ⓖ		Ⓖ and ⓖ

F2 (second generation) punnett square

Gametes	G	g
G	GG	Gg
g	Gg	gg

F2 Genotypes:	25% GG, 50% Gg and 25% gg
F2 Phenotypes:	75% green and 25% albino
Ratio:	3:1

Point to note

When an organism has a heterozygous genotype, it is often referred to as a hybrid. Plants and animals that are produced from genetically different parents often display increased productivity. This is referred to as **heterosis** or **hybrid vigour**.

Example 15.4

In guinea pigs, the allele for black coat (B) is dominant over the allele for brown coat (b). A pair of guinea pigs produces a litter of eight piglets; four of the litter are black and four are brown.

  (a) Give the genotypes and phenotypes of the parents.
  (b) Using a punnett square and labelling all genotypes and phenotypes, illustrate the cross.
  (c) What name is given to this type of cross? *(HL 2010)*

Answer

(a) **Parents' genotypes:**   Bb   ×   bb
     Parents' phenotypes: Black   Brown

     Gametes: ⓑ and ⓑ   ×   ⓑ

(b) **F1 punnett square**

Gametes	B	b
b	Bb	bb

     F1 Genotypes: 50% Bb and 50% bb
     F1 Phenotypes: 50% black and 50% brown
     Ratio: 1:1

(c) Back cross or test cross.

Incomplete dominance

In all of the examples above, one allele is dominant and the other allele is recessive. In the following example, there are two alleles of equal dominance. When they occur together in the genotype, the resulting phenotype is a blend of the two alleles. A common example of this occurs when you cross red snapdragons with white snapdragons – all the resulting offspring are pink.

Example 15.5

In sweet peas, a cross between a red-petalled plant and a white-petalled plant produces pink-petalled flowers in the progeny. Explain why this happens and show the cross using a diagram. *(HL 2005)*

Answer

The reason the offspring (F1) are all pink is as a result of incomplete dominance. For the parent plants to be red and white, they must be homozygous red (RR) and homozygous white (rr). When an allele for red petals (R) and an allele for white petals (r) occur together in the genotype, both alleles are equally dominant, and as a result the phenotype of the offspring is pink.

Parents' genotypes:	RR	×	rr
Parents' phenotypes:	Red		White
Gametes:	Ⓡ		ⓡ

F1	Rr
F1 Genotype:	100% Rr
F1 Phenotype:	100% pink

Example 15.6

Roan coat colour in Shorthorn cattle occurs as a result of incomplete dominance. Use a cross to show how roan coat colour arises from homozygous parents. *(HL 2011)*

Answer

This is a repeat of example 15.5. Roan coat colour arises when you cross a purebred red-coated Shorthorn with a purebred white-coated Shorthorn. Both alleles for red coat and white coat are equally dominant, so both are expressed in the phenotype of the offspring, resulting in the roan coat colour.

Parents' genotypes:	RR	×	rr
Parents' phenotypes:	Red coat		White coat
Gametes:	Ⓡ	×	ⓡ

F1	Rr
F1 Genotype:	100% Rr
F1 Phenotype:	100% roan coat colour

Example 15.7

Red flower colour in sweet pea plants is a homozygous dominant condition (RR). Pink flowering sweet pea plants were crossed with pink flowering sweet pea plants. The seeds from these plants were collected and sown and the new plants produced flowers as shown:

Number of plants with red flowers: 27
Number of plants with pink flowers: 56
Number of plants with white flowers: 29

(a) State the genotype of the original pink flowering parents.

(b) Explain how the three flower types shown above resulted from a cross between two pink-flowered plants.

(c) What offspring would result if a pink flowering sweet pea plant were crossed with a red flowering sweet pea plant? Describe this cross and state the genotype and phenotype of the offspring produced. *(HL 2003)*

Answer

(a) This cross is an example of incomplete dominance, as there are three phenotypes in the offspring. Therefore, the parents' genotypes must be Rr × Rr.

(b) The cross is easily explained by showing it as follows:

Parents' genotypes:	Rr	×	Rr	
Parents' phenotypes:	Pink	×	Pink	
Gametes:	Ⓡⓡ	×	Ⓡⓡ	

F1 punnett square

Gametes	R	r
R	RR	Rr
r	Rr	rr

F1 Genotype: 25% RR, 50% Rr and 25% rr
F1 Phenotype: 25% red, 50% pink and 25% white

(c) 50% of the offspring would be pink (Rr) and 50% would be red (RR).

Parents' genotypes:	Rr	×	RR
Parents' phenotypes:	Pink	×	Red
Gametes:	Ⓡⓡ	×	Ⓡ

F1 punnett square

Gametes	R	r
R	RR	Rr

F1 Genotype: 50% RR and 50% Rr
F1 Phenotype: 50% red and 50% pink

Example 15.8

In cereal trials for oats, the pure-breeding variety Barra, with a straw length of approximately 500 mm, was crossed with the pure-breeding variety Evita, with a straw length of approximately 800 mm. The resulting hybrid had an approximate straw length of 650 mm.

(a) Using B to represent the 500 mm gene and E to represent the 800 mm gene, show how this result arose.

(b) Using a punnett square or other suitable method, show the genotypes and matching phenotypes resulting from a cross between two of the new hybrids. *(HL 2012)*

Answer

(a) This cross is another example of incomplete dominance.

Parents' genotypes:	BB	×	EE
Parents' phenotypes:	500mm	×	800mm
Gametes:	Ⓑ	×	Ⓔ

F1 Genotype: 100% BE

F1 Phenotype: 650 mm straw length

(b) Cross between two of the hybrids BE

F1 x F1:	BE	×	BE
Gametes:	Ⓑ Ⓔ	×	Ⓑ Ⓔ

> **Top Tip!**
> This question specifies that a punnett square or other suitable method must be used. If a punnett square is not included in your answer, then it is likely that marks will be lost.

F2 punnett square

Gametes	B	E
B	BB	BE
E	BE	EE

F2 Genotype		Phenotype
25% BB	→	500 mm
50% BE	→	650 mm
25% EE	→	800 mm

> **Top Tip!**
> The question asks to show genotype and matching phenotype, so your answer must show this to ensure that all marks are awarded.

Dihybrid crosses

Dihybrid crosses involve the inheritance of two characteristics.

Example 15.9

In certain species of plants, the allele for straight stamen (S) is dominant to the allele for incurved stamen (s) and the allele for plain petal (P) is dominant to the allele for striped petal (p). If pollen from a homozygous straight stamen plain petal flower pollinates a flower with incurved stamens and striped petals:

(a) State the genotype of the seeds formed.
(b) Describe the phenotypes of flowers produced when the seeds germinate and grow.
(c) What ratio of offspring phenotypes could result from a cross between the F1 hybrid plant in (b) and a plant that is recessive from both traits?
(HL 2006)

Answer

(a) The seeds produced can be worked out by doing out the initial cross with the parents. As this is a dihybrid cross, both parents must have two alleles for each characteristic.

Point to note

The question does not tell us that the second parent is **homozygous** incurved stamens and striped petals. However, as these alleles are recessive, the parent must be homozygous (sspp) for these traits to be visible in the phenotype of the parent.

Parents' genotypes:	SSPP	×	sspp
Parents' phenotypes:	Straight and plain		Incurved and striped
Gametes:	SP	×	sp

Point to note

The gametes produced by these parents must have one gene from each **pair**. This fulfils Mendel's Law of Segregation.

F1	SsPp
Genotype of seeds formed:	100% SsPp

(b) Phenotype of the seeds when they germinate and grow: 100% straight stamens and plain petals.

(c) Cross between F1 hybrid from the above cross and a plant recessive for both traits:

Genotype of F1:   SsPp

Genotype of plant recessive for both characteristics: sspp

Cross: SsPp   ×   sspp

Gametes: × (sp)

Point to note

The parent SsPp will produce **four** different combinations of genes in its gametes. To identify the possible gametes produced, arrows can be used, as illustrated in Fig 15.1. First draw an arrow from the **first allele** to the **third and fourth allele**. This gives the first two gametes, which are then circled.

Fig 15.1

This step is repeated using arrows from the **second allele** to the **third and fourth allele**, giving the last two remaining gametes.

Fig 15.2

Point to note

Identification of all the possible types of gametes produced during a cross is fulfilling Mendel's Law of Independent Assortment.

The parent sspp produces only one type of gamete, as the alleles for each characteristic are identical.

F2 punnett square

Gametes	sp
SP	SsPp
Sp	Sspp
sP	ssPp
sp	sspp

Genotype: 25% SsPp, 25% Sspp, 25% ssPp and 25% sspp

Phenotype: 25% straight stamens and plain petals (SsPp)

                         25% straight stamens and striped petals (Sspp)

                         25% incurved stamens and plain petals (ssPp)

                         25% incurved stamens and striped petals (sspp)

Ratio of offspring phenotypes: 1:1:1:1

Example 15.10

A maize plant, heterozygous for the recessive alleles hairless tassel (h) and short anther (l), is self-fertilised and the seeds are collected. The genes for tassel type and anther length are not linked. Use a cross to illustrate what proportion of the offspring you would expect to show:

(a) Hairy tassel
(b) Short anther
(c) Hairy tassel and short anther. *(HL 2011)*

Answer

In the question, you are told that the maize plant is 'self-fertilised'. Therefore, the maize plant is crossed with itself.

Parents' genotypes: HhLl   ×   HhLl

Gametes:

The gametes are identified using the method from the previous example.

F2 punnett square

Gametes	HL	Hl	hL	hl
HL	HHLL	HHLl	HhLL	HhLl
Hl	HHLl	HHll	HhLl	Hhll
hL	HhLL	HhLl	hhLL	hhLl
hl	HhLl	Hhll	hhLl	hhll

Genotypes: **Phenotypes:**

$\frac{1}{16}$ HHLL

$\frac{2}{16}$ HHLl

$\frac{2}{16}$ HhLL

$\frac{4}{16}$ HhLl

9 hairy tassel and long anther

$\frac{1}{16}$ HHll

$\frac{2}{16}$ Hhll

3 hairy tassel and short anther

$\frac{1}{16}$ hhLL

$\frac{2}{16}$ hhLl

3 hairless tassel and long anther

$\frac{1}{16}$ hhll

1 hairless tassel and short anther

What proportion of offspring will have:

(a) Hairy tassel? Only those with Hh or HH in their genotype will give hairy tassels. Using the results above, 12 out of the 16 will have hairy tassels.

(b) Short anther? Only those with ll in their genotype will give short anthers; 4 out of 16 will have short anthers.

(c) Hairy tassel and short anther? Only those with the genotype HHll or Hhll will have hairy tassel and short anther in their phenotype; therefore 3 out of 16 will have this phenotype.

Sex determination

Sex is determined by a pair of sex chromosomes (the X and Y chromosomes). Females are XX and males are XY.

Males have two different sex chromosomes, the X and the Y chromosome. As a result they produce two different sperm cells: sperm that have an X chromosome in them and sperm that carry a Y chromosome. As all female egg cells have an X chromosome, it is the male sperm that is responsible for determining the sex of their offspring. Consequently, many AI stations in Ireland now offer sexed semen. Sexed semen has sperm carrying X chromosomes separated from sperm carrying Y chromosomes.

Sexed semen

In dairy herds, heifer calves are more desirable than bull calves, because heifer calves can be used as replacements or to expand the dairy herd. However, with conventional AI semen or with a stock bull, there is only a 50% chance of a heifer calf being produced.

Bull semen can be divided or sexed into two groups – sperm carrying Y chromosomes and sperm carrying X chromosomes. This is achieved by using an instrument called a flow cytometer, which can separate sperm cells based on their difference in total DNA. Sperm cells with an X chromosome have approximately 3.8% more DNA than sperm cells carrying a Y chromosome.

Advantages of sexed semen

- There is a 90% chance of producing a heifer calf using sexed semen.
- Sexed semen can be used to produce more heifer calves, which can be reared as replacement heifers in the dairy herd.
- It allows for the expansion of a dairy herd.
- It maintains biosecurity by allowing a farmer to keep a closed herd.
- It reduces the number of male dairy calves being born.
- It can reduce the risk of calving difficulties in maiden heifers, as heifer calves are smaller than bull calves.
- Sexed semen containing the Y chromosome can be used on genetically superior cows to produce bulls for breeding purposes.

Disadvantages of sexed semen

- It means a 10% chance that a male calf can be produced.
- Sexed semen is more expensive than conventional non-sexed semen.
- It results in reduced conception rates due to some sperm damage during the separation process. In addition, sexed semen has less sperm per straw than non-sexed semen straws.

Sex linkage or X-linkage

In males, the Y chromosome is much smaller than the X chromosome. As a result, the Y chromosome does not contain the same amount of genetic information as the X chromosome. The X chromosome carries a number of genes that are not related to sex determination. Some genes that are carried on the X chromosome have no corresponding copy on the Y chromosome (e.g. genes for colour vision and blood clotting in humans). These genes are known as sex-linked or X-linked, as they are only found on the X chromosome.

X-linked genes were first identified by Thomas Hunt Morgan when he was carrying out genetic crosses using fruit flies (*Drosophila melanogaster*). White eye in fruit flies, haemophilia and colour blindness in humans are all caused by recessive genes carried on the X chromosome. Sex-linked traits are more prominent in males than in females. If a male (having only one X chromosome) inherits a recessive gene for colour blindness or haemophilia, this gene is expressed in the phenotype, as there is no copy of the gene on the Y chromosome. Females having two X chromosomes need to inherit two copies of the recessive gene for it to be expressed in their phenotype.

Why fruit flies are used in the study of genetics

- Fruit flies are easy to keep.
- They produce large numbers of offspring.
- They produce a new generation every two weeks.
- They have only four pairs of chromosomes.
- Their mutations are well documented.

Questions

1 In tomato plants, the allele for purple stems (P) is dominant to the allele for green stems (p), and the allele for green fruit (G) is dominant to the allele for yellow fruit (g). A tomato plant heterozygous for stem colour and fruit colour is self-fertilised and the F1 seeds produced are planted the following year. Use a cross to illustrate what proportion of the offspring you would expect to show:
   (a) Purple stems
   (b) Yellow fruit
   (c) Purple stems and yellow fruit.

2 A purebred mouse with brown fur (B) was crossed with a purebred mouse with white fur (b). The resulting hybrid mice all had speckled fur.
   (a) With the use of a cross, show how this result occurred.
   (b) Two of the F1 hybrid speckled mice were crossed. Using a punnett square, show the genotypes and the matching phenotypes resulting from this cross.

Exam questions

1 Explain the following terms:
   (a) Recessive gene
   (b) Sex-linked gene
   (c) Multiple alleles
   (d) Continuous variation
   (e) Incomplete dominance
   (f) Sexed semen
   (g) Allele.

2 (a) The gender of offspring is determined by the male parent in mammals. Illustrate this statement in terms of chromosomes.

  (b) A broad-leaved red-flowered snapdragon was crossed with a narrow-leaved white-flowered snapdragon and all the offspring were broad-leaved with pink flowers.

    (i) Suggest why all the offspring were broad leaved.

    (ii) Suggest why all the offspring had pink flowers.

    (iii) List the phenotypes that may result from a cross between two plants heterozygous for both traits. *(HL 2008)*

3 Explain each of the following:

  (a) The appearance of roan coat colour in Shorthorn cattle

  (b) Continuous variation in many characteristics associated with higher organisms

  (c) Why some defective phenotypes are more common in males than in females. *(HL 2006)*

4 In guinea pigs the genes for hair colour and length are located on non-homologous chromosomes. The allele for black (B) is dominant to the allele for brown (b) and the allele for short hair (S) is dominant to the allele for long hair (s). If two guinea pigs, both heterozygous for hair colour and length, were mated, state:

  (a) The phenotypes that might appear in the offspring

  (b) The ratio of these phenotypes. *(HL 2004)*

5 In maize, the traits pigmy size (n) and crinkly leaf (r) are recessive to the traits normal size (N) and regular leaf (R). A maize plant, heterozygous for size and leaf shape, is self-pollinated and 160 seeds are subsequently collected and germinated.

  (a) Write the genotype of the parent using the above notation.

  (b) How many of the new plants would you expect to show:

    (i) Crinkly leaves

    (ii) Regular leaves

    (iii) Normal size and regular leaves

    (iv) Pigmy size and regular leaves. *(HL 2014)*

Key-points!

- A gene is part of a chromosome that contains information to produce a protein.
- Alleles are different forms of the same gene.
- Dominant genes are expressed in the phenotype when present in the genotype and are normally represented by a capital letter, e.g. B. Recessive genes are expressed only when there is no dominant gene present and are usually represented with a lower case letter, e.g. b.
- Genotype: This means the genes present in the organism and whether they are expressed or not, e.g. BB, Bb and bb. The phenotype is the outward appearance of the organism.
- Homozygous: The alleles present in the genotype are the same, e.g. BB and bb.
- Heterozygous: The alleles present in the genotype are not the same, e.g. Bb. Heterozygous genotype is commonly known as a hybrid.
- Law of Segregation: When gametes are formed, only one allele from a pair of alleles is carried into the gamete.
- Law of Independent Assortment: During gamete formation, members of a pair of alleles segregate and move into the gamete independently of any other pair of alleles.
- A monohybrid cross studies the inheritance of one characteristic.
- Dihybrid crosses involve the inheritance of two characteristics.
- When laying out genetic crosses in your answer book, always use headings: parents' genotype, gametes, genotypes and phenotypes. Use a punnett square to work out all the possible offspring genotypes produced by a cross.
- Incomplete dominance: Neither allele present in the genotype is dominant. This results in a blend of the two alleles in the phenotype, e.g. roan colour in Shorthorn cattle.
- Sex is determined by a pair of sex chromosomes (the X and Y chromosomes). Females are XX and males are XY.
- Sexed semen is used by some dairy farmers because there is a 90% chance of producing a heifer calf. This provides more heifer calves, which can be reared as replacements or for the expansion of the herd. Using sexed semen lessens the risk of calving difficulties, as heifer calves are smaller than bull calves. A disadvantage of this is that sexed semen is expensive and conception rates are lower.
- The X chromosome carries a number of genes that are not related to sex determination. Some genes that are carried on the X chromosome have no corresponding copy on the Y chromosome (e.g. genes for colour vision and blood clotting in humans). These genes are known as sex-linked or X-linked, as they are only found on the X chromosome.

16 Applied Genetics

Learning objectives

In this chapter you will learn about:

1 Selective breeding

2 Reproductive technologies

3 Mutations

4 Genetic modification

5 Polyploidy

Point to note

Applied genetics is the manipulation of the hereditary characteristics of an organism in order to improve or produce desirable characteristics in offspring. This can be done using selective breeding (inbreeding and crossbreeding) and genetic engineering.

Top Tip!

This section often appears in a genetics question and should not be ignored when revising the previous two chapters.

Selective breeding

Selective breeding can also be used to eliminate undesirable traits. Selective breeding is sometimes known as **artificial selection**. Selective breeding of animals produces **breeds** (e.g. Holstein, Jersey, etc.) and the selective breeding of plants produces **cultivars** or **varieties** (e.g. Kerr's Pink and Golden Wonders are varieties of potatoes). The selective breeding of plants and animals can be divided into **inbreeding** and **crossbreeding**.

Key definition

Selective breeding is the process of breeding animals or plants with desirable traits and to concentrate those desirable traits in their offspring.

Inbreeding

Advantages

- Fixes desirable genetic traits, such as high milk yields in purebred dairy cows
- Creates uniformity among the offspring
- Produces pedigree animals (purebred animals) whose lineage is known (ancestry) and are registered with a breed society or stud book
- Used to produce stock or purebred lines in plants.

Disadvantages

- Increases the inheritance of similar genes, leading to an increase in homozygous genotypes (BB or bb)
- Concentrates undesirable recessive traits
- Increases the chances of lethal genes occurring, which can result in the death of the organism
- In Holsteins this has led to an increase in calving intervals
- May make animals more susceptible to disease
- Leads to a loss in genetic diversity.

> **Key definition**
>
> **Inbreeding:** The mating of closely related animals or plants.

Crossbreeding

Advantages

- Offspring often inherit favourable genes from both parents, which leads to increased productivity. This is known as hybrid vigour.
- Crossbreeding often leads to better health traits and lifespan in the offspring.
- It reduces the risk of recessive genes appearing in the phenotype.
- It increases the number of heterozygous pairs of genes.

> **Key definition**
>
> **Crossbreeding** (outbreeding) involves the mating of animals or plants from two different breeds, varieties or species.

> **Key definition**
>
> **Hybrid vigour (heterosis)** is the increased productivity displayed by offspring from genetically different parents.

Disadvantages

- When horses are crossed with donkeys, the resulting offspring (mules) are infertile.
- Crossbreeding results in loss in uniformity of the offspring.

- There is a loss of hybrid vigour, with subsequent crossing of the hybrids or crossbred animals.
- Crossbred animals cannot be registered with a breed society or breed register, as they are not purebred.

F1 hybrid seed varieties

F1 hybrids are produced by crossbreeding two genetically different purebred parents. The hybrids are usually stronger, have greater disease resistance and produce higher yields.

- The parent plants are inbred over several generations.
- Parent plants are called breeding stock.
- Parent plants are crossed (usually by hand pollination).
- This produces the seeds that are a hybrid.

Advantages

- F1 hybrids benefit from hybrid vigour.
- F1 hybrids are uniform in phenotype.

Disadvantages

- F1 hybrids are expensive to produce.
- The parent plants (breeding stock) must be crossed every year.
- If the F1 hybrids are crossed to form an F2, there is a loss in uniformity and in hybrid vigour.

Reproductive technologies

Reproductive technologies have led to an increase in the number of offspring that can be produced from genetically superior plants and animals, an increase that would otherwise not be possible naturally. Micropropagation, grafting and cuttings are used extensively in horticulture to increase the number of plant offspring (see pp.32–33).

Artificial insemination (AI)

AI is a routine procedure used on many farms (particularly dairy farms) to increase the genetic merit of the herd.

How are AI straws produced?

Initially the semen is collected from the bull. The semen is diluted using an extender (usually a mixture of egg yolk and glycerol), which protects against cold shock and damage during freezing. The extender also contains glucose, which is a source of energy for the sperm cells and a buffer to prevent any pH changes of the solution. The diluted sperm is packed into a plastic straw and stored in liquid nitrogen at −196°C. Before insemination, the straws are thawed in warm water.

Advantages of AI

- AI allows maximum use of superior bulls.
- Bulls have been performance and progeny tested.
- AI allows a wide choice of bulls.
- AI prevents the spread of sexually transmitted diseases.
- The semen can be sexed to produce only heifer calves (see p.101).
- The cost of a straw is small in comparison to the cost of keeping a bull.
- AI increases the number of cows served by a genetically superior bull than would otherwise be possible by natural means.

> ## Key definitions
>
> **Performance testing:** The evaluation of a bull's performance by comparing its weight gain and food conversion ratio (FCR) with other bulls kept under similar feed and housing conditions.
>
> **Progeny testing:** The evaluation of the performance of a bull's offspring compared to other bulls' offspring kept under similar feed and housing conditions.

Disadvantages

- Successful heat detection is crucial.
- More labour and management skills are required compared to natural service with a stock bull.
- AI has a lower conception rate compared to using a fertile stock bull.
- Inseminations must be carried out by a trained AI technician.
- Semen must be stored properly; otherwise it will not be viable.
- Farmers may still need to keep a stock bull for mopping up at the end of the breeding season. (Mopping up involves a stock bull detecting and servicing any cows or heifers not in calf.)

- Artificial insemination (AI) is used on many farms. It has a number of advantages, including: it allows for the maximum use of superior bulls, bulls have been performance and progeny tested, there is a wide choice of bulls and it is cheaper than the cost of keeping a bull. Successful heat detection and lower conception rates are disadvantages of AI.

- Performance testing: The evaluation of a bull's performance by comparing its weight gain and food conversion ratio (FCR) with other bulls kept under similar feed and housing conditions.

- Progeny testing: The evaluation of the performance of a bull's offspring compared to other bulls' offspring kept under similar feed and housing conditions.

- EBI: A single-figure profit index given in euro of profit per lactation for the animal's progeny compared to an average dairy cow. The objective of the EBI is to identify genetically superior sire and dam lines in the dairy herd and to use this to improve the average dairy production through selective breeding.

- Genomic selection evaluates bulls and heifers on the basis of their DNA profile. The animal's DNA profile can then be used to predict its EBI. Genomic selection identifies high EBI sires at a young age without having to wait a number of years for that sire's offspring to be progeny tested.

- Embryo transplantation involves the collection of embryos from a donor animal and implanting these embryos into a surrogate mother or recipient. The donor animal is given hormone injections to bring about super ovulation. The donor eggs can be fertilised using AI inside the uterus or, alternatively, *in vitro*. The embryos are then transferred to a surrogate mother.

- Cloning produces genetically identical animals. There are many disadvantages to cloning, including a high failure rate in cloning animals, a reduction in biodiversity and the emergence of ethical issues surrounding the use of cloning.

- A mutation is a permanent change in the DNA sequence of a gene in an organism. Mutations in genes are sources of new alleles. Mutations are rare and random events. Factors that cause mutations are called mutagens. X-rays, radiation, radon gas and colchicines are all known mutagens.

- Genetic modification involves the insertion of beneficial genes into the chromosomes of plants and animals from unrelated species. Plants and animals produced by genetic modification are known as transgenic species or genetically modified organisms (GMOs). Genetically modified plants have increased crop yields and are resistant to herbicides, pests and diseases.

- Polyploidy describes cells that contain more than two sets of chromosomes. Polyploidy occurs as a result of abnormal cell division. It is more commonly found in plants, e.g. wheat and rye grass.

Soil Formation and Classification

17

Rock types

Rocks are divided into groups based on how they are formed. There are three groups of rocks: igneous, sedimentary and metamorphic. All three groups provide the parent material from which the mineral matter in our soils originates.

Igneous

A liquid called magma is found underneath the earth's crust. Magma is molten (melted) rock. When magma cools it solidifies and forms rock. When magma appears above the earth's surface it is called lava. This also cools to form rock. The type of rock that is formed when magma or lava solidifies is called **igneous rock**.

As magma cools, it forms crystals that consist of minerals. If magma cools quickly the crystals will be small, but if it cools slowly the crystals formed are large. The three most common crystals formed are quartz, feldspar and mica. Their properties determine the characteristics of the rock in which they are found and in turn the soil that is formed when that rock is weathered. Quartz is acidic, while feldspar is alkaline.

Granite and basalt are the two most common igneous rocks found in Ireland. Granite contains a lot of quartz and therefore is an acidic rock. The soils formed from granite are also acidic. Basalt is less acidic, as it contains only a small amount of quartz. It does contain feldspar, which makes it smoother and more fine grained. The soils that are formed from basalt take the same form.

Sedimentary

Millions of years ago, layers of sediment were deposited at the bottom of seas and lakes. These layers built up and slowly compacted in the process. As they compacted they solidified to form what is known as sedimentary rock.

Mineral sediments are of different sizes. The largest particles (quartz) were washed up on shores and are commonly known as sand. Smaller particles known as clay were brought further out to sea for deposition. Clay particles are a result of the weathering of igneous rock. The shells of fossils that contain lime were deposited in deep water. Each of the three types of sediment was compacted over time to form a different type of rock: sandstone, shale and limestone, respectively.

Table 17.1 Characteristics of sedimentary rocks

Particle type	Rock formed	pH
Sand (quartz)	Sandstone	Acidic
Clay	Shale	Less acidic
Fossils and shells	Limestone	Alkaline

Metamorphic

Metamorphic rocks are formed from igneous or sedimentary rocks. Heat or pressure change the rock. Metamorphic rocks, like igneous and sedimentary rocks, have an influence on the acidity or alkalinity of the soils formed from them. If the metamorphic rock is acidic, the soil formed when it is weathered will also be acidic.

Table 17.2 Metamorphic rock formation

Rock type	Rock group	Metamorphic rock formed
Limestone	Sedimentary	Marble
Shale	Sedimentary	Slate
Granite	Igneous	Gneiss
Sandstone	Sedimentary	Quartzite

Weathering and decomposition of rocks

Weathering of rock takes place when rock is broken down by physical (mechanical) or chemical means.

Physical weathering

Table 17.3 Physical weathering of rocks

Weathering effect	Description
Heating and cooling	Rock minerals expand with increased temperatures. Expansion of minerals at different rates causes rocks to shatter. Minerals will also contract as they cool, causing further breakdown.
Freezing/frost action	Cracks in rock are filled by water, which freezes and expands. Rock shatters, creating more cracks that fill with water and continue the same process.
Root activity	Roots of trees penetrate cracks in rocks, putting pressure on rock and causing it to break.
Animal activity	Digging and burrowing cause the breakdown of rock over time.
Grinding action/ erosion	Rocks and rock particles are moved by water, wind and gravity. They erode rock material as they are transported. Glaciers also level land and move rocks, causing breakdown.

Chemical weathering

Table 17.4 Chemical weathering of rocks

Weathering effect	Description
Hydrolysis	Hydrogen ions in water react with rock minerals, forming hydroxide compounds that release minerals into the soil.
Oxidation and reduction	Oxidation takes place in dry conditions in the presence of oxygen, e.g. haematite is formed by oxidation. Reduction takes place in wet conditions where oxygen is absent, e.g. iron is dissolved and removed from rock.
Hydration	Hydration occurs through the addition of water to rock minerals. It combines with minerals that expand, causing rock to break down.
Solution and carbonation	Minerals dissolve in water as it percolates through rock. If water reacts with carbon dioxide it forms carbonic acid, which dissolves alkaline minerals in rock.

Organic parent materials

- Organic parent materials consist of the remains of plants that have partially decomposed.
- These remains accumulate in wet, waterlogged conditions and often in lakes.
- The wet, waterlogged conditions in which these plant remains are found lack the oxygen necessary for decomposition to occur.
- Peat is the main material that is produced from these plant remains.
- An area where peat accumulates is known as a bog. There are three types of bog in Ireland: blanket bogs, raised bogs and basin peats/fens.

The formation of basin peat

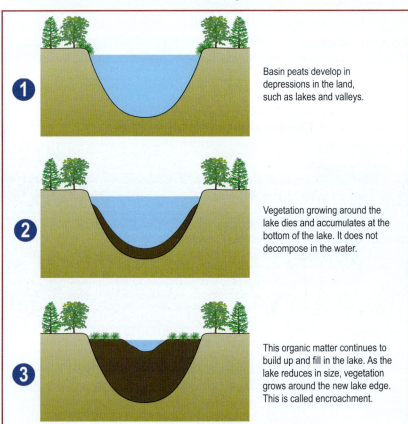

1. Basin peats develop in depressions in the land, such as lakes and valleys.

2. Vegetation growing around the lake dies and accumulates at the bottom of the lake. It does not decompose in the water.

3. This organic matter continues to build up and fill in the lake. As the lake reduces in size, vegetation grows around the new lake edge. This is called encroachment.

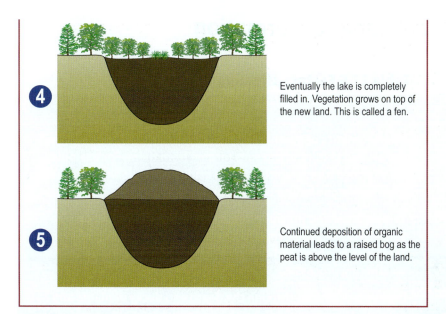

Eventually the lake is completely filled in. Vegetation grows on top of the new land. This is called a fen.

Continued deposition of organic material leads to a raised bog as the peat is above the level of the land.

Fig 17.1 *Basin peat formation*

Blanket bogs

- Develop in areas of high rainfall and low evaporation
- Found in mountainous areas
- Not as deep as basin peats
- Acidic with low fertility; hence limited agricultural use.

Table 17.5 Basin peats/fens, raised bogs and blanket bog characteristics

Characteristic	Basin peat/fen	Raised bog	Blanket bog
Depth	2 m	8–12 m	2.6 m
Shape	Flat	Dome shaped	Sloped or flat depending on landscape
pH	6.0	4.0–6.0	5.0
Location	Valleys, lakes	Lakes	Mountains and lowland on the west coast

Factors affecting soil formation

Table 17.6 Factors affecting soil formation

Factor	Effect
Parent material	Characteristics of parent material, e.g. acidity and texture, affect the pH and texture of the soils formed from them. For example, soils formed from granite have an acidic pH, while those formed from sandstone have a coarse, sandy texture.
Climate	Temperature and precipitation have the greatest effect on soil formation. Water contributes to the weathering of rock. Temperatures heat and cool rock, which also contributes to weathering processes.
Living organisms	Humus is produced through the death and decay of plants and animals. Microorganisms aid the decomposition of this material in the soil. Soils lacking in vegetation also lack organic matter. Organic matter contributes to the structure and fertility of a soil. Fibrous plant roots help bind soil together. Alkaline plant material reduces acidity in the soil, increasing its suitability for cultivation.
Topography	Refers to the slope of a landscape. Steep slopes are heavily eroded and lead to thin soils on hillsides, with topsoil eroded and deposited in valleys, leading to deep, fertile valley soils.
Time	Ireland's soils are young, as they were formed after the Ice Age. There is a high level of parent rock material available for weathering and soil formation, contributing to the overall fertility of the soil.

Point to note

Do not confuse factors affecting soil formation and physical and chemical weathering. Weathering primarily refers to the breakdown of rock. The factors affecting soil formation are external factors that contribute to the soil's formation and its characteristics.

Soil profiles

The materials provided by parent rock and organic matter for soil formation form layers in the soil known as horizons. Soils have a number of horizons, each with their own characteristics. A soil profile shows all of the horizons in a soil, from the uppermost layer to the bedrock.

- **O horizon:** This is not always present due to the absence of vegetation. It consists of organic material.

- **A horizon:** This is commonly known as topsoil. It contains minerals and may have organic matter mixed through it, but it can experience the effects of leaching so it may be lacking in minerals in certain conditions.

- **B horizon:** This is known as subsoil. It is normally a lighter colour than topsoil, except where minerals have been leached and have accumulated in this horizon.

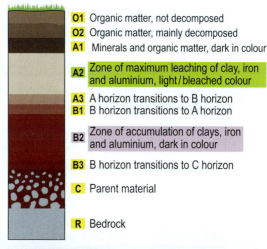

O1	Organic matter, not decomposed
O2	Organic matter, mainly decomposed
A1	Minerals and organic matter, dark in colour
A2	Zone of maximum leaching of clay, iron and aluminium, light/bleached colour
A3	A horizon transitions to B horizon
B1	B horizon transitions to A horizon
B2	Zone of accumulation of clays, iron and aluminium, dark in colour
B3	B horizon transitions to C horizon
C	Parent material
R	Bedrock

Fig 17.2 Soil profile

- **C horizon:** This contains parent material and is rocky in nature. It is generally light coloured.

- **R horizon:** This is bedrock and is solid.

Soil classification

The soils found in Ireland are categorised into 10 different groups:

- Podzols
- Brown podzolics
- Brown earths
- Grey brown podzolics
- Gleys
- Blanket peat
- Basin peat
- Rendzinas
- Regosols
- Lithosols

Podzols

- Podzols are found overlying acidic parent material such as sandstone.
- They are mainly used for forestry or rough grazing because of their acidic nature.
- They are prone to **leaching** of minerals.
- Acid leaching of minerals causes the leaching of iron and aluminium from the A horizon. This causes bleaching of the A horizon. The minerals accumulate in the B horizon and form an iron pan.
- The iron pan is impermeable to water, which can cause waterlogging. The iron pan can be broken up with a subsoiler or deep ploughing.

- **O horizon present:** Organic matter has not decomposed due to acidic conditions.
- **A horizon:** Thin A1 horizon and thick A2 horizon, bleached in colour due to leaching of minerals.
- **B horizon:** Red-brown colour due to the accumulation of minerals. Iron pan is formed at B2 horizon.

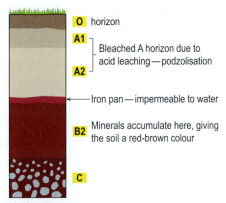

O horizon

A1 ⎫
A2 ⎭ Bleached A horizon due to acid leaching — podzolisation

Iron pan — impermeable to water

B2 Minerals accumulate here, giving the soil a red-brown colour

C

Fig 17.3 Podzol

Brown podzolics

- **A horizon:** Large quantity of organic matter in the A1 horizon. The A2 horizon is thin and shows little development.
- **B horizon:** Red-brown in colour due to the accumulation of minerals, particularly iron.

Brown earths

Brown earths are found in lowland areas. They are very suitable for crop production. They are found overlying limestone/lime-rich parent materials and have a high pH. They require little lime or fertiliser and have good drainage. Very little leaching takes place in these soils. They are dark brown in colour and do not appear to have distinct horizons.

- High levels of organic matter give the soil a darker appearance at the surface (topsoil).

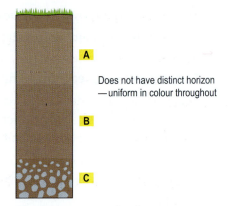

A

Does not have distinct horizon — uniform in colour throughout

B

C

Fig 17.4 Brown earth soil

- Uniform brown colour throughout showing little leaching of minerals.
- Very fertile soils.

Gleys

Gleys are poorly drained soils that form in waterlogged conditions, where iron is reduced, to give a mottled appearance. There are two types of gleys, categorised by their method of formation. Formation of a gley is known as **gleisation**. Gleys have poor structure. They can be improved by drainage but their use is limited. Gleys are confined to grazing and planting of some broadleaf tree species. Gleys are not leached.

- **A horizon:** There is no definition in the A horizon and A1 and A2 horizons are not identified. The A layer has limited structure due to the vegetation present.
- **B horizon:** There are also no defined horizons within the B horizon. Oxidation and reduction of minerals give it a mottled appearance.
- **Groundwater gley:** Forms in depressions in the landscape.
- **Surface water gley:** Found overlying land impervious to water.

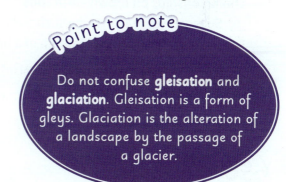

Point to note

Do not confuse **gleisation** and **glaciation**. Gleisation is a form of gleys. Glaciation is the alteration of a landscape by the passage of a glacier.

Exam questions

1   Describe how you would identify limestone as a parent material in soil.
(HL 2011)

2   (a) Name one type of soil pan.
    (b) Outline how the named soil pan is formed.
    (c) State one problem associated with the named soil pan.
    (d) Say how the named soil pan could be removed.   *(HL 2011)*

3   Describe gleisation and its role in the development of a soil profile.   *(HL 2011)*

4   Compare limestone and granite as parent materials in soil formation.
(HL 2012)

5   Explain how the aspect of a field may affect the temperature of a soil in early spring.   *(HL 2014)*

6 (a) What are the two main factors involved in the formation of metamorphic rocks?

   (b) Name two metamorphic rocks and in each case state which rock type it develops from.

   (c) Explain one way in which parent material influences the type of soil that eventually develops. *(HL 2014)*

7 (a) Give two methods by which organic matter may be added to a soil.

   (b) Outline the importance of maintaining a satisfactory level of organic matter in a tillage soil. *(HL 2014)*

8 Highlight the main differences between glaciation and gleisation. *(HL 2014)*

9 The National Ploughing Association of Ireland often holds its ploughing championships on brown earth soils.

   (a) Suggest two reasons why such soils are suited to tillage.

   (b) Draw a large labelled diagram of a brown earth soil profile. *(HL 2012)*

10 Granite is an igneous rock. True or false? *(OL 2012)*

11 List the principal factors influencing soil formation. *(HL 1994)*

Key-points!

- Rocks that provide parent material are categorised on how they are formed.
- The three categories of rock are: igneous, sedimentary and metamorphic.
- Weathering of rocks, which leads to soil particle formation, can be physical or chemical.
- Physical weathering includes heating and cooling, frost action, animal activity and erosion by wind, water or gravity.
- Chemical weathering includes hydrolysis, carbonation, oxidation and reduction.
- Organic parent materials (plant remains) decomposing in waterlogged, anaerobic conditions lead to the formation of peat over time.
- Soil formation is affected by climate, parent material, living organisms, topography and time.
- A soil profile shows all the horizons in a soil, from the uppermost layer to the bedrock.
- Leaching is a process where soluble matter such as minerals dissolves in water filtering through soil and is carried downwards.
- Gleisation is the formation of a soil in waterlogged conditions where iron is reduced in the soil and accumulates in the B horizon, giving it a mottled appearance.

Physical Properties of Soil 18

Soil consists of solid material that is derived from parent rock (mineral) material and organic matter. Together, the mineral and organic material comprises 50% of soil volume. The remaining 50% consists of air and water that occupy the soil pores. Half the pore space is normally filled with water and the other half with air. In times of heavy rainfall water volume may increase, leading to a reduction in air, and in times of drought air volume increases and water levels decrease.

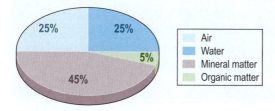

Fig 18.1 *Composition of soil*

Soil composition

Mineral matter

Parent rock material is broken down into mineral particles that are classified by size. The five types of particle are in order of decreasing size: gravel, coarse sand, fine sand, silt and clay.

Table 18.1 Soil mineral particles and their properties

	Gravel and sand (coarse and fine)	Silt and clay
Particle size	Large soil particles	Small soil particles
Pore space between particles	Large pore spaces between particles	Small pore spaces between particles
Drainage	Free draining due to large pore spaces	Poor drainage due to small pore spaces
Aeration	Well aerated due to large pore spaces	Poor aeration due to small pore spaces
Waterlogging/ drought	Can be prone to drought in prolonged periods of dry weather	Do not suffer from drought, will retain water in dry weather but can become waterlogged after prolonged rainfall
Fertility/ion exchange	No contribution to fertility or ion exchange	Clay is a source of K, P, Ca and Mg ions and its large surface area allows for **ion exchange** to take place

Point to note

Ion exchange: This process takes place in soil where ions are attracted to soil particles (clay) and are held on the surface of these particles. This is known as **adsorption**. The clay particles also contain ions of their own and they release these particles in the exchange. The smaller the particle, the more ion exchange that takes place. Colloidal clay particles are the smallest type of clay particles and have the greatest capacity for ion exchange.

Organic matter

Organic matter consists of the remains of plants and animals. Organic matter that has decomposed is called humus. Humus particles are small in size.

Key definition

Humus: The dark-coloured, decomposed plant and animal matter found in soil. It is rich in nutrients and contributes to soil structure.

Similar to mineral matter, the size of the particles of organic matter has an effect on their contribution to the soil's properties.

Effect of organic matter on soil

- Large particles of organic matter create large pore spaces, which improve drainage.
- Small particles provide a source of nutrients for plant growth.
- Small particles have an important role in ion exchange.

 Experiment

To determine the organic matter content of a soil

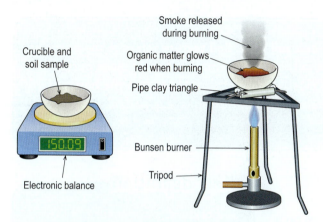

Fig 18.2 *Organic matter experiment*

1   **Weigh an empty crucible** and **record its mass**.

2   Add a **dry sample of soil** to the crucible and record its mass.

3   Subtract the mass of the crucible from the combined mass of the crucible and soil sample to **calculate the mass of the soil**.

4   Put the crucible on a pipe clay triangle on a tripod stand.

5   **Heat the soil** in the crucible with a **Bunsen burner**. The humus (organic matter) should **glow red** as it burns and smoke will be produced. Continue to burn off the humus until there is **no more smoke** and it does not glow.

6   Remove the crucible from the tripod with tongs and **reweigh**, noting its mass.

7   **Calculate the loss of mass** in the soil by subtracting the mass of the crucible and burned soil from the mass of the crucible and soil before burning.

Calculation of percentage of organic matter in soil:

$$\frac{\text{Mass of organic matter}}{\text{Mass of original soil sample}} \times \frac{100}{1} = \text{Percentage organic matter}$$

Physical properties of soil

The physical properties of soil play a large role in determining its suitability for crop growth. The physical properties of soil are:

- Soil texture
- Soil structure
- Soil porosity (air and water)
- Soil colour
- Soil temperature.

> ## Point to note
>
> Do not confuse **soil texture** and **soil type. Soil texture** refers to the particles that make up soil, e.g. sand, silt, clay or a combination of these particles (loam). **Soil type** refers to a classification of a soil based on the horizons found in the soil and the characteristics it exhibits, e.g. podzol, brown earth, gley.

Soil texture

Soil texture has a huge influence on a soil's characteristics. It is a permanent property of the soil that cannot be changed. The proportion of sand, silt and clay particles in a soil will influence the drainage, aeration and fertility in the soil and how easy it is to cultivate. The proportions of sand, silt and clay in a soil determine the soil texture.

> ### Key definition
>
> **Soil texture** is a measure of the proportion of different sizes of mineral particles (sand, silt, clay) that are found in a sample of soil.

> ### Key definition
>
> **Loam soil:** A soil that contains equal amounts of sand, silt and clay.

Experiment

To determine the soil texture of a soil sample by the feel method

1. Take a **dry sample of soil** and **rub it between your thumb and fingers**. Take note of its grittiness or smoothness.

2. **Wet the soil sample** with some water and rub it between your finger and thumb, again noting its grittiness or smoothness. Also note the plasticity (ability to be shaped/moulded) of the sample. Note if the wet sample is sticky or not.

3 **Roll the sample into a ball**. Record if this is possible or not.

4 **Roll the sample into threads** on a flat surface. Record if this is possible or not. If the soil can be rolled into threads, **attempt to make a ring** out of the thread. Record your observations.

Result

Soils with a high sand content will not form threads and cannot be moulded. Clay soils, which are sticky, can be moulded into a ball and those with high clay content can form threads or ribbons.

Experiment

To determine the soil texture of a soil sample by sedimentation

1 Add a sample of soil to a beaker of water and stir it with the stirring rod to break up any large lumps of soil.

2 Pour the mixture of soil and water into a graduated cylinder, rinsing all soil from the beaker into the cylinder. Add enough water to cover the soil completely.

3 Place a stopper on the cylinder and shake it to mix the soil and water thoroughly.

4 Leave to settle for a few hours/overnight.

5 Observe the layers that have settled in the graduated cylinder. Sand settles at the bottom, silt above the sand layer and clay on top of the silt.

6 Using the graduation marks on the cylinder, record the amount of sand, silt and clay in the soil sample as a percentage of the total soil solids.

7 Use a soil triangle to classify your soil sample.

Experiment

To determine the soil texture of a soil sample using a soil sieve

1 **Place a soil sample in an oven** to dry it out completely.

2 When the soil is dry, **crush it** with a pestle and mortar.

3 **Weigh** an empty weighing boat. Place the crushed sample into the boat and reweigh. Subtract the mass of the empty boat to calculate the mass of the soil.

4 **Place the crushed soil sample in the largest soil sieve**. Place a cover on the sieve and **shake**.

5 Remove the cover from the sieve and separate out each sieve.

6   Weigh the empty weighing boats.

7   Pour the contents of each sieve into separate pre-weighing boats.

8   **Weigh each sample** in turn.

9   **Calculate** each separate sample of sand, silt and clay as a percentage of the total soil mass.

10 Use a **soil triangle** to classify your soil sample.

Table 18.2 Soil textural properties			
	Sandy soils*	Loam soils**	Clay soils***
Drainage	Well drained, free draining	Good drainage	Poor drainage
Aeration	Well aerated	Good aeration	Poor aeration
Fertility	Low fertility	Good fertility	Fertile, retain nutrients
Tillage capabilities	Easily tilled	Easily tilled	Not suited to tillage due to plasticity
Temperature	Warm up quickly in spring	Will warm up in spring	Do not warm up due to lack of aeration; cold soils
Drought/ waterlogging	Prone to drought, do not get waterlogged	Will retain water but will not become waterlogged or be prone to drought	Retain water during drought but are prone to waterlogging and poaching by animals

*Sandy soils: Sand, loamy sand
**Loam soils: Loam, sandy loam, silt loam, clay loam
***Clay soils: Clay, silty clay, silty clay loam

Soil structure

Soil structure describes the arrangement of soil particles within a soil. Sand, silt and clay particles, which are the primary particles soil is composed of, form clusters in the soil known as aggregates or peds. The coming together of these aggregates determines the soil pore space. A good soil structure has a large volume of pores – 50% of the total soil – which are occupied by air and water.

Good soil structure is necessary for:

- Drainage of excess water
- Retention of water for plant growth

- Air movement within the soil
- Root penetration
- Emergence of seedlings.

As the primary soil particles aggregate, pores are formed between the particles within the aggregates. These are known as micropores. As the aggregates cluster together, more pores are formed between the aggregate units. These are known as macropores. Both micropores and macropores are necessary for good soil structure. A well-structured soil containing approximately 50% pore space will contain both micropores and macropores. A poorly structured soil typically does not form aggregates. As a result, the only pore space within this soil is between the primary soil particles and may be as low as 20%.

Aggregate formation

An aggregate is formed when sand, silt and clay particles cluster together. Pores are formed within the aggregate between the soil particles and are known as micropores. Larger pores, known as macropores, are formed between aggregates. Aggregates are held together by the clay particles and other polymers. The process by which the particles join together is known as flocculation. A well-structured soil should ideally have 50% pore space, including both types of pore.

Key definition

Flocculation: The clustering together of soil particles to create larger structures called floccules.

 Experiment

To show flocculation in a soil

1   Add 1 g of **clay** to 100 ml of **deionised water** and **mix thoroughly**.

2   Pour 10 ml of the clay–water suspension into each of four test tubes.

3   Add 1.0 ml of **hydrochloric acid** to the first test tube.

4   Add 1.0 ml of **sodium chloride** to the second test tube.

5   Add 1.0 ml of **calcium chloride** to the third test tube.

6   Add 1.0 ml of **aluminium chloride** to the fourth test tube.

7   Place a **stopper** on each test tube and **shake** to mix.

8   Observe the test tubes and record the level of flocculation in each one at five-minute intervals.

9   Determine which reagent (chemical) was the most effective flocculant.

Structural development of a soil

All of the activities that influence soil structure can be classified either as cementation or separation processes.

Key definitions

Cementation: This is where soil particles bind together. An example of this is when silt and sand particles are cemented together in aggregates during flocculation by clay particles.

Separation: This is where soil aggregates are separated within the soil. Large cracks may develop in the soil, which damages its overall structure.

Factors affecting structural development

- **Freezing and thawing:** Water in the soil expands and contracts, causing a change in the soil volume. This leads to aggregation of soil.
- **Wetting and drying:** This causes the soil volume to change as it expands and shrinks. As the soil dries out, the particles are cemented together. When the soil is wet again, the soil breaks up and cracks may form.
- **Soil organic matter:** Organic matter provides a substrate for building aggregates. The presence of organic matter in the soil will lead to aggregation of the soil, particularly in the upper horizons.
- **Plant root activity:** Small roots compact the soil and bind it together. The roots of larger plants and trees can break up the soil, forming cracks in the structure.
- **Animal activity:** Small burrowing animals, particularly earthworms, contribute to soil cementation, forming aggregates. Earthworms also contribute to the organic matter in the soil through the ingestion and egestion of soil.
- **Cultivation and tillage:** Agricultural activities such as ploughing and harrowing break up soil and encourage aggregation.

Soil porosity

Porosity refers to the total volume of the soil occupied by soil pores. A soil with good structure should have 50% of its volume occupied by soil pores. These pores are filled with air and water. The number of pores present in a soil and the size of the pores are also important factors in determining the characteristics of a soil.

Importance of soil air

- Air is necessary in the soil for plant root respiration. Soil air has almost the same composition as atmospheric air. The main difference is that there is a higher level of carbon dioxide in soil air than in atmospheric air and there is a lower level of oxygen in soil air than in the atmosphere.
- Plant roots take in oxygen when they are respiring and release carbon dioxide. This leads to a depletion of oxygen in the soil and a build-up of carbon dioxide.
- To prevent a depletion of oxygen in soil and a build-up of carbon dioxide, oxygen needs to diffuse from the atmosphere into the soil, and carbon dioxide from the soil to the atmosphere.
- If diffusion does not occur, the plant roots may be starved of oxygen and carbon dioxide will build up to toxic levels. Plant roots will be unable to respire and this will have a negative effect on plant growth.
- A soil with good structure and large pore spaces will allow the diffusion of gases to occur. Poor structure may result in a lack of diffusion and crop failure due to a lack of soil pores, a lack of oxygen and carbon dioxide toxicity. Soil aeration can also be improved by using a subsoiler, which breaks up compacted soil.

 Experiment

To compare the total pore space in a structured soil and a structureless soil (to calculate the total pore space of a soil sample)

1 Take a **dry sample of soil** and add 50 g of the sample to a **graduated cylinder**.

2 Tap the cylinder to remove any large air pockets in the soil.

3 **Record the volume of soil** in the cylinder.

4 Take another 50 g sample of the same soil and **crush it with a pestle and mortar**. Add this soil to a second graduated cylinder.

5 Measure out 50 ml of **water** and **add it** to the first cylinder. Repeat for the second cylinder.

6 Allow the cylinders to **stand for 1 hour**. **Record the total volume** of soil and water in each cylinder.

7 **Calculate the percentage** pore space in each soil and compare the results.

Soil water

Water is held in soil by adsorption and capillary action. Adsorbed water is held on the surface of the soil particles. This water is not available to plants and cannot be removed from the soil by their roots. Adsorbed water is also known as hygroscopic water.

Key definition

Hygroscopic water (adsorbed water): Water that forms a thin film around a soil particle and is held on the surface of the particle by force of attraction. It cannot be removed from the soil and is not available to plants.

Capillary action occurs when water is drawn into pores in the soil and is drawn upwards through the soil against the force of gravity. The water molecules are attracted to the soil particles and held in the soil by adsorption. The water molecules are also attracted to other water molecules in the soil. The smaller the pores in the soil, the more water will be held in the pores and the further it will travel upwards through the soil.

 Experiment

To demonstrate capillary action in a sandy soil and a clay soil

1   Plug the ends of two tubes with **cotton wool** or cover the ends of each tube with muslin cloth and hold in place with rubber bands.

2   Fill the first tube with **sandy soil**. Fill the second tube with an equal amount of **clay soil**.

3   Stand both tubes in a water trough.

4   **Leave the tubes in the water trough for a few hours**.

5   Observe the tubes and **note any rise in water level** in each tube. Use a ruler to measure the level the water has risen to. Compare the level in the sandy soil with the clay soil to determine which soil had the greatest capillary action.

6   Cress seeds may be added to the surface of each soil, as they will germinate if the water reaches a level that is available to the seeds.

Capillary water

- Capillary water is held in the pores within the soil aggregates and between the soil aggregates (micropores and macropores).

- Water in macropores is available for plant uptake. Water in micropores is not available for plant uptake.

Gravitational water

- Gravitational water is moved through soil by gravity, and is found in cracks and large pores.
- It is only available for a short period of time, e.g. after heavy rainfall, and drains away quickly.
- Air replaces water in large soil pores when gravitational water has drained away.

Water availability in the soil

- **Saturation:** When the large pores are full of gravitational water, the soil is described as saturated. This may occur after heavy rainfall.
- **Field capacity:** This is the water present in the soil after the gravitational water has been drained away. The large capillary pores contain air and the small capillary pores contain water. Plant uptake reduces the level of water in the soil. This water is replaced regularly from rainfall. However, if there is a prolonged period of dry weather and water is constantly removed from the soil by plants and is not replaced, eventually all the capillary water will be used up. When no more water can be removed from the soil, the soil is said to be at its permanent wilting point.

Key definitions

Field capacity: The amount of water in a soil after the gravitational water has drained away.

Permanent wilting point: The point at which no more capillary water can be removed from a soil (by plant roots). Plants will die from drought if the soil in which they are growing reaches its permanent wilting point.

Available water capacity: This is the amount of water between the field capacity and permanent wilting point that is available for absorption by plant roots.

Available water capacity =
Field capacity – Permanent wilting point

Top Tip!

The terms described above have appeared as definitions in the soil question on past exam papers.

Available water capacity in soils

Soils that retain a high volume of water, such as clay soils, do not necessarily have a high available water capacity. This is because much of the water retained in clay soils is retained in capillary pores and is hygroscopic water, which is unavailable to plants. Thus, a clay soil may have a high field capacity but also a high wilting point.

In contrast, loam and clay loam soils have a much lower permanent wilting point, giving a higher available water capacity. This means that there is a greater volume of water available for plant uptake in these soils.

 Experiment

To compare the infiltration rate (drainage) in a sandy soil and a clay soil

1   Set up the apparatus as shown in Figure 18.3. Line a **filter funnel** with **filter paper** and fill it with **sandy soil**. Repeat with the second funnel, but fill it with an equal amount of **clay soil**.

2   Using a graduated cylinder, measure out 20 ml of water and pour it into a beaker. Repeat with a second beaker.

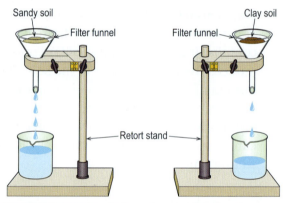

Fig 18.3 *Comparing drainage in a sandy soil and a clay soil*

3   Pour each beaker of water into one of the soil samples at the same time.

4   Drainage and infiltration rate can be measured in two ways:

(a) Using a stopwatch, time how long it takes for the first drop of water to pass through the soil and be collected in the beaker below the funnel for each sample.

OR

(b) Using a stopwatch **for a set period of time**, e.g. 5 minutes, 10 minutes, **measure the volume of water** that passes through each soil sample in the time allowed. Compare the results of both samples.

Result

The soil with the best drainage/infiltration rate will have the higher volume of water pass through it in the time allowed. The time taken for a drop of water to pass through this soil will also be the shorter of the two.

Soil colour

In terms of physical properties, the colour of a soil indicates the humus and mineral content of a soil.

- A soil that is a dark brown-black colour is usually rich in humus. These types of soils have high fertility and nutrient content and a high humus content, which leads to good soil structure. Dark-coloured soils also absorb more sunlight and so are warm soils.
- Soils that are light coloured or grey tend to be low in fertility and nutrients and lacking in humus. These soils can suffer from leaching, where the minerals are washed out of the soil or accumulate in a lower horizon in the subsoil.
- Red colouring in soil indicates the presence of iron. Often iron is leached from the upper layers of the soil and accumulates in the lower horizons, where it forms an iron pan that may be impermeable to water and roots. This will be characterised by a thin red layer in the subsoil.

Soil temperature

Air that is found in pores in the soil is more easily heated than water. Therefore, it is more advantageous to have a well-drained sandy soil or a loam soil for crop growth, as this soil will warm up quicker in springtime. Soil temperature is an important factor in crop growth, as cold temperatures will slow or stunt the growth of a crop. The rate of chemical reactions doubles with every 10°C rise in temperature (Van't Hoff's law), so the warmer the soil, the faster the growth rate.

Exam questions

1   Describe a laboratory or field experiment to demonstrate soil flocculation.
(HL 2011)

2   Explain how a named soil texture influences:
   (a) Pore spaces
   (b) Water movement
   (c) Fertility. *(HL 2012)*

3   Describe an experiment to estimate the percentage of clay in a soil sample.
(OL 2012)

4   (a) List **four** physical properties of soil.
   (b) Explain the necessity for the presence of oxygen in the soil.
   (c) Describe the factors affecting the availability of oxygen in the soil.
(HL)

5   Describe the conditions under which soil compaction is likely to occur.
(HL 1993)

6   Outline the importance of maintaining a satisfactory level of organic matter in a tillage soil. *(HL 1994)*

7   Outline a laboratory method used to compare the structure and texture of any **two** contrasting soil types. *(HL 1995)*

8   In the case of a named soil type, describe the importance of each of the following: capillarity, leaching, field capacity. *(HL 1997)*

Key-points!

- Soil consists of 45% mineral matter, 5% organic matter, 25% air and 25% water.
- Soil mineral particles include (in decreasing order of size) gravel, sand, silt and clay.
- Sand provides good drainage and aeration to a soil but has little fertility.
- Clay retains water and is fertile, but has poor aeration and is prone to waterlogging.
- A loam soil contains equal amounts of sand, silt and clay and has good aeration, drainage and fertility. Loams are not prone to waterlogging or drought and are easily cultivated.
- The physical properties of soil include texture, structure, porosity (air and water), colour and temperature.
- Soil texture influences structure and porosity in a soil.
- Soil structure is improved by the formation of aggregates in a process called flocculation.
- Flocculation is the clustering together of soil particles to create larger structures called floccules.
- Structural development of a soil is determined by cementation and separation processes such as freezing and thawing, animal activity and cultivation operations.
- Soil air is necessary for plant root respiration. For continued respiration, diffusion of oxygen into the soil and carbon dioxide into the atmosphere is necessary to allow proper growth and development of plants.
- Field capacity: The amount of water in a soil after the gravitational water has drained away.
- Permanent wilting point: The point at which no more capillary water can be removed from a soil (by plant roots). Plants will die from drought if the soil they are growing in reaches its permanent wilting point.
- Available water capacity: The amount of water between the field capacity and permanent wilting point that is available for absorption by plant roots.

Biological and Chemical Properties of Soil

19

Chemical properties of soil

There are two chemical properties that are important in determining the characteristics of a soil:

- Cation exchange capacity
- pH.

Cation exchange capacity

- Cations are positively charged ions, such as H^+, K^+ and Ca^{2+}.
- Positively charged cations are attracted to negatively charged humus and clay particles.
- They are held on the surface (adsorbed), as the opposite charges of the particles attract each other. Clay and humus particles can release cations that are adsorbed onto their surfaces and replace them with other cations.
- The ability of soil particles to attract, retain and release cations is called cation exchange.

 Experiment

To demonstrate cation exchange capacity in a soil

1 Add 5 g of dry, sieved soil to a filter funnel.

2 Using a dropper, add **potassium chloride** solution to the soil, drop by drop. **Collect the water** that filters from the soil in a beaker. This is known as the **leachate**.

3 **Test the leachate for calcium** by adding 10 drops of **ammonium oxalate** to the leachate. If a **white precipitate** is formed, calcium is present.

4 Discard the leachate and repeat the experiment by adding more KCl to the soil and testing the leachate for calcium. **Repeat until the leachate does not test positive** for calcium.

Result

The soil that initially contained calcium ions has undergone cation exchange and the calcium ions have been replaced by potassium ions.

pH

pH refers to the concentration of hydrogen ions in a solution and their activity. The solution in this case is the soil solution.

> ### Key definition
>
> **pH:** A measure of the concentration of the hydrogen ions in a solution. It can also be expressed as the negative log of the hydrogen ion concentration: $-\log_{10}[H+]$.

The acidity of the soil is determined by the concentration of acidic ions adsorbed on the surface of the soil colloids. Hydrogen and aluminium ions (H^+ and Al^{3+}) are acidic ions and the soils in which they dominate will also be acidic. Calcium and magnesium (Ca^{2+} and Mg^{2+}) are alkaline ions and the soils in which they dominate will be alkaline.

To determine the pH of a soil

1 Add 20 g of a soil sample to a beaker. Add approximately 25 ml of **distilled water** to the soil and stir for five minutes.

2 Turn on a **pH meter** and insert the electrode in a beaker of distilled water (pH 7) to ensure the probe is clean and reading the pH accurately.

3 Insert the electrode into the soil and water mixture. Note the pH reading on the meter. Clean the electrode with distilled water after use.

Importance of pH on soil activity

Most crops will grow in a pH range from 5.5 to 8.5. Some crops will grow at pH levels slightly above or below this range. The optimum pH level for crop growth is between 6.5 and 7.5. Outside these ranges, a very low or very high pH can reduce the availability of nutrients to plants, certain ions may become abundant in the soil to the point where they are at toxic levels and the activity of some microorganisms may decrease because of unsuitable environmental conditions.

Biological properties of soil

Key definitions

Soil biomass: The total mass of living material in a habitat.

Humus: The dead and decomposed remains of plants and animals.

Humification: The process by which soil organic matter is converted to humus.

Soil organisms

The majority of humus-forming organisms are microscopic in size. They feed on plant and animal remains, producing humus. The humus releases nutrients into the soil that are then available for plant uptake. This allows nutrients to be continuously recycled. Organisms that can be seen by the naked eye are described as macroorganisms.

Macroorganisms: The earthworm

The optimum environmental conditions for earthworm populations are in moist soils rich in organic matter, with a pH close to neutral. Earthworms prefer soils with a pH range of 6 to 8. Earthworm populations are also affected by temperature and prefer warm soil conditions above 12°C.

To determine the population of earthworms in a field or pasture

1   Mark out an area of a field or pasture with a **quadrat** (1 m², 0.25 m², etc.).

2   **Remove all vegetation** and ground cover within the quadrat using a shears or **scissors**.

3   Make up a **solution of warm water and washing-up liquid**.

4   **Apply the solution** to the area inside the quadrat with a watering can.

5   **Wait for a few minutes** for the earthworms to come to the surface.

6   **Count each worm** that comes to the surface and place the worm in a bucket or suitable container so that it will not be counted a second time. Do not count worms that surface outside the quadrat.

7   **Record the number of worms** that were observed.

8   **Repeat** the experiment in other areas of the field.

9   **Calculate an average** number of earthworms per quadrat.

Results

Calculate the area of the field. Divide the area by the size of the quadrat. Multiply the answer by the average number of worms per quadrat to calculate the earthworm population of the field.

Types of microorganisms

- **Bacteria:** Single-celled organisms that are responsible for converting soil organic matter into humus. They are also responsible for converting nitrogen into usable forms (nitrogen fixation and nitrification) and converting usable nitrogen into atmospheric nitrogen, which is not available for plant use (denitrification).

- **Actinomycetes:** These are mycelial bacteria that have thread-like extensions radiating from their single-cell structure. They are responsible for the humification of soil organic matter.

- **Fungi:** Fungi range from microscopic in size to large mushrooms. They are responsible for the humification of soil organic matter and some species form symbiotic relationships with other living organisms in the habitat. Some fungi are parasitic and can have a detrimental effect on a crop when they attack it.

Nutrient recycling: the carbon cycle and the nitrogen cycle

The carbon cycle

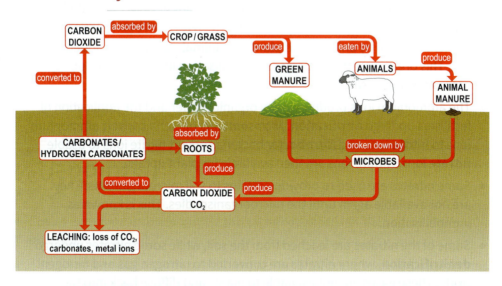

Fig 19.1 *The carbon cycle*

- Plants take in CO_2 from the atmosphere during photosynthesis and convert it to carbohydrate. Plant roots respire, producing carbon dioxide.
- Plants are eaten by animals, which respire to produce carbon dioxide and also produce animal manure. Plants produce manure, known as green manure, when they die.
- Microorganisms in the soil break down plant and animal manures. They respire, producing carbon dioxide.
- The CO_2 produced by plant roots and soil microorganisms is converted to carbonate ions in the soil. These can be taken up by plant roots but can also be lost due to leaching.
- Some of the carbon dioxide produced in the soil diffuses back into the atmosphere, where it can be used by plants during photosynthesis.

The nitrogen cycle

- Nitrogen may be applied to the land in the form of artificial fertiliser. N-fertiliser contains compounds such as nitrates, urea and ammonia. The **nitrates** (NO_3^-) are available immediately for plant uptake. Urea and ammonia must be converted to nitrates by the process of **nitrification**.

20 Soil Fertility and Crop Nutrition

Macronutrients and micronutrients

Macronutrients are used in large quantities by plants and micronutrients are used in small quantities. Both are needed for plant growth.

- **Macronutrients:** Nitrogen, phosphorus, potassium, calcium, magnesium, sulfur
- **Micronutrients:** Iron, zinc, manganese, copper, boron, molybdenum, chlorine, nickel.

All of the above elements are called essential elements because plants would not be able to grow or complete their life cycles without them.

All of the elements listed except for carbon, hydrogen and oxygen are extracted from the soil by plants. The three most important elements are the macronutrients nitrogen (N), phosphorus (P) and potassium (K).

Table 20.1 Functions and deficiency symptoms of macronutrients

Element	Functions	Deficiency symptoms
Nitrogen (N)	• Component of chlorophyll, which is needed for photosynthesis • Component of amino acids, which are needed to create protein • Component of DNA, which is responsible for growth and reproduction in plants • Component of ATP, a compound responsible for the control of metabolic energy in the plant • Promotes rapid plant growth • Leaves are dark green when sufficient N is present • Seeds have a high protein content when there is sufficient N	• Slow growth, small plants • Pale green or yellow due to a lack of chlorophyll • Necrosis (death) in older leaves as N is used in younger leaves • Elongated roots for attempted N uptake
Phosphorus (P)	• Uptake is largely dependent on the pH of the soil • It is immobilised and unavailable to plants at pH levels below 5 and above 7.5 • Required for optimum growth and reproduction • Involved in energy transfer in the plant • Production and development of new cells • Transfer of DNA to new cells • Seed formation and development • Promotes vigorous growth and early maturing, increased disease resistance, improved flower formation and stem strength	• Stunted growth • Lack of fruit or flowers • Wilting • Discoloured blue-purple leaves • Delayed maturity • Stunted roots
Potassium (K)	• Protein synthesis • Translocation of carbohydrates • Regulation of plant stomata and water use • Promotion of disease resistance • Activation of plant enzymes • Leads to increased crop yields and root growth	• Reduced crop yield • Scorching of leaves (chlorosis) along leaf margins • Slow growth • Poorly developed root system • Weak stalks, leading to lodging in cereals • Low sugar content in fruit

Element	Functions	Deficiency symptoms
Calcium (Ca)	Needed for cell wall formation	No development of terminal buds
Magnesium (Mg)	Part of the chlorophyll molecule	Chlorosis of lower plant leaves
Sulfur (S)	Contained in amino acids for protein formation	Chlorosis of upper plant leaves

Table 20.2 Deficiencies caused by a lack of micronutrients

Micronutrient	Deficiency disease
Iron (Fe)	Chlorosis, leading to reduced yield/poor-quality fruit in pears and raspberries Anaemia in pigs
Zinc (Zn)	Reduced yield in cereals, stunted growth and reduced flowering in legumes
Manganese (Mn)	Grey speck in oats, marsh spot in peas, speckled yellows in sugar beet
Copper (Cu)	Swayback in sheep
Boron (B)	Heart rot/crown rot in sugar beet
Molybdenum (Mo)	Whiptail (narrow distorted leaves) in cauliflower
Cobalt (Co)	Pine disease in cattle and sheep

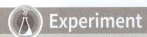 Experiment

To test a soil for the presence of macronutrients and micronutrients

These tests are designed to test for the presence of nitrates, phosphates, sulfates and chlorides in a soil sample.

1   Set up a filter funnel. Add soil to the filter funnel. Pour deionised water through the soil and collect it in a beaker as it filters through.

2   Pour the filtrate into four test tubes.

Table 20.3 Tests for macronutrients and micronutrients

Nutrient	Test	Result (positive test)
Nitrate	Add an iron sulfate solution to the test tube of filtrate. Add 5 drops of sulfuric acid with a dropper down the side of the test tube.	A brown ring will form in the test tube if nitrate is present.
Phosphate	Add a solution of ammonium molybdate to a test tube of filtrate. Add a few drops of nitric acid.	A yellow precipitate is formed if sulfates are present.
Sulfate and sulfite	Add a solution of barium chloride to a solution of the filtrate.	A white precipitate is formed if sulfates or sulfites are present.
Chloride	Add a few drops of silver nitrate to the solution of the filtrate.	A white precipitate is formed if chlorine is present.

 Experiment

To show the importance of macronutrients on plant growth

1 Set up four seed trays. Each polystyrene tray has holes in it to hold the seedlings.

2 Each tray should have an equal number of seedlings placed in it.

3 Place each seed tray into a separate water trough.
A different mineral solution is added to each trough as follows:
    Trough 1: Solution contains all mineral nutrients (control).
    Trough 2: Solution contains all mineral nutrients except nitrogen.
    Trough 3: Solution contains all mineral nutrients except phosphorus.
    Trough 4: Solution contains all mineral nutrients except potassium.

4 Leave all trays in sunlight for two weeks.

5 Observe any change in the seedlings.

6 Continue observations for one month.

Point to note
This experiment can be used to show the effects of any one specific macronutrient by comparing a plant given all nutrients with a plant deficient in one nutrient only.

Result

Plants lacking a specific nutrient will display symptoms of the deficiency diseases in Table 20.1.

Availability of soil nutrients

Most nutrients are available between pH 6 and 7. This is the optimum pH range for crop growth in a wide range of crops. In soils that are acidic, the availability of nutrients can be increased by raising the pH of the soil. This is normally achieved by liming.

Liming

Liming involves spreading ground limestone on the soil. Ground limestone contains calcium and magnesium, both of which are alkaline. The calcium (Ca^{2+}) and magnesium (Mg^{2+}) ions replace acidic hydrogen and aluminium ions through cation exchange. This reduces acid leaching and makes soils more suitable for crop growth. Liming is a medium-term activity, as it takes approximately two years for the full effects of lime to be seen on the land.

Ground limestone

- Ground limestone for agricultural use should consist of crushed natural limestone containing calcium carbonate or magnesium carbonate.
- Moisture content should be no greater than 2.5%.
- Total neutralising value should be no less than 90%.
- All ground limestone should pass through a 3.35 mm sieve and not less than 35% of it should pass through a 0.15 mm sieve.

Reasons for soil testing

- Soil testing allows a farmer to determine the nutrients available in their land and to determine how suitable an area is for crop growth.
- Farmers engaged in intense crop production may test their soils more often to optimise crop production.
- Soil tests are essential in order to be able to apply the correct fertiliser to the soil and in the correct quantities.
- It will also help to determine the suitability of a soil for the production of a particular crop.

Guidelines for taking a soil sample

1. Divide the area to be sampled into regions 2–4 ha in size.
2. Take samples from a wide range of areas, accounting for differences such as different soil types, previous cropping history or slopes.
3. Avoid taking samples from places that are not typical of the area, such as entrances and exits to fields, around drinking troughs, beside ditches or marsh land.

4 Do not sample for P and K for at least three months after the last P and K application.

5 Do not sample for lime for at least two years after the last application.

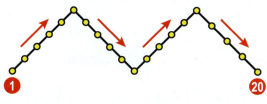

Fig 20.1 *Soil sampling pattern*

6 Samples should be taken using a soil auger. At least 20 samples should be taken in a W shape across the field. The samples should be 10 cm in depth.

Exam questions

1 Explain the factors to be considered when taking soil samples for analysis.
(HL 2011)

2 Describe an experiment to investigate the presence of nitrogen in a soil sample.
(HL 2011)

Key-points!

- Macronutrients and micronutrients are essential for healthy plant growth.
- Plants lacking in nutrients will be susceptible to deficiency diseases.
- Availability of nutrients is highest in soil between pH 6 and 7.
- Soil tests can be carried out to check the availability of plant nutrients.
- Liming can be carried out to increase soil pH in the medium term.
- Soil sampling is carried out to get a representative sample of soil for soil testing.

21 Fertilisers, the Environment and Organic Farming

Fertilisers and manures

Fertilisers and manures are any artificially or naturally produced materials that can be added to soil to provide one or more of the elements that are essential for plant growth. Most fertilisers contain nitrogen (N), phosphorus (P) or potassium (K), or a combination of the three. They are the most important elements needed for plant growth.

Key definitions

Fertiliser: An inorganic manufactured material that may contain one or more of the essential elements required for crop growth.

Manure: An organic material that consists of the wastes of plants and animals.

Fertilisers and essential elements

> ## Key definition
>
> **Straight (simple) fertiliser:** A fertiliser that contains only **one** of the essential elements.
>
> **Compound fertiliser:** Any fertiliser that contains two or more nutrient elements. Compound fertilisers are often produced by the combination of two or more straight fertilisers.

Table 21.1 Simple/straight fertilisers

Fertiliser name	Nutrient	Percentage nutrient present
Urea	N	46
Calcium ammonium nitrate (CAN)	N	27.5
Ground rock phosphate	P	12
Superphosphate	P	7
Muriate of potash	K	50
Sulfate of potash	K	42

Important fertilisers

Calcium ammonium nitrate (CAN)

- It is the most widely used straight nitrogen fertiliser in Ireland.
- It contains two forms of nitrogen: nitrate and ammonium ions.
- Ammonium ions are acidic and can lower the soil pH.
- Calcium in CAN is alkaline and acts as a buffer against the ammonium ions, preventing the soil pH from becoming too acidic.
- It is a fast-acting fertiliser, as nitrate can be taken up by crops immediately.
- Ammonium ions are slow acting, as they must first be converted to nitrate.
- CAN must be stored in airtight conditions, as it is hygroscopic and any moisture retention will result in the granules caking together.

Urea

- It contains a higher concentration of nitrogen than CAN, so less fertiliser is needed.
- There is a reduction in costs and labour in comparison to CAN.

- It is a slower-acting fertiliser than CAN.
- Urea is converted to ammonium form and then to nitrate before it can be used by crops.
- One of the other disadvantages of urea as a nitrogen fertiliser is that it undergoes volatilisation.
- It is hygroscopic, so it must be stored in airtight containers.

Disadvantages of volatilisation

- Ammonia is lost to the atmosphere, so fertiliser is wasted.
- High levels of ammonia gas at ground level can cause toxicity in germinating seedlings.
- Volatilisation can be avoided by spreading urea when soil is moist and rain is due.

Ground rock phosphate

- Mainly used in the forestry sector.
- Conifers grown on acidic soils are suited to the slow release of phosphate caused by the reduction in phosphorus availability at low pH values.

Compound fertilisers

The main advantage of compound fertilisers is that only one fertiliser may be needed for application to a crop or grassland, as it provides all of the nutrients required by the crop. Compound fertilisers may contain all three main minerals or just two of the minerals.

Naming compound fertilisers

All compound fertilisers are labelled with three numbers. These numbers represent the percentages of N, P and K present in the fertiliser mix.

Table 21.2 Uses of N-P-K fertiliser	
N-P-K fertiliser	Common use
10-10-20	Grassland/potatoes/cereals
18-6-12	Grassland/cereals
27-2.5-5	Cereal crops/intense grazing
7-6-17	Root crops

Fertiliser application

Fertiliser may be applied in one of three ways:

- **Placed in soil:** The fertiliser is applied to the land when the seeds are sown. The seed drill sows the seed and applies the fertiliser in a band close to the seed so nutrients are available to the crop.
- **Broadcast:** Fertiliser is spread (broadcast) onto the soil using a fertiliser spreader and then harrowed into the soil. This may take place prior to sowing.
- **Top dressing:** Fertiliser is spread onto an established crop.

Manures

Table 21.3 Comparison of farmyard manure and slurry

Farmyard manure (FYM)	Slurry
<ul><li>Consists of animal dung, animal urine and straw from winter bedding</li><li>Cheap source of nutrients</li><li>Cost-effective way of recycling animal waste</li><li>Reduces the need to purchase artificial fertilisers</li><li>Adds organic matter to the soil</li><li>Improves soil structure and fertility</li><li>Can be used by organic farmers</li><li>Spread with a muck spreader</li></ul>	<ul><li>Liquid manure that contains animal dung and urine</li><li>Contains less organic matter because of the absence of straw</li><li>Liquid composition allows it to be absorbed faster and release nutrients faster than FYM</li><li>Spread with a slurry spreader</li><li>Can contribute to the spread of pests and diseases and weed dispersal, such as dock leaves</li></ul>

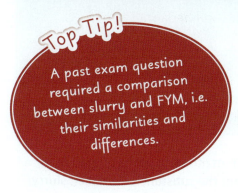

Top Tip!

A past exam question required a comparison between slurry and FYM, i.e. their similarities and differences.

Table 21.4 Sources and effects of pollution in agriculture

Source of pollution	Effect of pollution
Silage/hay wrap	• Littering
Fertiliser run-off from fields	• Contamination of groundwater, streams, rivers and lakes
Silage effluent	• Eutrophication of water, leading to algal blooms and fish kills
Sheep dip	• Build-up of toxins in the food chain (through the use of pesticides, herbicides and fungicides)
Slurry (cattle, pigs and poultry)	
Farmyard manure	
Pesticides, herbicides and fungicides	
Milk	
Run-off from milking parlours	

Top Tip!

Listing sources of pollution or ways to prevent pollution has appeared on the Ordinary Level exam paper.

Key definitions

Eutrophication: The enrichment of a habitat or environment with nutrients.

Effects: Nutrients from fertilisers, slurry, silage effluent and milk promote excessive growth of algae in aquatic habitats, known as algal bloom. Algae die, producing dead organic matter that is decomposed by bacteria aerobically. This uses up oxygen in the water. Other aquatic organisms (fish) die due to the lack of oxygen. The death of a large number of fish in this manner is called a fish kill.

Biochemical oxygen demand (BOD): The amount of dissolved oxygen needed to break down 1 litre of an organic material in a water sample.

Some organic materials are more pollutant than others in terms of their BOD value. The higher the value, the more pollutant the substance. Fertiliser, slurry, silage effluent and milk have high BOD values.

Fish kills may also occur due to rising temperatures in water during the summer months. Oxygen gas is less soluble in water with a rise in temperature. As oxygen levels fall, fish may be deprived of oxygen and die. This is a natural form of fish kill.

Preventing pollution: spreading fertilisers and the nitrates directive

In order to prevent waste, run-off and water pollution, fertilisers should not be spread under the following conditions:

- If land is waterlogged, flooded, snow-covered or frozen
- If heavy rain is forecast within 48 hours, or if the ground is steeply sloped
- On land within 1.5 m of a watercourse
- During winter months (dates vary by region).
- Applies also to spreading of manure

Autumn ploughing is prohibited under the nitrates directive; land cannot be left bare because this leads to leaching.

Protecting and enhancing the environment

A diverse range of living organisms is important in an ecosystem in order to provide resources such as food, but also for recycling wastes and nutrients. If habitats are destroyed, ecosystems can collapse and disappear rapidly, which in turn eradicates various plants, animals and other living organisms.

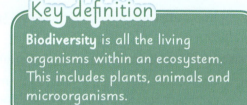

Key definition

Biodiversity is all the living organisms within an ecosystem. This includes plants, animals and microorganisms.

Ways in which farmers can enhance biodiversity on their farms include:

- Traditional hay meadows: Allow flowers and grasses to produce seed to benefit wildlife (REPS).
- Nature corridors: Protect and enhance field margins, which are an important source of plant diversity and wildlife habitat.
- Hedgerow maintenance: Hedgerows are retained and managed. Cutting is prohibited during the bird nesting season.
- Minimise the use of chemical fertilisers and pesticides (Organic Farming Scheme).
- Forestry: Plant both coniferous and deciduous trees, with an emphasis on planting broadleaf species (FEPS).
- Retain existing lakes, marshes, woodland, bogs and watercourses in areas designated for forestry (FEPS).

Importance of hedgerows in agriculture

- Play an important role in maintaining biodiversity within our ecosystem
- Provide a home for many birds, mammals and insects (natural habitat of these organisms)
- Provide a source of food and shelter for these animals and insects
- Provide shelter for livestock
- Natural land boundaries/enclosures
- Aesthetically attractive
- Better growth of plants on the sheltered side of the hedge
- REPS requirement.

Organic farming

- Animals are reared on land free from chemicals (fertilisers, pesticides and herbicides).
- Animals are free range and have had suitable living conditions while on the farm.
- Crops have not been genetically modified.
- Soil structure has been protected by means of rotations and the additions of green manures, farmyard manures and mulches.
- As there are no organic or chemical pollutants produced, waterways are not at risk of pollution.
- Habitats are maintained, thus promoting and encouraging biodiversity.

Exam questions

1 (a) Explain the term *BOD*.
   (b) Name **one** agricultural pollutant with a high BOD.
   (c) Explain how the named pollutant affects water quality.
   (d) Suggest **two** key elements of a waste management strategy for the
       named pollutant.   (HL 2011)

2 2010 was designated by the United Nations the International Year of
   Biodiversity. Explain the term *biodiversity*.   (OL 2011).

3 Describe how the problem of water pollution from silage effluent may
   be prevented.   (HL 1990)

4 Describe ways in which wild animals and plants can be conserved while
   at the same time employing modern agricultural practices.   (HL 1990)

5   State **two** reasons why fertilisers may become unavailable to plants following spreading in spring.   (OL 1999)

6   With regard to fertilisers and manures on Irish farms:
     (a) Name **four** types of fertilisers.
     (b) State **two** reasons why farmers use them.
     (c) Describe **three** methods of their application on land.
     (d) Describe **three** precautions that are necessary to prevent problems with pollution associated with their application onto the land.   (OL 2003)

7   Give a full explanation why it is not recommended to spread nitrogen fertiliser on grassland in late autumn.   (HL 2014)

8   Calcium ammonium nitrate (CAN) is the most widely used fertiliser on Irish farms.
     (a) What is the main plant nutrient found in CAN?
     (b) Describe an experiment to show the effect of CAN on grass growth.   (OL 2014)

Key-points!

- Fertilisers are artificially produced materials that provide a source of nutrients when applied to soil.
- Simple and compound fertilisers are used to provide nutrients to the soil.
- Manures are organic materials (plant and animal wastes) that provide a source of nutrients when applied to soil.
- CAN and urea are the most popular nitrogen fertilisers in Ireland.
- Fertiliser can be applied in a number of ways: placed in soil, broadcast or used as a top dressing.
- Farmyard manure and slurry are the most common manures used on farms.
- Slurry, silage effluent, fertilisers and pesticides can all cause pollution on farms, particularly of water sources, if not applied or disposed of properly.
- Eutrophication is the enrichment of water with nutrients.
- Biodiversity is all the living organisms within an ecosystem. This includes plants, animals and microorganisms.

22 Types of Grassland

Learning objectives

In this chapter you will learn about:

1 Grassland ecology

2 Categories of grassland

3 Characteristics of grass

4 Constituents of grass

5 Growth of grass

6 Experiment: To determine the dry matter content of grass

7 Experiment: To estimate sucrose concentration in grass

8 Grass and clover species for leys

9 Seed mixtures

Grassland ecology

Grassland is semi-natural vegetation that thrives in the temperate climate of Ireland but ultimately is controlled by human activity. If grassland was not grazed by livestock or cut for silage or hay, eventually small shrubs and trees (bramble and blackthorn) would invade the land and become the dominant species. Over a longer period of time, this scrubland would be replaced by the natural vegetation of the country – deciduous forest. The larger trees would create a canopy that would block out light to the smaller shrubs, preventing their growth.

Short, leafy grass species are favoured over tall, stemmy species for grazing, as they are more palatable and nutritious for livestock. If grassland is not grazed efficiently, the taller grass species can become dominant in grassland, lowering its overall feeding value. Grassland is categorised based on the grasses present for use in grazing and winter fodder conservation.

Table 22.1 Characteristics of grassland

Characteristic	Definition
Botanical composition	Variety of grasses, plants and other vegetation present
Stocking rate	The number of animals that can be stocked on an area of land
Production levels	Amount of herbage produced by the pasture: high production levels lead to high production levels in livestock (e.g. weight gain, milk production)

Categories of grassland

- **Rough mountain and hill grazing:** Poor-quality grass found in mountainous areas, which is often acidic and difficult to cultivate.
- **Permanent grassland:** Grassland that is never ploughed, but can be improved with liming and fertilisation.
- **Leys:** A field or pasture sown by the farmer that is used for grazing by livestock. They are temporary in nature and are reseeded regularly.

Table 22.2 Categories of grassland

Category	Botanical composition	Stocking rate	Production levels
Rough mountain/ hill grazing	Highly variable, many poorer grasses such as bent grasses and fescues	Low: livestock cannot be stocked at a high density due to low nutritional value of grass	Low: grasses are not productive and do not lead to high production levels in livestock
Permanent grassland	Variable – can contain poor grasses as well as highly productive grasses such as perennial ryegrass	Higher stocking rate than rough mountain grazing due to improved grazing conditions	Higher production levels than mountain grazing, as grassland is of better quality and can be improved through fertilisation and liming
Leys	One or two species, such as perennial ryegrass and clover, dominate, which are sown by the farmer	High, as good-quality grassland can support a large number of livestock	High, as the best grasses are sown in leys

Characteristics of grass

The most important characteristics of grass are its palatability, productivity and digestibility. Grass species with the highest levels of palatability, productivity and digestibility are the most desirable for grazing and conservation.

- **Palatability:** A measure of how pleasant the grass tastes. Cattle and sheep are selective grazers and will eat only the grasses that are most palatable to them. If there is a variety of grasses in a pasture, livestock will eat the palatable grasses and ignore the unpalatable species. As the unpalatable species go uneaten, they continue to develop and begin to dominate the pasture. The productivity and quality of the pasture are therefore lowered. The most palatable species of grass to grazing animals is perennial ryegrass.
- **Productivity:** This is a measure of the quantity of plant material (herbage) produced by the grass. The higher the productivity, the more grass is available to livestock for consumption. Higher stocking rates are also possible on more productive grasses. Again, perennial ryegrass has one of the highest levels of productivity of all the grass species.
- **Digestibility:** This represents the proportion of food that can be assimilated and used by the body in comparison to the amount of food consumed. Ideally, digestibility levels should be high, as this means there is little waste. The higher the digestibility of a food (in this case, grass), the more meat and milk can be produced from that grass.

Constituents of grass

The constituents of grass include sugar, protein, cellulose and fibre. Sugar and protein are highly digestible, so grass with high levels of sugar and protein is desirable for grazing and conservation.

Growth of grass

Vegetative stage

- Grass enters the vegetative stage of growth in spring, after germination.
- The plant photosynthesises, producing large amounts of carbohydrate in the form of sugar and starch, which is stored in the leaves.
- More than 80% of the grass can be digested by a ruminant animal.

Reproductive stage

- Grass enters the reproductive stage in mid-May and begins to produce flowering stems.

- Fibre is needed in the stem to support the seed head and is produced at the expense of protein and carbohydrate.
- As fibre levels increase, protein and carbohydrate levels drop (by 0.5% per day), decreasing the overall digestibility of the grass, which can drop from 80% to 50% in one month.

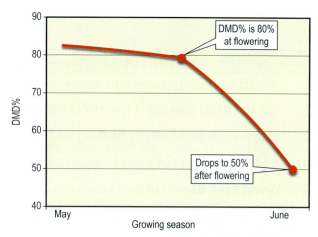

Fig 22.1 *Changes in DMD levels of grass over the growing season*

Key definitions

Dry matter (DM): The matter remaining in a sample of food after the water has been removed.

Dry matter digestibility (DMD): The amount (percentage) of dry matter that can be digested by an animal.

Dry matter intake (DMI): The amount of feed an animal consumes, excluding its water content.

Top Tip!

Questions are frequently asked in the exam about the carbohydrate levels in grass at harvesting and their effect on the quality of the silage.

If the DMD value for grass or silage is low, the dry matter intake of the animal will increase, as it has to consume more feed to get the nutrients it requires. Leafy grass will have a high DMD value, as it contains a high level of carbohydrates and protein, whereas stemmy grass has a low DMD value, as the stems consist of fibres. Cutting grass for silage at the leafy stage is crucial, as the sugars and proteins are contained in the leaves of the plant. The sugars and proteins are converted to fibre as the stems develop, leading to a low DMD during conservation.

To determine the dry matter content of grass

1 Dry off any excess water on a sample of grass using tissue paper.

2 **Cut the grass into short lengths** of equal size using a **scissors**.

3 **Weigh** each of the empty **beakers** and record the mass.

4 **Add a sample of cut grass** to each beaker.

5 **Weigh each beaker of grass** and record its mass.

6 Place all the beakers in an **oven at 100°C**.

7 Remove beakers from the oven using tongs and **reweigh every 10 minutes until a constant mass is achieved**.

8 Record your results and **calculate the DM content** of the samples.

9 Calculate the average DM content of the grass.

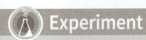 Experiment

To estimate sucrose concentration in grass

1 Obtain a sample of grass. **Dry off any excess water** from the grass with a tissue. Water will dilute the sugar concentration.

2 Place the sample of grass in a polythene bag. **Remove the air** from the bag and seal it.

3 **Place the bag in a freezer overnight**. Freezing the grass causes the cells to burst. Sap is released from the cells into the bag.

4 Remove the bag from the freezer. Open the bag, being careful not to spill the sap.

5 Look through the eyepiece of a refractometer to check that it is clear.

6 Place a drop of **distilled water** on the plate, close the cover and adjust the meter to zero so as to calibrate the refractometer.

7 Place a **few drops of sap** on the plate of the **refractometer**, close the cover and look through the eyepiece.

8 **Take a reading of the sucrose percentage** from the scale that is visible.

9 Take two further readings and get an average value for the readings.

Grass and clover species for leys

A variety of strains of ryegrass and clover are the most common seed mixtures sown in leys. The most common grass sown is perennial ryegrass and it is usually sown with white clover.

Perennial ryegrass

- Suited to well-drained soils with a pH > 6.0
- Needs fertile soils and benefits from nitrogen fertilisation
- Will persist for many years in a well-managed pasture
- Identified by the presence of spikelets on alternate sides of the stem (see photo in Figure 34.1).

Advantages of perennial ryegrass

- Higher palatability, productivity and digestibility in comparison to other grasses
- High DM production
- Long growing season means reduced costs for winter feed
- High stocking rate can be maintained because of high productivity levels
- Good tillering ability leading to sward dominance, good ground cover and weed prevention.

Italian ryegrass

- Biennial plant that must be resown every two years
- Requires similar soil conditions to perennial ryegrass
- Identified by the awns on its spikelets.

Advantages of Italian ryegrass

- Longer growing season than perennial ryegrass (PRG)
- Produces 20% more herbage than PRG
- High production levels that make it particularly suitable for silage production.

Hybrid ryegrasses

These are grasses that are produced as a result of a cross between different species of ryegrass, usually perennial ryegrass and Italian ryegrass. The aim is to produce a strain of grass with hybrid vigour. This would combine the persistence of PRG with the longer growing season and high production levels of IRG.

White clover

- Perennial plant with white flowers
- Smooth stems lacking in hairs (glabrous)
- Produces stolons and spreads quickly within a sward
- Included in seed mixtures for leys, for grazing or for conservation as silage.

Advantages of white clover

- Good source of protein
- Its ability to fix nitrogen reduces the need for artificial fertiliser, which also reduces costs
- Increased level of productivity, palatability and digestibility of the sward
- Reduces the use of chemicals, particularly in organic farming
- Meets REPS requirements
- High mineral content
- Provides good ground cover, which controls the spread of weeds.

Red clover

- Used in seed mixtures sown for silage production
- Perennial plant and can be recognised by its purple flowers
- Leaves and stems of red clover are hairy
- Grows in similar conditions to white clover.

Advantages of red clover

- Highly digestible
- Highly productive – provides a high yield of silage and can be cut a number of times in a season
- Can fix nitrogen, so there is little need for fertiliser, which reduces costs
- Tap roots improve aeration and soil structure.

Seed mixtures

A seed mixture is a combination of a number of different species of grass and clover or a combination of different strains of the same species of grass, often mixed with clover. Most seed mixtures are comprised of strains of perennial ryegrass combined with white clover.

Reasons for using a seed mixture

- Uniform seed mixtures result in a pasture that all heads out at the same time. Otherwise, a surplus of grass would be available at one point in the grazing season and a scarcity at another point.
- Seed mixtures combining different strains of grass species result in heading-out dates being staggered, ensuring fresh grass for grazing throughout the grazing season.

Key definition

Heading dates: The heading date of a grass species is the time when the ear emerges on the grass plant. Grass species are categorised as early, intermediate and late heading.

Table 22.3 Heading dates

Category	Heading date	Use
Early	Mid-May	Provide grazing in spring (March/April)
Intermediate	Late May	Provide a good silage yield from May to July
Late	Early June	Provide silage in June to late July and long-term grazing

Seed mixtures for grazing

- Seed mixtures usually include a number of strains of perennial ryegrass (early, intermediate and late heading varieties).
- Early heading PRG will provide grass for grazing in spring.
- The mid- and late-season varieties will provide grazing pasture throughout the summer and may extend the grazing season into late autumn.
- Excess grass produced may be cut for silage.

There are a number of advantages associated with using this type of seed mixture for grazing pasture:

- There is a constant supply of grass over the grazing season from spring to autumn.
- There is always a fresh supply of leafy grass with a high DMD value, as heading dates vary. This ensures the sward has a good feeding value.
- There will not be a dip in production levels at any point in the grazing season, as there would be if only one strain of grass was used.

- The whole sward will not go stemmy at the same time, leaving unpalatable, poor-quality grass.

Seed mixtures for silage

- The best-quality silage will be achieved if all the grass has a similar heading date, as grass growth will be uniform.
- A seed mixture is used with only one strain of grass or a number of strains of the same type of grass with similar heading dates.
- All the grass is ready for silage at the same time and can be cut a number of times in one season.

Questions

1 Explain, using specific examples, why seed mixtures used for silage should differ from those required for permanent pasture.

2 List, giving reasons, the grass species you would include in a seed mixture for the establishment of the following:
   (a) Short-term grass sward
   (b) Permanent pasture.

3 List the species in a seed mixture you would select for a short-term grass sward intended for silage. Give reasons for including the species you name.

4 Explain how the botanical composition of a grass sward may influence its feeding value for livestock.

Exam questions

1 Explain how the composition of a sward in a permanent ley differs from a temporary ley. *(HL 1992)*

2 Farmers often sow a mixture of seed varieties in their leys. The seeds germinate and undergo establishment even though the varieties have different heading-out dates. Explain the three terms. *(OL 2011)*

3 What does the term *dry matter digestibility (DMD)* mean? *(OL 2005)*

4 What approximate DMD value should high-quality silage be? *(OL 2005)*

5 Explain why old, poorly managed grassland is unsuitable for the production of good-quality silage. *(OL 2011)*

6 Give two reasons for including clover in a seed mixture for pasture. *(HL 2008)*

Key-points!

- Grassland is categorised by its botanical composition, stocking rate and production levels.

- The three main categories of grass are rough mountain and hill grazing, permanent grassland and leys.

- The characteristics of grass that are used to determine its value are palatability, productivity and digestibility.

- Dry matter digestibility (DMD) is one of the most important factors when determining the feeding value of grass.

- Perennial ryegrass, Italian ryegrass, white clover and red clover are the main species used in grass seed mixtures.

- Seed mixtures are created to produce a good-quality grazing pasture with a constant supply of grass or a pasture for silage production.

23 Grassland Management

Livestock units

A livestock unit is used to determine how much grazing and winter fodder are needed on a farm. It is a measure of livestock grazing. One livestock unit (1 LU) is the equivalent of one dairy cow or one suckler cow. One livestock unit requires 12 tonnes (1 tonne = 1,000 kg) of herbage annually. This value can be used to determine the total quantity of herbage required on the farm for the herd.

1 dairy/suckler cow	= 1.0 LU	Cattle 1–2 years	= 0.6 LU
Cattle < 1 year	= 0.4 LU	Sheep	= 0.15 LU

Rotational grazing systems

- Animals are moved around a number of different grazing fields or areas.
- Livestock graze on fresh grass constantly.
- Rotation allows for regrowth of grazed areas. Regrowth takes approximately three weeks.

- The best rotational grazing systems operate on the basis that a herd will not return to a paddock during this time to allow the grass to regrow and reach the vegetative stage of growth.
- Grass is at its most digestible and is highly palatable during this growth stage.

Paddock grazing

Land is divided into 20 to 30 paddocks of equal size. The herd grazes down one paddock each day and then moves to the next paddock. Grazed paddock is fertilised and livestock do not return to the paddock for at least three weeks to give time for recovery and regrowth.

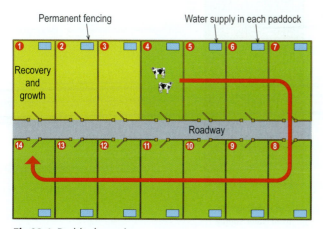

Fig 23.1 *Paddock grazing*

Table 23.1 Advantages and disadvantages of paddock grazing

Advantages	Disadvantages
Fresh, highly digestible leafy grass is available every day for grazing.	Expensive to set up. Roadways/access to each paddock need to be created. Fencing and a water supply are needed for each paddock.
No grass is wasted.	Labour intensive: Livestock need to be moved each day and grazed paddocks fertilised.
Excess grass produced can be saved as silage.	If paddocks are small, it can be difficult to cut grass for silage.

Top Tip!

Compare/contrast two methods of grazing is a common question on rotational grazing methods.

Strip grazing

A paddock is divided into strips using a **movable electric fence**. A strip is created that is big enough to provide enough grazing to the herd for 24 hours. The herd is moved forward to a fresh strip of grass each day. A back fence is used to prevent movement of livestock into the pasture that has previously been grazed. Livestock are moved around strips in a rotational manner until they return to the first strip three to four weeks later. Each time stock is moved, the previous strip is fertilised. Strip grazing can be used with a fixed or movable water supply.

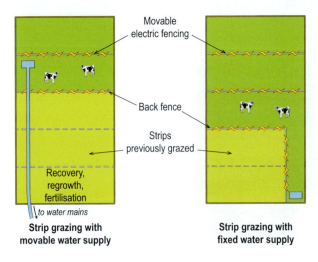

Fig 23.2 Strip grazing

Table 23.2 Advantages and disadvantages of strip grazing	
Advantages	**Disadvantages**
Fresh, leafy grass is available for grazing each day.	Labour intensive: Livestock, fencing and water supply (if movable) have to be moved each day.
No wastage of grass, as each strip is grazed bare.	The use of a fixed water supply means part of a field has to be left as access to the water supply. This land cannot be used for grazing and can be damaged by constant use.
Grass is not damaged while regrowing, as it is not accessible to livestock.	

Set stocking

Livestock have access to all grazing land over one continuous area for the grazing season.

Table 23.3 Advantages and disadvantages of set stocking	
Advantages	**Disadvantages**
Low-cost system: Minimal fencing and water troughs required.	Grazing is not optimised in summer, when growth is at its peak, as livestock are not confined to one grazing area.
Low stocking density means that poaching is reduced.	Grass turns stemmy, as it is not fully grazed, thus reducing the feeding value of the grass and encouraging the growth of poor-quality grasses with a lower digestibility value.
Low labour requirement.	If disease is present in the pasture, livestock are constantly exposed to it.

Block grazing

Block grazing consists of dividing up large fields into smaller blocks. Livestock graze a block for approximately one week before moving to the next block. Electric fencing can be used to strip graze blocks. Livestock return to a block after three weeks.

Table 23.4 Advantages and disadvantages of block grazing	
Advantages	**Disadvantages**
Cheaper than paddock grazing.	Grazing of blocks is not as efficient as paddock or strip grazing.
Less fencing needed.	
Less labour required and less movement of animals.	

Zero grazing

Zero grazing is a system where cattle are housed all year round. Grass or other forage crops **are cut and brought to the livestock**, where they are fed indoors. **Cattle do not graze the land**.

Advantages of zero grazing

- Land is not poached by animals.
- Energy is used for live weight gain and milk production rather than movement.
- There is less chance of lameness, as livestock are not walking on roads.
- Feed intake increases with constant access to fresh grass.
- The need for silage decreases due to the intake of fresh grass cut from distant fields that was previously inaccessible to livestock. All fields are accessible for grazing.
- While slurry production increases, this can be spread on the land, reducing the need for artificial fertilisers and thus reducing costs.
- Topping of grass is unnecessary, as all grass is cut at the same time.

> **Points to note**
>
> **Topping:** Mowing grass to a height of 5 cm to 7 cm. It is carried out post-grazing to remove any remaining grass. Topping cuts grass to the correct post-grazing height and encourages tillering. It can also be used to control weeds.
>
> **Tillering:** The development of side shoots in a plant. When the main shoot of the plant is grazed, this encourages the production of side shoots, or tillers. This increases the quantity of herbage produced. Tillering can be encouraged by grazing pasture with sheep or light stock such as calves. Topping can also encourage tillering.

Creep grazing

Creep grazing makes use of a creep gate or gap in a fence to allow calves or lambs access to another field. This field is disease free and has fresh grass available for grazing. The gate prevents the older animals from entering the field, but allows the young animals to graze and return to their mothers to suckle. It can be used in conjunction with rotational grazing.

Leader-follower system

The leader-follower system is used in conjunction with paddock grazing, where the young animals (calves) are grazed one field ahead of the older animals. Young animals have access to the freshest, leafiest, most digestible grasses, as they are always put on fresh pasture. When they are moved to the next paddock, the older animals are moved into the paddock the young animals have just left and graze down the grass that remains. It also means that the young animals are always on fresh, clean grass, so there is less chance of them picking up disease from the grass or from the older animals that have a better immune system.

Top Tip!

Definitions for **tillering, topping** and the **leader-follower system** and their advantages are often asked at both Higher and Ordinary Level.

Mixed grazing

Mixed grazing is the grazing of cattle and sheep together in the same field or paddock.

Advantages of mixed grazing

- Production levels are increased by 10% to 15% in both cattle and sheep.
- Tillering is increased as sheep graze grass closer to the ground. It also reduces the need for topping.
- There is less waste of grass due to the sheeps' close-grazing habit.
- Cows will not eat around their own dung. Sheep will eat this grass, ensuring there is no waste and preventing grass from becoming patchy, stemmy and unpalatable.
- Cows are less selective grazers than sheep, so will eat grass species that sheep will not consume.
- Mixed grazing can reduce the risk of worm infestation in cattle and sheep, as the stocking rate for each is lower when mixed, thus lowering the risk of infection. In addition, some worms are host specific, so the risk of infestation by endoparasites is reduced.

Exam questions

1   Explain the term *leader-follower* as a grazing system.   (OL 2009)

2   Grazing pasture can be improved by **tillering** and **topping**. Explain each of the highlighted terms.   (OL 2010)

3   Outline the main features of strip grazing.   (HL 2011)

4   (a) Explain the term *tillering*.
    (b) Mention **two** ways by which the farmer can encourage the tillering process.
    (c) Give **two** reasons for the process of topping grassland during the grazing season.   (HL 2008)

5 Explain the leader-follower grazing system and give **two** reasons why it is used by farmers. *(HL 2008)*

6 To measure how intensively a farm is being managed, the term *livestock unit per hectare* is used. Explain the term *livestock unit* and give an appropriate value for the livestock unit per hectare for an intensively managed dairy farm. *(HL 2007)*

7 During 2013 many farmers in Ireland experienced a fodder crisis. Describe any two circumstances, and their effects, that could contribute to a widespread shortage of fodder. *(HL 2014)*

8 In 2013 a larger number of farmers than in recent years returned to haymaking as a method of conserving grass.
   (a) Give the main reason for the return to haymaking.
   (b) Describe the main steps in conserving grass as hay and give a scientific reason behind each step. *(HL 2014)*

9 Outline **four** grassland management practices used to achieve high-quality silage. *(HL 2014)*

Key-points!

- A livestock unit is used to determine how much grazing and winter fodder are needed on a farm.
- Rotational grazing is a method of grazing that involves moving livestock from one pasture to another in a regular pattern to provide a constant supply of fresh grass.
- Paddock grazing and strip grazing are both forms of rotational grazing.
- Topping is carried out to remove ungrazed grass to prevent stemmy patches from building up in a pasture.
- Tillering is the development of side shoots in a plant.
- Zero grazing means livestock are kept indoors and grass is cut fresh and brought to the sheds for feeding.
- Creep grazing allows young livestock into a good-quality pasture while preventing access to it by older livestock. The young livestock can still suckle their mothers.
- The leader-follower system means young livestock graze one paddock ahead of the older livestock, where they will always be put on new, leafy, disease-free pasture first.

Sowing and Reseeding Grassland

24

Learning objectives

In this chapter you will learn about:

1 Reasons for reseeding grassland
2 Benefits of reseeding grassland
3 Methods of sowing and reseeding grassland

Reasons for reseeding grassland

There are a number of reasons for reseeding grassland. Overall, the aim is to improve the quality of the grass sward. There are also a number of specific reasons for reseeding:

- **Weed infestation:** Weeds reduce the productivity of a pasture.
- **Low ryegrass content/high content of poor-quality grasses:** When poor-quality grasses begin to dominate a pasture, the productivity, palatability and digestibility of the sward decrease.
- **Addition of clover:** Clover will increase the protein content of the pasture as well as fixing nitrogen in the soil if included in a seed mix.
- **Activity of animals:** Livestock may have poached the land, leading to poor-quality pasture. Livestock may also overgraze or undergraze the land. Undergrazing can lead to poorer-quality grasses becoming dominant. Overgrazing a pasture down to the roots can prevent the grass from growing back properly and hinder its ability to tiller.
- **Poor soil fertility:** Perennial ryegrass has an optimum growth rate at a pH of 6.5, so it may be necessary to lime the land to raise the pH to a suitable level. Phosphorus is important in the development of plant roots, and a soil deficient in phosphorus will lead to poor root development in the grass sward.

Benefits of reseeding grassland

- Improvement of grass quality
- Improvement of silage quality
- Increased meat and milk production
- Higher output – allows increased stocking density on land
- Better response to N fertilisers
- Longer grazing season – reduces the need for winter fodder
- Excess grass as a result of increased productivity – could be cut for silage and sold.

Methods of sowing and reseeding grassland

Direct sowing

Land is ploughed, which has the advantage of burying the weed seeds. It is harrowed to create a fine seedbed. Seed can be sown using a seed drill or by broadcasting the seed onto the soil surface and covering with a harrow.

- **Fertiliser application:** In leys sown in autumn, N fertiliser is not applied until the following spring. In spring-sown leys, fertiliser can be applied during seedbed preparation and harrowed into the soil.
- **Time of sowing:** Seed has to be sown by September in an autumn-sown ley, as frost and winter weather conditions could kill the seedlings. In spring, seed should be sown before May. This will prevent seedlings from being killed off due to drought. It will also provide a longer growing season for seed establishment.

Undersowing

This method of sowing is most commonly used on farms growing tillage crops. It is particularly suitable for tillage/grassland rotations. Undersowing means grass seed is sown with a tillage crop (e.g. barley, wheat). It is not suitable for winter cereals. Grass seed is sown

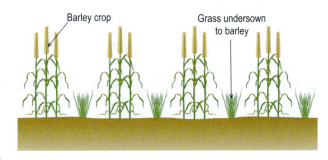

Barley crop

Grass undersown to barley

Fig 24.1 *Undersowing*

with the spring cereal. The cereal can be described as a **nurse crop**. The land is prepared for the cereal crop and the cereal seed is then sown. Cereal varieties with a short straw should be chosen to reduce the risk of lodging. Lodging will damage the grass. The grass seed is then sown immediately afterwards. Both grow at the same time. When the cereal is harvested in summer, the grass remains and establishes itself in the field.

Point to note

Nurse crop: An annual crop sown along with a perennial crop such as grass. The nurse crop is harvested, which then allows the perennial crop to become established. Nurse crops in Ireland are usually cereals but may also be leguminous crops such as peas.

Benefits of undersowing/nurse crops

- Nitrogen leaching can be prevented or reduced, as the grass will take up any excess nitrogen following the cereal harvest.
- Soil erosion can be prevented, as the grass is established after the cereal has been harvested.
- Having grass growing alongside the cereal can provide good ground cover and prevent weed infestation.

Drawbacks of undersowing

- As two crops are growing simultaneously, they are in competition for water, nutrients and space.
- Undersowing grass to a cereal will lead to a reduction in yield in the cereal crop, as it competes with the grass.
- Herbicide use must be restricted if clover is sown with the grass seed.
- This method is not suited to intensive cereal farming where high crop yields are required.

Direct drilling/direct seeding/slurry seeding

This involves the use of a direct drilling machine. This machine cuts a slit in the soil and drops a seed into it. The land does not have to be ploughed beforehand. Direct drilling is most successful if the land to be seeded/reseeded is grazed bare or if a herbicide is applied beforehand. Glyphosphate should be applied to the land to remove broadleaf weeds such as dock leaves. Seeds have the best chance of germination and establishment if they are drilled into bare land. This technique is known as slurry seeding if slurry is applied to the land directly after sowing.

Benefits of direct seeding

- This method is of most benefit on soils where ploughing is not possible or is difficult.
- Soils that are easily poached or are shallow are particularly suitable for direct seeding.

Slit seeding/stitching in

This method of reseeding is very similar to direct seeding. The main difference is that the grassland is not killed off. Seed is always sown into old grassland. Slit seeding should take place in spring (March or April), when grass growth is not at an optimum level. This will give the new seed a chance to establish itself in the sward without having to compete with the old sward during the rapid growth periods in the summer months. The old sward should be tightly grazed before seeding. Nitrogen fertiliser may be sown with the seed to encourage establishment.

Benefits of slit seeding

- These is no need to plough the land.
- Land has not been taken out of use for a prolonged period of time.
- These is an increase in production level, quality and yield in grass.
- If the seed does not establish itself, the old sward will continue to grow.
- This method can be used on poached/shallow soils not suited to ploughing.

Exam questions

1   State the most suitable method of sowing grass seed in each of the following situations:
    (a) A farmer wants to plant barley but also have grass available for grazing when the barley is harvested.
    (b) A farmer wants to sow grass seed on land that is shallow or not easily ploughed.   (OL 2011)

2   Explain the term *nurse crop*.   (HL 2012)

3   Describe **two** methods by which a named seed mixture could be introduced into a pasture without ploughing the area involved.   (HL 2004)

4   (a) Name two species of grass commonly sown on Irish farms.
    (b) Clover is used in grass seed mixtures. Give two benefits of clover   (OL 2014)

Key-points!

- Reseeding takes place to improve the quality of a pasture due to weed infestation, poor-quality grasses, damage to grass or poor soil fertility.

- Undersowing is where grass is sown with a cereal crop and is allowed to grow when the cereal is harvested.

- Direct sowing is where the land is ploughed and harrowed and grass seed is sown.

- Stitching-in allows grass to be sown into old grassland that has been grazed bare or killed off with a total herbicide.

- Slit seeding involves sowing grass seed into old pasture but without killing off the pasture beforehand.

25 Silage and Hay Production

Conservation of grass as a winter feed

Excess grass produced in summer months is saved as silage or hay for winter fodder, as there is no grass growth during winter months. Silage and hay are far cheaper sources of winter feed than concentrated animal feeds. Concentrated feeds can be used to supplement silage and hay for winter feeding. Grass conservation can only take place if bacterial activity in the grass is inhibited. Bacteria would spoil saved grass, rendering it useless. Silage and hay making use different methods of conservation.

- **Silage:** Fermentation of carbohydrates in the grass produces acids that lower the pH of the grass and inhibit all microbial activity. Properly fermented and preserved silage can be stored for a few years.
- **Hay:** Grass is dehydrated to remove the majority of the water present. In the absence of water, microbial activity is inhibited.

Factors influencing silage production

- Silage should be cut when the weather is good, in mid- to late May and again in July or August.
- Silage is cut from permanent grassland or ryegrass-sown leys.
- The heading dates of the grasses in these fields can also determine when the silage is cut. An early heading grass may be cut in May, but it will not be possible to cut a late heading grass until June.
- Grass should be cut when digestibility is high to ensure the highest possible feeding value for the silage. Dry matter digestibility is approximately 75% at the heading-out stage in perennial ryegrass.
- Grass should contain a high level of carbohydrate to ensure proper fermentation of the grass.

Key definitions

Heading out: This is when half of the grass plants have produced seed heads.

Ensiling: This is the process of storing grass or another crop in a silo, clamp or pit for preservation as silage.

Optimising carbohydrate levels in grass

- Water dilutes carbohydrate concentration in grass. Do not cut grass during or after rainfall.
- Cut grass at the vegetative stage, when it is leafy and there is a high carbohydrate concentration.
- Wilt the grass for one to two days after mowing. Wilting reduces water content, therefore increasing carbohydrate content.
- Use double chop machinery to cut the grass in smaller pieces. Carbohydrate is more accessible to bacteria for fermentation when the grass is more finely chopped.
- Cut grass in the afternoon, as the grass has been photosynthesising, giving a higher carbohydrate content.
- Adding a sugar or molasses solution increases carbohydrate content in the ensiled grass. This will ensure fermentation takes place.

The biochemistry of silage making: the fermentation process

- Fermentation of carbohydrates in grass is carried out by **anaerobic bacteria**.
- All the oxygen is removed from the cut grass by rolling it in the pit. This also prevents the grass from respiring.
- Respiration uses up carbohydrate and lowers the nutritional value of the silage.
- Bacteria respire anaerobically, converting carbohydrate into acid.
- The acids lower the pH, which inhibits bacterial activity and which preserves the grass as silage.
- The carbohydrate concentration (high/low) in the cut grass determines which bacteria will produce the acids in the fermentation process and which acids are produced.

Table 25.1 Comparison of lactic acid silage and butyric acid silage

	Lactic acid silage	Butyric acid silage
Carbohydrate concentration	High	Low
Bacteria present	*Lactobacillus*	*Clostridium*
Acid produced	Lactic acid	Butyric acid
Silage quality	Good	Poor
Nutritional value	Good	Poor
Palatability	Palatable to stock	Unpalatable to stock
Storage duration	A number of years	A few months

Silage making

Silage can be produced in two ways: in a pit/clamp or in round bales.

Pit silage

- Pit silage is more common on large-scale farms.
- A pit can be expensive to construct and is not financially viable for smaller farmers.
- The pit also needs to have a leakproof storage tank for effluent and channels to bring effluent from the pit to the tank.

- Grass is mowed and left in rows called swathes. It is allowed to wilt.
- It is then picked up by a forage harvester that cuts the grass and blows it into a trailer.
- The cut grass is brought to the silage pit or clamp and heaped. The pit should be easily accessible for winter feeding.
- A tractor is then used to roll over the layer of grass to remove any air from it. If additives are being used in the silage-making process, they can be added to each layer that is rolled. Some additives may have been added during the harvesting process.
- The pit is sealed with heavy-duty black polythene sheeting. The polythene keeps the pit airtight to allow for anaerobic respiration to take place. It also prevents water from getting into the silage.
- The polythene should be weighed down to keep it in place. Tyres can be used for this purpose. The polythene sheet should be inspected after two or three weeks and tightened and resealed, as the silage may subside during this time.

Round bale silage

- Grass for round bales should be mown and wilted for one or two days, to 30% DM.
- Swathes of grass are then collected by the baler and turned into bales.
- They are wrapped in polythene by the wrapper. Baling and wrapping can be carried out using separate baling and wrapping machines or by one integrated machine that completes both tasks. The bales should then be transported to where they are to be stored. Care should be taken in transport to prevent damage or tears to the polythene. Any damage should be rectified immediately.
- Bales should be stored standing on the flat part of the bale. This has a thicker layer of polythene and is less likely to burst. The thicker layer of polythene is also better able to withstand attack from birds.
- To comply with REPS, bales should not be stored closer than 20 m from a watercourse and stacked no more than two bales high.

Advantages of round bale silage

- Less dependent on weather conditions
- Quality of baled silage can be as good as pit silage, usually better when well managed
- Lower aerobic spoilage losses compared to pit silage
- Ideal for conservation of surplus grass and grass harvested in autumn

- Lower dry matter losses during production and storage (< 5% to 10%) than pit silage
- Flexible storage system – bales can be stored in the field or easily transported to any location on the farm
- Less expensive for the small farmer, where construction of a silage pit cannot be justified
- Low transport and storage cost
- If bales are wrapped properly, there is no effluent, which lowers the risk of pollution; effluent storage facilities and disposal are unnecessary
- Excess round bales can be sold.

Disadvantages of round bale silage

- High unit costs
- Not suitable for very wet silage
- Labour/time at feeding out
- Prone to damage if not properly handled
- Plastic waste disposal cost and compliance with waste regulations.

Silage additives

Additives are used in silage-making where carbohydrate concentration in the ensiled grass is low.

Table 25.2 Additives in silage production	
Additive	**Mode of action**
Sulfuric acid	• Acids lower the pH of the silage, inhibiting fermentation and preventing bacterial activity • Applied at a rate of 3 litres/tonne • Can reduce silage palatability and corrode machinery • Mainly used by silage contractors
Molasses	• Added to ensiled grass to increase carbohydrate concentration • The extra sugar is used in fermentation • Increases palatability of silage for livestock
Bacterial inoculants	• Speed up fermentation process and reduce pH in the pit • Work faster than acids • Can aid in protein preservation
Enzymes	• Break down grass fibres to provide additional carbohydrates for fermentation

Silage effluent

- Fermentation results in the production of a liquid known as silage effluent.
- Effluent is nutrient rich and contains nitric acid.
- It can cause pollution if it seeps into a watercourse, so it should be stored in a leakproof underground tank.
- Effluent can be diluted and spread on the land as a fertiliser, which reduces disposal costs. It should not be spread near waterways.
- Wilting grass before conservation reduces the amount of effluent produced.

Assessing silage quality

Silage can be assessed for quality by examining its **colour, texture, smell, pH and DM content**. Most of these tests can be done at the silage pit. A sample of silage can also be tested in the laboratory if more appropriate.

Table 25.3 Comparison of lactic acid and butyric acid silage					
Silage type	Colour	Texture	Smell	pH	DM content
Lactic acid	Yellow-green	Soft but firm. Fibres do not wear easily.	Sharp, acidic, vinegar.	< 5.0. Ideally should be between 3.8 and 4.2.	Liquid cannot be removed by hand. DM > 25%.
Butyric acid	Dark green	Wet and slimy.	Putrid or rancid.	> 5.0. Acidic but has not been properly preserved, only clostridial bacteria present.	Liquid can be wrung out with two hands. DM 20% to 25%. Liquid can be squeezed out with one hand. DM < 20%.

- **Colour:** Begin with a visual assessment of the silage. Note its colour.
- **Texture:** Rub the sample between your fingers. Note the feel of the leaves and the stems.
- **Smell:** Smell the silage and record the smell.
- **pH:** Squeeze liquid from silage and put a pH meter probe into the liquid to read the pH. Alternately, if liquid cannot be squeezed from the silage, place a small amount of silage (20 g) in a beaker with 20 ml distilled water. Stir the silage and water. Place the pH meter probe in the water and record the pH.

- **DM content:** Squeeze a sample of silage with one hand. Note if any liquid can be removed from it. Repeat by wringing out a sample of silage with two hands and note if any liquid can be removed from it.
- **DM assessment in lab:** Place 50 g silage in a microwave for 30 seconds. Remove from the microwave and weigh it. Multiply its mass by 2 to calculate dry matter.

Top Tip! Assessing silage quality can be examined by experiment or by a comparison of two silage samples under the headings listed.

 **Experiment**

Determining the leaf-to-stem ratio of a silage sample

1   Take a sample of silage and weigh it.

2   Separate the leaves from the stems and divide into two piles.

3   Weigh two dishes. Place the leaves in one dish and the stems in another.

4   Reweigh each dish and record the weight of leaves and stems.

5   Calculate the ratio of leaves to stems.

6   The higher the ratio of leaves, the better the quality of the silage, as leafy silage has a higher feeding value.

Hay making

About 18% of conserved grass in Ireland is used for hay making. Its popularity has declined over the years, with more farmers choosing to make silage. As hay making is heavily reliant on good weather conditions, silage making has become a safer choice. However, hay has the advantage of being a clean, easily transported winter feed that produces no effluent.

Hay production

- Grass should ideally be cut in late May/early June, but having the grass at the correct growth stage is most important. DMD should be high.
- Do not allow livestock to graze the field prior to harvest. Fertilise grass with N-P-K fertiliser, such as 18-6-12.
- Cut grass for hay only when a prolonged period of dry weather is expected.
- Warm, sunny, dry weather is needed to remove the moisture from the crop. The moisture levels at storage should be less than 20%.
- A **rotary mower** is used to cut the grass and leave it in rows.

- A **rotary tedder** (hay bob) shakes the grass, allowing air to pass through it and speeding up the drying process.
- Ted grass twice before baling. Gather the grass into rows for baling using the tedder.
- Collect the dried grass with the **baler** and make bales. Secure bales with net wrap or baling twine. Bales should be moved into storage in a hay shed as soon as possible to avoid getting wet.

Exam questions

1   Explain the contrasting approaches used in the conservation of grass for winter feed as:
    (a) Silage
    (b) Hay.   (HL 2001)

2   There will always be a role for hay in Irish farming.
    (a) Defend this statement.
    (b) Outline **three** principal steps in conserving grass as hay.   (HL 2012)

3   Describe a lab or field method to assess the quality of grass silage.   (HL 2012)

4   Explain the significance of the leaf-to-stem ratio in relation to silage quality.
                                                                            (HL 2010)

Key-points!

- Grass is fermented, producing acid that preserves the grass as silage.
- Grass can also be dehydrated, which preserves the grass as hay.
- The higher the carbohydrate level in the grass at cutting, the better-quality silage is produced.
- Silage can be assessed by its colour, smell, texture, taste, pH, DM percentage and leaf-to-stem ratio.
- Silage can be preserved in a pit, which requires an effluent tank to store the liquid effluent that seeps from the silage.
- Silage can also be preserved in round bales.
- Additives can be added to silage, such as molasses or acid to help in the preservation process.
- Hay production must take place in dry, sunny weather when there is enough time available to dry out the grass.

26 Principles of Crop Production

Certified seed

Seeds must pass identity and purity tests to be classified as certified seed. The main advantage of using certified seed is that the germination rate is guaranteed and therefore a high yield can be guaranteed.

Properties of certified seed (cereals)

- Must have a minimum germination rate of 85%
- Must have a minimum analytical purity rate of 98%
- Must have undergone treatment with fungicide/pesticide
- Must be completely free from wild oat seed.

Experiment

To determine the percentage germination of certified seed and uncertified seed

1 Count out 100 grains of certified seed and 100 grains of uncertified seed. Do not mix the two samples.

2   Place each sample in a separate labelled beaker. Add water and leave to soak for 24 hours.

3   Using labelled seed trays, lay out damp filter paper on the tray or use a suitable growth medium. Lay the seeds from each sample in separate trays.

4   Place the trays in darkness for one week. Check on the trays regularly to ensure the filter paper has not dried out. If it has, add some water to it.

5   After one week, count the number of germinated seeds.

Result

To calculate the germination rate, calculate the number of seeds germinated as a percentage of the total sown for each sample.

Winter and spring seed varieties

Some varieties of cereal seed are not suitable to the colder conditions experienced during winter and would not survive winter frosts. Winter and spring variety seeds give farmers flexibility in when to sow a crop. Winter and spring varieties can be sown in rotation. Farmers can use winter varieties to spread the work in a mixed-farming system.

Table 26.1 Characteristics of winter and spring variety seeds

Winter variety seeds	Spring variety seeds
Frost resistant	Not frost resistant
Sown September to November	Sown February to April
Harvested from mid-July onwards	Harvested from August onwards
Longer growing season	Shorter growing season
Higher yield due to longer growing season	Lower yield due to shorter growing season

Advantages of sowing winter variety cereals

- In a mixed farming system (tillage and livestock), labour may be spread out over the year by sowing winter varieties, as the farmer will be busy with calving and lambing in springtime.
- Winter varieties have a longer growing season and as a result a higher yield – by as much as 20%.
- Harvesting dates for winter varieties are earlier, so they can be harvested in good weather conditions.

- Poor weather conditions in spring may delay sowing, germination and establishment of a crop. This can lead to a delay in harvesting and lower yields than winter varieties.

Crop rotation

Advantages of crop rotation

- **Prevention of the build-up of pests and diseases:** Different crops are affected by different pests. Rotating a crop annually prevents a build-up of pests of that crop. If a different type of crop is sown (e.g. cereal followed by root), the chances of being damaged by pests of the crop are reduced.

- **Prevention of the build-up of weeds:** Similar to pests, crops have particular weeds associated with them. A crop rotation will help control weeds and prevent an infestation in the crop.

- **Nutrient management:** Growing the same crop continuously means the soil will be depleted of certain nutrients. Rotation gives the soil a chance to replenish those nutrients, as different crops will use nutrients in different quantities. In addition, some crops add nutrients to the soil (legumes add nitrogen to the soil).

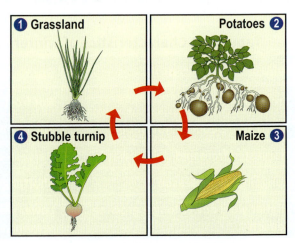

Fig 26.1 *An example of a four-year crop rotation.*

- **Soil structure:** Crops with fibrous root systems help bind soil together, preventing soil erosion. Grass can be ploughed back into soil, contributing organic matter to the soil.

Direct control (chemical control) of weeds, pests and diseases

Direct control (chemical control) is the use of chemicals to control or eradicate weeds, pests and diseases. There are three types of chemical control: herbicides, fungicides and pesticides.

Key definitions

Herbicide: A chemical that kills plants or inhibits their growth.

Fungicide: A chemical that kills or inhibits the growth of fungi.

Pesticide: A chemical used to kill pests (particularly insects and rodents).

Types of herbicide

- **Selective herbicides:** These herbicides control or kill certain species of plant life without harming other plant species. Many are designed to kill off broad leaf weeds, which absorb more of the chemical than narrow leaf cereal and grass species.

- **Non-selective herbicides:** These are also known as total herbicides. They kill all plant life and do not distinguish between weeds and crops. An example of a total herbicide is Roundup.

- **Pre- and post-emergent herbicides:** Herbicides work in a number of ways. Pre-emergent herbicides prevent germinating weeds from establishing themselves in a crop and are applied before weeds have germinated. Post-emergent herbicides kill weeds after they have germinated. They should be applied after the weed has germinated and can be seen in the crop.

Modes of action

- **Contact herbicide:** These chemicals only kill the foliage they come into contact with, so complete coverage of the plant is important.

- **Translocated herbicide:** These chemicals are absorbed by the plant and are translocated to the stem, leaves and roots. The herbicide kills off each part of the plant it comes into contact with. This type of herbicide is particularly suitable for perennial weeds.

- **Soil-acting herbicide:** These are also known as residual herbicides. They are applied to the soil and absorbed by the germinating weed seedlings, killing them off as they grow.

Types of fungicide

- **Contact fungicides:** They will only kill the fungi they have come into contact with, so it is important to apply the fungicide to the entire plant.
- **Systemic fungicides:** These are absorbed by the plant and translocated to the stem, leaves and roots. They kill any fungal infection they come into contact with.
- **Translaminar fungicide:** This is sprayed on the crop and absorbed by the upper leaf surface and translocated to the lower leaf surface, giving it protection from fungal attack.
- **Protective fungicides:** These are used as a preventative measure. They are sprayed on the crop before attacks occur to protect them from any possible fungal attack. Spray in dry weather to prevent the fungicide from being washed away by rain.

Pesticides

Insecticides are used to kill insects that are pests of plant crops and animals. Crops may be sprayed with a solution of the pesticide. The pesticide may remain on the surface of the plant or be absorbed by the plant's foliage. When an insect pest eats the plant foliage, it will ingest the insecticide and will die. The insect may also be killed by contact with the insecticide.

Non-chemical control of weeds, pests and diseases

Indirect control

This is the implementation of agricultural practices that do not eradicate pests and diseases directly, but instead discourages their establishment.

> **Point to note**
>
> **Biological control:** The control of a pest organism by the introduction of a predator or parasite of that organism. A common example is the ladybird, which is the natural predator of the aphid.

There are five methods of controlling pests, weeds and diseases indirectly:

- **Crop rotation** prevents the build-up of pests, weeds and diseases of a specific crop by sowing dissimilar crops in the same place in subsequent years.
- **Sowing resistant crop varieties** helps to prevent attack from pests and diseases, as these varieties are not affected by the disease.

- **Growth encouragement** promotes the growth of healthy crops, which prevents growth of weeds and attack by pests and diseases. Growth in plants is favoured by availability of nutrients (fertilisers), proper seedbed preparation and timely sowing of seed.
- **The timely harvesting of the crop** ensures that the crop is less susceptible to attack. Over-ripe crops increase the risk of damage by pests and diseases.
- **Stubble cleaning** is the cultivation of the land with ploughs and harrows after harvest. Harrowing the land encourages weeds to germinate. When the weeds have germinated, the land is harrowed again and the weeds are killed.

Exam questions

1   Give the scientific explanation for the treatment of cereal seeds with fungicide before sowing.   *(HL 1998)*

2   (a) List **three** advantages of crop rotation.
    (b) Name **two** crops that can be grown as a suitable root break in a cereal rotation.
    (c) State any **one** use for **one** of the crops you have mentioned.   *(HL 2008)*

3   What is the difference between a selective herbicide and a total herbicide?
                                                                                   (OL 2011)

Key-points!

- Certified seed must have a minimum germination rate of 85%, 98% purity, be free from wild oats and be treated with a fungicide and pesticide.
- Non-selective herbicides (total herbicides) kill all vegetation they come into contact with. Selective herbicides kill certain species of plant life without killing other species.
- Fungicides are used to kill or control the spread of fungal diseases in plants.
- Pesticides are used to eradicate or control pests that attack plants, such as insects, slugs, snails and rodents.
- Indirect (biological) control is the control of a pest organism by the introduction of a predator or parasite of that organism.
- Stubble cleaning is the cultivation of the land with ploughs and harrows after harvest. Harrowing the land encourages weeds to germinate. When the weeds have germinated, the land is harrowed again and the weeds are killed.

27 Cereal Crops

Learning objectives

In this chapter you will learn about:

1 Cereal crop varieties

2 Cultivation of barley

3 Popularity of barley and other cereal crops

4 Maize and advantages of maize silage

5 Experiment: To calculate the 1,000 grain weight of a cereal

Cereal crop varieties

The Gramineae family includes the cereals barley, wheat, oats and maize. Of these crops, barley is the most widely grown cereal in Ireland.

Table 27.1 Uses of cereal crops	
Crop	**Uses**
Malting barley	Malting and brewing, alcohol production; straw is used for animal bedding
Feeding barley	Production of animal feed; straw is used for animal bedding
Wheat	Flour production (baking), animal bedding, mushroom composting
Oats	Animal feed (horses), human consumption
Maize	Maize silage (winter feed), human consumption

Cereal crop varieties are chosen based on a number of characteristics:

- Yield
- Shortness of straw
- Strength of straw
- Earliness of ripening
- Disease resistance
- Winter hardiness (for winter varieties only).

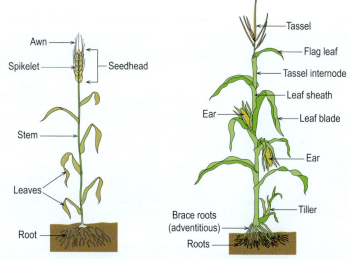

Fig 27.1 Barley

Fig 27.2 Maize

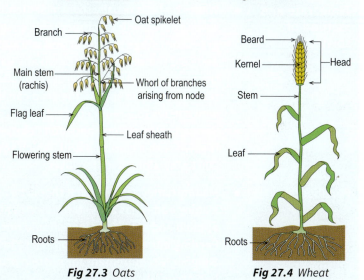

Fig 27.3 Oats

Fig 27.4 Wheat

Table 27.2 Cereal varieties commonly sown in Ireland

Crop	Varieties
Barley	Amarena, Saffron, Quench
Wheat	Cordial, Einstein, Sparrow
Oats	Barry, Evita, Husky
Maize	Fergus, Destiny, Kougar

Cultivation of barley

Table 27.3 Cultivation of barley	
Soil suitability	• Malting barley: Deep sandy loam soils and grey brown podzolics, pH 6.5. • Feeding barley: Brown earth and loam soils, pH 6.0–6.5.
Climate	• Dry conditions needed for harvesting. • Moisture is important for barley growth, as drought leads to a lower yield and a poorer-quality grain. • South-east Ireland has the most suitable climate for barley growing.
Preparation of seedbed	• Land should be autumn ploughed and then harrowed with a one-run harrow. • For spring barley, land may also be rolled after sowing seed to ensure good seed-soil contact.
Time, rate and method of sowing	• Winter barley is usually sown in September, with the optimum sowing date being 1 October. This ensures it will reach the grass corn stage by winter and will survive the winter frost and cold temperatures. If sown any earlier it will grow past the grass corn stage and grow too tall. When growth recommences in spring, the crop can be prone to lodging, which leads to a reduced yield. • Spring barley is sown between February and April. Barley is sown with a combine drill, which sows seed at a rate of 200 kg/ha along with fertiliser.
Fertilisers	• Malting barley: Only P and K should be applied at sowing. Malting barley has a low N requirement, so N should not be applied and split dressings should not be used. • Feeding barley: N can be applied to feeding barley, as it has a higher N requirement for protein production. N is supplied by CAN or 10-10-20.
Weed control	• Selective herbicides are used to control weeds. The crop should be sprayed at the 3–5 leaf stage. Crop rotation and stubble cleaning also help to control weeds.
Rotation	• Feeding barley: Soil-borne pests and diseases do not seriously affect barley, so it can be sown continuously. Rotation may help to increase yield. • Malting barley: As it has a lower N requirement than feeding barley, it should not be sown after grass/legumes in a rotation.

| Harvest and storage | • Barley is harvested with a combine harvester. When the crop is ripe, the ear will bend over and lie parallel to the stem. The grains will be hard and dry and the golden colour of the crop fades. Grain should have low moisture levels; otherwise it will have to be dried out. |
| | • Grain that is kept in storage is treated with propionic acid. Acid treatment prevents the grain from being attacked by pests, fungi and bacteria. It is stored in large, ventilated sheds. |

Point to note

Lodging is the tendency of cereal crops to bend over so that they lie more or less flat on the ground. This makes it impossible to harvest the crop and reduces the yield.

Table 27.4 Yields of cereal crops

Crop	Tonnes/ha	Harvest date
Winter barley	7–9	July
Spring barley	6–7	August
Winter wheat	9: Low yield	Mid-July to early August
	11: High yield	Mid-July to early August
Spring wheat	8.5	Mid-August to September
Winter oats	7.5	July to August
Spring oats	6.5	August to September

Table 27.5 Weeds, pests and diseases of cereal crops

Disease/pest name	Crops affected	Symptoms and treatment
Powdery mildew	Barley, wheat, oats	• Fungal disease • Affects the leaves of the plant • Forms grey-white patches of fungus on the leaves • Underside of the leaves turns yellow • Treated by spraying a fungicide

Disease/pest name	Crops affected	Symptoms and treatment
Barley yellow dwarf virus (BYDV) / red leaf in oats	Barley	• Viral disease transmitted by aphids • The leaves turn bright yellow
	Oats	• Yield is reduced • Controlled by the use of an aphicide
Leaf blotch (leaf scald) / *Rhynchosporium*	Barley	• Fungal disease • Causes large yield losses • Diamond-shaped chlorotic patches on leaves • Controlled by the use of a fungicide
Leaf blotch / *Septoria*	Wheat	• Fungal disease • Yellow spots on the leaves that elongate to form larger yellow-brown patches • Spray with a protective fungicide and plough in wheat stubble
Take all (root and crown rot)	Wheat	• Fungal disease • Stunted growth with white heads on wheat • White heads empty of grain • Roots may also be blackened • Spraying with a fungicide or using seed dressings can help to control this disease
Leaf rust (brown rust)	Barley	• Orange-brown circular spores that are found on leaf surfaces • Premature death of leaves • Reduction in yield • Controlled by the use of a fungicide spray
Eyespot	Oats, maize	• Fungal disease • Leaves of the plant will display brown spots, each surrounded by a yellow circle • Spray crop with a fungicide when they are 1 metre tall (maize)
Wireworms	Barley, wheat, oats, maize	• Feed on the seeds, roots and stems of plants • Reduce the yield of the plant • Cause lodging
Leatherjackets	Barley, wheat, oats	• Cause damage by eating the roots and underground stems of the plant • Can be controlled by spraying the crop with a pesticide

Popularity of barley and other cereal crops

Barley is the most widely grown cereal crop in Ireland. There is substantially more barley grown than wheat, oats or maize. There are a number of reasons for its popularity and the smaller area of land sown under other cereal crops.

- Barley is suited to the Irish climate, whereas wheat does not grow as well in our cool, wet climate.
- Barley is higher in protein and fibre than wheat and is therefore a more valuable animal feed.
- Much of the wheat produced in Ireland is not suitable for flour making, the principal product of wheat.
- Varieties of wheat suited to the Irish climate are not always suitable for milling.
- As the wheat varieties grown in Ireland are not suitable for high-grade milling, the price received for wheat grain is not as favourable.
- Oats, which are used for feeding horses, have declined as the role of the horse has declined in agriculture.
- Maize grown in the open requires warm temperatures, so most maize in Ireland is grown under plastic and harvested using specialist machinery, incurring extra costs.

Maize

Maize is a relatively new cereal crop to Ireland. However, its popularity as a crop for animal feed is increasing annually. Maize silage is an alternative winter feed option to grass silage and concentrates for livestock farmers.

Advantages of maize silage

- It has a higher dry matter yield than first-cut grass silage (15–20 tonnes/ha vs 7–8 tonnes/ha).
- It has a higher dry matter content than first-cut grass silage (28–32% vs 20–22%).
- With its higher DM value, maize produces little or no effluent, thus reducing storage and disposal costs and reducing the potential to pollute.
- Feeding maize silage to beef and dairy cattle increases their dry matter intake and live weight gain, thus reducing the need for feed concentrates.
- No additives are needed, as the sugar content of the maize is so high.
- Maize contains high levels of starch and protein and is palatable to livestock.

To calculate the 1,000 grain weight of a cereal

Note: This experiment can be carried out using any cereal grain (e.g. barley, wheat, oats).

1 Examine the seed sample and remove any damaged seeds, straw, etc.

2 Count out 1,000 seeds or count out a specified number of seeds, e.g. 100 seeds.

3 Weigh the seed sample and record the mass.

4 Count out a second sample of the seeds and repeat the procedure eight times.

5 Calculate the average mass of the seed samples.

6 For samples that contained fewer than 1,000 seeds, multiply by the relevant factor to get 1,000 grain weight. For example, for 100 seed weight, multiply by 10 to calculate the 1,000 grain weight.

Point to note

The 1,000 grain weight is used to calculate seeding rates for crops. If the 1,000 grain weight is known and the germination and establishment rates of the seed are known, it is possible to calculate how much seed will be needed for sowing.

Exam questions

1 Give **four** reasons why the area under **wheat** cultivation is much less than the area under **barley** cultivation in Ireland. *(HL 2012)*

2 Give a scientific explanation for the occurrence of bare patches of ground in a recently sown cereal crop. *(HL 2012)*

3 Mention **three** features that distinguish the production of malting barley from feeding barley. *(HL 2007)*

4 Describe **four** signs of ripeness in a cereal. *(HL 2011)*

5	Describe in detail the production of a named cereal crop under each of the following headings:
   (a) Soil suitability
   (b) Preparation of the seed bed
   (c) Sowing the seed
   (d) Use of fertiliser
   (e) Harvesting
   (f) Straw yield.   *(HL 2014)*

6	Compare the growing of malting barley and feeding barley under the following headings:
   (a) Soil type
   (b) Rotation
   (c) Fertiliser regime
   (d) End use.   *(HL 2011)*

7	Account for the increasing popularity of maize silage as a feed for dairy cows. *(HL 2010)*

Key-points!

- Cereal crop varieties are chosen based on a number of characteristics: yield, shortness of straw, strength of straw, earliness of ripening, disease resistance and winter hardiness (winter varieties only).

- Malting barley is used in alcohol production, while feeding barley is used for the production of animal feeds.

- Lodging is the tendency of cereal crops to bend over so that they lie more or less flat on the ground. This makes it impossible to harvest the crop and reduces the yield.

- Barley is the most popular cereal crop, as it is more suited to the Irish climate. Wheat varieties grown in Ireland are not suitable for flour production.

- Maize silage is a suitable winter feed, as it has a high protein content, a high DM content, is palatable to livestock and produces no effluent.

28 Potatoes, Roots and Catch Crops

Learning objectives

In this chapter you will learn about:

1 Potatoes and root crops

2 Sugar beet

3 Catch crops

Potatoes and root crops

The potato is one of the most important crops in Ireland. It is a stem tuber. Sugar beet was once the mainstay of the Irish sugar industry, but currently is only grown by a small number of farmers for winter fodder. Kale and stubble turnip are popular catch crops, which can be used for winter feed and are often described as fodder crops.

Table 28.1 Crops and crop families

Crop	Family
Potato	Solonaceae
Sugar beet	Chenopodiaceae
Kale	Cruciferae
Stubble turnip	Cruciferae

Classification of potatoes

Potatoes are classified as:

- **First earlies:** Planted in early spring (February to March). They are not frost resistant and are grown in southern coastal areas (Cork, Wexford). They are harvested immature from May onwards. They have a low yield but command a high price.

- **Second earlies:** Sown in spring, but harvested later than first earlies. As a result they have a higher yield than the first earlies but have a lower price.

- **Maincrop:** Sown in spring and harvested when fully mature in September to October. They have a high yield and are used to supply consumers until May of the following year.

Table 28.2 Potato varieties and characteristics

Category	Variety	Characteristics
First earlies	Home Guard Epicure	Good eating quality, good yield Good eating quality and yield
Second earlies	British Queen Maris Piper	Excellent eating quality Good yield
Maincrop	Kerr's Pink Golden Wonder Cara	Good eating quality, high yield Excellent eating quality, low yield Low dry matter, poorer eating quality, very high yield

Potato seed production

Seed potato production is centred in Donegal. Aphids are a carrier of many potato diseases. Their population is kept low by the cool, windy conditions of Donegal reducing the risk of disease. Donegal is also isolated from the rest of the country, which helps to prevent the spread of disease in the seed crop.

Seed potatoes must be free from potato cyst nematode and viruses such as leaf roll, virus Y and leaf mosaic virus. Certified seed potatoes have a high germination rate, a high yield and are true to type.

Top Tip!

Cultivation of potatoes or a root crop is a common question on the Ordinary Level paper. It also appears frequently on the Higher Level paper.

Cultivation of potatoes

Soil suitability

- Deep, well-drained loam and sandy loam soils.
- pH 5.5 to 6.0.
- Irrigation may be needed in dry summers, as drought affects tuber development and reduces yield.

Rotation

- Ware potatoes should only be grown one year in four.
- Seed potatoes should only be grown one year in five.
- Rotation prevents the build-up of potato cyst nematode.

Preparation of seedbed

- Land is ploughed in spring to a depth of 22 cm and rotovated.
- Seedbeds are 172–182 cm wide and will accommodate two drills.
- Stones and clods are removed by a destoning machine and placed in a line at the side of the seedbed.

Sowing

Potatoes are sown 10 cm below the ridge. The size of the potato seed determines the space between seeds.

Table 28.3 Seeding rate for potatoes

Seed size	Spacing	Sowing rate
35–45 mm	20–25 cm	60,000
45–55 mm	30–35 cm	40,000

In large commercial operations, a potato planter is used to plant seed.

Sprouting

Sprouting (also known as chitting) can be carried out before planting. Potatoes are exposed to light in order to develop shoots. This gives the potatoes a head start and speeds up growth, plant emergence and yield and is essential in early potato production.

Fertiliser application

- 10-10-20 is one of the most popular fertilisers in potato production for providing N, P and K. It is broadcast onto the soil during the cultivation process.
- Commercial growers place the fertiliser in a band on either side of the drill. Fertiliser is evenly distributed and it ensures uniform growth.
- Fertilisers can have negative effects. Too much N depresses the dry matter content of the tuber, producing watery potatoes. Excess phosphate also depresses dry matter. Sulfate of potash (source of potassium) increases dry matter.

Weed control

Contact and residual herbicides can be used to kill established and emergent weeds. Contact herbicides kill off the potato plant foliage as well as the weeds, but the plants will grow back quickly. Shading by the potato plants prevents weeds from establishing.

Earthing up

This involves making ridges deeper by covering haulms with more soil. It prevents exposure of the growing tubers to sunlight, which prevents greening in potatoes. Green potatoes contain poisonous alkaloids and cannot be sold. It also prevents blight spores from being washed down into the soil and onto the tubers.

Harvest and storage

Potatoes are harvested from early May (first earlies) to late October (maincrop). Haulms are killed off with a herbicide. This makes harvesting easier and allows the tuber skins to toughen. Potatoes are harvested with an elevator digger.

Potatoes are stored in well-ventilated, leakproof, frostproof sheds. Potatoes are stocked up to 1.8 m high. If allowed to overheat, the potatoes will start to sprout. This can be prevented by spraying sprout inhibitor.

Yield

- First and second earlies: 7–10 tonnes/ha.
- Maincrop: 30–40 tonnes/ha.

Potato pests and diseases

Table 28.4 Potato pests and diseases	
Disease	**Symptoms, prevention and treatment**
Potato blight	Fungal disease, **Phytophthora infestans**. Prevalent in humid weather conditions. Symptoms include: • Yellow spots that turn black on leaves • White furry growth on the underside of leaves • Spores are then washed into soil, where they infect and rot the tubers. It can be prevented by spraying the crop with a fungicide. Crops should be sprayed every 10 days when warnings are issued.

Disease	Symptoms, prevention and treatment
Blackleg	Bacterial disease, *Erwinia carotovora*. Causes the soft rot of tubers and can prevent emergence of the potato plant if seed is infected. Symptoms include: • Yellow leaves • Stems turn black at ground level. Cool, wet weather favours the spread of the bacteria causing the disease, as do poor-draining soils. It can be prevented by sowing disease-free certified seed, removing infected plants and tubers and ensuring all potatoes are removed from the soil at harvest. Rotation is also effective at controlling blackleg.
Wireworms	Can affect potatoes if planted after pasture. They eat tubers, reducing yield and quality. They can be controlled by spraying an insecticide.

Sugar beet

Main product: Sugar.

By-products and their uses

- **Molasses:** Used in animal feeds and to increase palatability of silage. It is also a silage additive, stimulating the fermentation of grass.
- **Beet tops:** Animal feed that can be grazed *in situ*, as tops are separated from root and remain in the field at harvest.
- **Beet pulp:** Used as animal feed, it is the remains of the crop left after the sugar extraction process.

Deficiency diseases

- Heart rot (crown rot) caused by a lack of boron (B)
- Speckled yellows caused by a lack of manganese (Mn).

Sugar beet also needs sodium (Na), as it is related to sea beet, a salt-loving coastal plant.

Yield

- Roots: 40 tonnes/ha.
- Tops: 25 tonnes/ha.

Feeding sugar beet tops

Sugar beet tops can be fed to livestock *in situ*. However, they contain oxalic acid, which causes scour in animals. To reduce the concentration of oxalic acid in the beet tops, they should be wilted for one week before allowing livestock to graze them. Wilting reduces the oxalic acid concentration.

Top Tip!
Questions on the advantages or reasons for growing catch crops have appeared numerous times on the exam.

Catch crops

> **Key definition**
>
> **Catch crops** are fast-growing crops grown between two main crops when land would otherwise lie idle.

Advantages and disadvantages of catch crops

Table 28.5 Advantages and disadvantages of catch crops

Advantages	Disadvantages
• Reduced feed costs, reduced need for expensive concentrates • High crude protein content in some crops (kale) • Help prevent soil erosion and nitrogen leaching • Break crop between grass and cereals • Early bite for dairy cows when grazed in February	• Labour intensive if strip grazed or zero grazed • Must be supplemented with hay/silage if crop is low in fibre • Vulnerable to disease and pest attacks; crop rotation must be used • Costly to replace productive pasture with catch crop unless reseeding • Brassicas are low in iodine and can inhibit uptake of iodine in livestock • Risk of poaching if grazed *in situ* in wet winter months

Cultivation of kale and stubble turnip

Table 28.6 Cultivation of kale and stubble turnip

	Kale	Stubble turnip
Soil suitability	Free-draining loam/sandy loam soils, pH 6.0–7.0	Free-draining loam, pH 6.5
Rotation	Grow 1 in 5 years	Grow 1 in 3 years

	Kale	Stubble turnip
Growth period	5–6 months	12–14 weeks
Sowing	Spring/autumn	All year round, but is not winter hardy
Pests and diseases	Both kale and stubble turnip are susceptible to club root, a soil-borne fungus that attacks members of the Cruciferae family. Flea beetles also attack both crops, leaving circular holes in the leaves. Can be controlled by spraying insecticides.	
Uses	Strip grazed fodder for livestock	Feed for finishing lambs (spring crop) Winter fodder (summer crop)
Yield	6–12 tonnes/ha	38–40 tonnes/ha

Exam questions

1   Give a reason for **each** of the following practices in potato cultivation:
   (a) Sprouting
   (b) Burning off the haulms
   (c) Earthing up
   (d) Using certified seed.   (HL 2012)

2   Outline **four** reasons for losses occurring in potatoes during storage.
                                                                     (HL 2012)

3   Highlight the main differences between a nurse crop and a catch crop.
                                                                     (HL 2012)

4   First early potatoes are usually grown in coastal areas of the east and south of Ireland. Give **two** reasons why these areas are suitable for early potato production.   (OL 2012)

5   Give **two** advantages and **two** disadvantages of strip grazing in the feeding of fodder roots to sheep.   (HL 2011)

6   Identify the type of organism that causes each of the following diseases and explain how each disease could be controlled or prevented:
   (a) Club root in turnips
   (b) Leaf roll in potatoes.   (HL 2008)

7   Give **two** reasons why the intake of fodder crops (e.g. rape and kale) in the diet of a farm animal should be limited.   (HL 2007)

8   Describe the production of a named catch crop on a tillage farm.   (HL 2007)

Key-points!

- Potatoes are classified as first earlies, second earlies or maincrop. First earlies are harvested immature with a low yield but command a high price. Second earlies and maincrop have a higher yield but lower price.

- The seed potato industry is located in Donegal, where cool, windy conditions keep aphid populations low. Aphids carry viral diseases such as leaf roll and potato mosaic virus.

- Potatoes need deep, well-drained loam soils and should be grown in rotation, planting no more frequently than one year in four.

- Sprouting prior to planting speeds up growth and plant emergence, increases yield and is essential in early potato production.

- Haulms are burnt off before harvesting to make harvesting easier and it allows tuber skins to toughen.

- Sugar beet tops must be wilted before feeding to cattle to reduce the levels of oxalic acid in the tops, as it causes scouring.

- Catch crops are fast-growing crops grown between two main crops when land would otherwise lie idle.

- A break crop is sown between two similar crops, possibly as part of a rotation including grass and cereals.

29 General Principles of Animal Production

Learning objectives

In this chapter you will learn about:

1 Animal nutrition and feeds
2 Experiment: To compare the digestibility of rolled barley vs whole barley when fed to cows
3 Metabolisable energy and food conversion ratios
4 Maintenance and production diets
5 Conformation
6 Body condition score (BCS)
7 Care and management of newborn animals
8 Factors that contribute to mortality at birth
9 Criteria for the culling of stock
10 Criteria for the selection of breeding stock

Animal nutrition and feeds

Cattle, sheep and pigs must have a diet that incorporates all the nutrients.

Table 29.1 Nutrients and their functions

Nutrient	Function
Carbohydrate	Energy and fibre (roughage)
Protein	Growth and repair of cells, energy
Fat	Insulation and energy
Vitamins	Control of many metabolic processes

Nutrient	Function
Minerals	Bone and teeth building, energy production, milk production
Water	Solvent, aids in temperature regulation, lactation and other metabolic processes

Protein is an important component of any animal's diet, as it is used to produce muscle, milk, etc. Protein is composed of amino acids. In monogastric animals, such as pigs, several of these amino acids must be present in their diet, e.g. lysine. These are referred to as essential amino acids. Ruminant animals (cattle and sheep) do not have any dietary requirement for amino acids because the microorganisms in their rumen have the ability to synthesise all amino acids (essential and non-essential).

Table 29.2 Essential and non-essential amino acids	
Essential amino acids	**Non-essential amino acids**
• Cannot be manufactured in the monogastric animal's body • Must be obtained in the animal's diet • Examples: Lysine and methionine	• Can be manufactured in the body from other amino acids • Examples: Alanine and glutomine

Animal feeds can be divided into bulky feeds and concentrate feeds.

Bulky feeds

Bulky feeds are high in water or fibre (roughage). Feeds such as hay, haylage and straw are high in fibre.

> **Top Tip!**
>
> **Haylage** is commonly used as a winter feed for horses. It is cut like hay but left to dry for a shorter period of time (until the moisture content is between 30–40%). Haylage is wrapped, similar to silage, and a mild fermentation preserves it.

Fibre has a number of important roles in the diet of ruminant animals (cattle and sheep).

- Fibre is required to develop the rumen in calves and lambs (scratch factor). It is normally introduced in the first week of the animal's life.

- Fibre is required for the correct functioning of the rumen in older animals.
- Fibre prevents acidosis in cattle and sheep.
- An increase in fibre in a dairy cow's diet increases the butterfat content of the milk.

Concentrate feeds

Concentrate feeds are low in water and fibre. Concentrate feeds are formulated rations to give the correct balance of protein, carbohydrate, minerals and vitamins.

Cereals often make up a substantial proportion of the formulated ration. Barley, wheat and maize are commonly used. The advantages of using cereals include:

- They are high in carbohydrates and energy.
- Their seed coats contain fibre.
- They can be used to supplement poor-quality silage.
- They ensure production targets are met.

> **Point to note**
>
> Carbohydrate (for energy) and protein are important in dairy and beef production for milk production and live weight gain (LWG). Formulated rations for pigs will have less fibre than cattle and sheep. Pigs are monogastric animals and are unable to digest fibre. Pigs' rations also have lysine added, an essential amino acid required by pigs.

Concentrated rations often have added vitamins and minerals included to prevent deficiency diseases.

There are a number of other ways an animal's diet can be supplemented with minerals:

- Dusting mineral supplements into silage
- Providing mineral licks
- Dressing the pasture
- Adding them to drinking water
- Providing an oral dose or a mineral bullet.

Barley is commonly used in both pig and ruminant rations. In a ruminant ration, the barley is rolled. This breaks the seed coat, allowing the ruminant's digestive system to completely break down the contents of the seed. In pig ration, the barley must be ground down so that it can be easily digested.

Experiment

To compare the digestibility of rolled barley vs whole barley when fed to cows

1. House two similar cows (similar age, breed) indoors for the duration of the experiment.

2. Feed one cow 500 g of rolled barley and the other cow 500 g of whole barley.

3. Cows are also provided with water and hay or silage.

4. Collect dung separately from both cows.

5. Wash dung through a sieve with water.

6. Collect and count any whole grain barley.

Result

The cow fed whole barley seeds will have more undigested barley grains in its dung than the cow fed rolled barley.

The testing of animal feeds for the presence of nutrients is summarised in Table 29.3 below. Deionised water can be used as a control for each of these tests.

Top Tip!

These tests can be used for testing any food product for nutrients, e.g. showing the presence of protein in milk or the presence of starch in potatoes. They are not confined to just testing animal feeds.

Table 29.3 Testing animal feeds for nutrients

Nutrient	Reagents added	Result
Starch (carbohydrate)	Iodine solution	Blue-black colour if starch is present. Iodine remains orange-red in absence of starch.
Glucose (carbohydrate)	Benedict's reagent Heating required	A brick-red colour if glucose is present. Benedict's reagent remains blue in absence of glucose.
Fats	Rub on brown paper	Translucent spot remains if fat is present.
Protein	Copper sulfate and sodium hydroxide	Violet/purple colour if protein is present. Remains blue if protein is absent.
Vitamin C	DCPIP	Changes from blue to colourless in the presence of vitamin C.

Metabolisable energy and food conversion ratios

Energy that is not converted into muscle gain or milk is often lost through:

- Undigested materials in faeces
- Production of urine
- Formation of methane gas by ruminant animals
- Production of heat (to keep the animal warm).

Food conversion ratio is also known as **food/feed conversion efficiency**.

Animals with a **low FCR** are efficient converters of feed to LWG. FCR is extremely important in pig production. Factors that affect FCR in relation to pigs will be dealt with in Chapter 30.

Point to note

Food conversion ratio (FCR) is a measure of an animal's efficiency at converting a mass of food into live weight gain (LWG). It is expressed as a ratio of the food consumed to the live weight gained.

Top Tip!

It is important to be familiar with FCR values for various agricultural animals.

Table 29.4 FCR values for pigs, poultry, cattle and sheep

Animal	FCR value
Pigs: Weaners	1.75:1
Pigs: Fatteners	3.25:1
Poultry	2:1
Cattle/sheep	8:1

Effect of age on food conversion ratio (FCR)

FCR values increase with age. In other words, the efficiency with which an animal converts food/feed into live gain weight (LWG) decreases as the animal gets older. A young animal (lamb, calf or piglet) has a low FCR value, as it will convert most of the food it consumes into bone and muscle growth. As the animal gets older, and in particular as it reaches its slaughter weight, its FCR value increases. The reason for this is that fat deposition has started and this requires more energy than the production of lean muscle, therefore decreasing food conversion efficiency.

How to improve the food conversion ratio

- Use high-quality feeds or increase the amounts of concentrates in the diet of the animal. The higher the quality of the feed, the more efficiently the animal will convert it to body tissue. In addition, if the feed is palatable, it will increase the animal's intake of the feed, leading to a lower FCR.
- Use a breed that confers low FCR values. In pig production, Large White is used to confer a good FCR value onto their offspring. In cattle and sheep, breeds with fast growth rates tend to have better or smaller FCR values.
- Good disease and parasite control: Diseases and parasites can increase FCR value. Nutrients are diverted away from LWG and used by the immune system to fight a disease. In addition, diseases normally reduce feed intake.
- Housing and temperature control: Cattle housed outdoors over the winter months utilise feed less efficiently than those housed indoors. As it is colder outside, animals divert more of their feed intake into heat production to keep themselves warm. Temperature control is vital in pig production. The houses in a pig production unit are maintained at appropriate temperatures for good FCR values (dry sow house at 20°C, weaner house at 24°C and fattener house at 22°C).

Maintenance and production diets

Key definitions

Maintenance diet: The amount of feed that allows an animal to maintain a constant body weight.

Production diet: The extra amount of feed required to produce 1 kg of LWG, 1 litre of milk, 1 kg of wool or to produce a calf or a lamb.

The diets of cows, sheep and pigs change throughout the course of the year. In sheep production, ewes are placed on a low plane of nutrition (commonly called a maintenance diet) prior to flushing. Prior to mating, giving birth and producing milk, the ewes are placed on a high plane of nutrition (production diet). Production diets normally include the feeding of concentrates and/or good-quality pasture to the animals.

Conformation

Conformation is important in the grading of beef carcasses under the EUROP classification system (see Chapter 33).

In beef production, beef breeds have a block-shaped conformation, with wide shoulders and hindquarters that are well fleshed. Dairy breeds have a wedge-shaped conformation, with narrow shoulders and not well-fleshed shoulders and hindquarters.

Key definition

Conformation: The shape of an animal and the distribution of fat and muscle around its body.

Factors affecting conformation in beef production

- **Breed:** Continental beef breeds have the best conformation, while purebred dairy breeds have the worst.
- **Sex:** Bulls have the best conformation, followed by steers (castrated males) and heifers. Cows have the worst conformation.

Body condition score (BCS)

Body condition scoring is commonly referred to as the **ratio of lean meat to fat on an animal's body**. The fat reserves on the animal are assessed both visually and by feeling along the back of the animal. BCSs range from 1 to 5 for sheep, cattle and pigs. An older system of BCS for pigs graded pigs from 0 to 9. A condition score of 1 indicates extreme thinness, while a score of 5 indicates an extremely fat animal.

Point to note

Body condition scoring of cattle, sheep and pigs allows the animal producer to assess the level of fat reserves that an animal has at various production stages.

Top Tip!

It is important to be familiar with the BCS for animals at various stages in their production cycles.

Table 29.5 Body condition scores for dairy, sheep and pigs at service and at giving birth

Animal	BCS at service (mating)	BCS giving birth
Dairy cow	2.9	3.25
Ewe	3.5	3–3.5 for single lamb 3.5–4.0 for twin lambs
Pigs	2.0–2.5	3.0–3.5

Effect of body condition score (BCS) on fertility and giving birth

- Animals with a BCS less than what is recommended at service will often be delayed going back into oestrus.
- There is an increased risk of metabolic disorders and disease if the BCS is too low or is greater than 4.
- Animals with a BCS greater than those recommended at birth are more likely to have difficulties when giving birth.

Point to note

The following section deals with the care of newborn animals, culling and the selection of replacement stock. Many of the principles involved are common to dairy, beef, sheep and pig production. For this reason, they have been grouped together. If any production has a particular requirement, that requirement will be referenced to that production system.

Care and management of newborn animals

The care and management of any newborn animal is virtually the same for all farm animals.

Top Tip!

Husbandry is a term that is sometimes used in exam questions. The term 'husbandry' means the care, management and breeding of animals.

- Have an experienced person on hand.
- Call the vet if the animal is having difficulties giving birth (calf/lamb etc. wrongly positioned in the uterus).
- Clear mucus away from the mouth and nose of the newborn.

- Once born, rub the newborn with straw or allow the mother to lick the newborn to stimulate the circulatory system.
- Dip the navel in iodine to prevent navel ill/joint ill.
- Feed the newborn colostrum.
- Vaccinate the newborn.
- **Calves and lambs:** Tag all newborn calves and lambs.
- **Bonhams only:** Teeth of bonhams are clipped to prevent damage to the sow's teats. Tails of the bonhams are docked to prevent tail biting. Bonhams are also given an injection of iron to prevent anaemia.

Key definition

Colostrum: The first milk secreted by mammals after giving birth. It is high in nutrients and antibodies and is essential for the survival of the newborn animal.

Point to note

The ability of the newborn animal to absorb the antibodies present in colostrum directly into its bloodstream is greatest in the first 24 hours. After this time period, the digestive system of the newborn will break down the antibodies.

Benefits of colostrum

- It is highly nutritious. Colostrum has a higher percentage of protein and fat than normal milk.
- It is easily digestible.
- It provides the newborn with antibodies that protect it from disease.
- The high fat content has a laxative effect, helping to clean out the newborn animal's digestive system.
- It warms up the newborn.

Factors that contribute to mortality at birth

Many of these factors are common to all agricultural animals.

- Newborn animal did not get colostrum (or enough colostrum).
- Mother and newborn animal have not been vaccinated.
- Not dipping the navel in iodine can result in navel ill.
- Milk fever (hypocalcaemia).

- Lack of supervision at birth.
- **In sheep production:** Lambing outdoors increases the risk of chilled lambs and abandoned lambs. In addition, lambs are vulnerable to predators. Twin lamb disease can occur if ewes are not properly steamed up prior to lambing.
- **In beef and dairy production:** Using the wrong bull can lead to calving difficulties.
- **Pigs and bonhams only:** Not providing iron injection to bonhams. Bonhams being crushed by sow as farrowing did not take place in a farrowing crate.

Criteria for the culling of stock

In all production units, the reasons for culling breeding stock are often the same.

- **Age**.
- **Health problems:** Lameness and disease (TB and brucellosis in cattle, chronic foot rot in sheep).
- **Problems with milk production:** Mastitis, poor milk yield and animals that have lost part of their udder function. In dairy productions, cows with a high somatic cell count (SCC) should be culled.
- **Problems with fertility:** Decrease in fertility, animals with birthing difficulties (lambing difficulties and calving difficulties). In sheep production, barren ewes are often culled.
- **Grading up:** Improving the genetic merit of the herd or flock.

Criteria for the selection of breeding stock

Replacement heifers for the dairy herd

- Correct body condition score (BCS for a first-time heifer should be at 3.25 at mating)
- Dairy breed: Holstein-Friesian, Jersey, British Friesian, etc.
- Good health: Good teeth, feet and a well-formed udder with four teats
- Good conformation
- Come from a mother with a high milk yield, good fertility and easy calving
- Offspring of a good EBI (Economic Breeding Index) bull
- Disease free
- Docile.

> **Point to note**
>
> These criteria could also be used to select a replacement heifer for a suckler herd. In addition, a replacement suckler heifer should be the offspring of a cross between a dairy and a beef animal. As a result, the heifer would possess a good milk yield and good conformation.

Selection of replacement ewes for breeding

- Age of the ewe
- Health of the ewe: Good teeth, feet and udder
- Disease free
- Body condition score of the ewe
- Good conformation
- No jaw defects; an undershot or overshot jaw will affect the ewe grazing
- A ewe that will consistently produce twins (prolific).

Exam questions

1   What is meant by *condition scoring* in cows? Give the recommended condition scores for a dairy cow at service **and** at calving.   *(HL 2011)*

2   Describe **four** qualities a farmer would look for when selecting replacement heifers for a dairy herd.   *(HL 2011)*

3   **Food conversion efficiency** (FCE) decreases with age in farm animals.

   (a) Explain the meaning of the highlighted term **and** give an example of FCE for a **named** farm animal.

   (b) Explain why FCE decreases with age in an animal.

   (c) Explain how a farmer might improve the FCE of the herd.   *(HL 2011)*

> **Top Tip!**
>
> Question 3 has asked for a named farm animal. This must be provided in your answer.

4   Explain why a young animal should receive colostrum in the first day of life. List **three** benefits of colostrum to the young animal.   *(HL 2011)*

5   Highlight the main differences between essential and non-essential amino acids.   *(HL 2011)*

6   Describe a laboratory investigation to show the presence of **one named** component of fresh milk.   *(OL 2011)*

> **Top Tip!**
>
> A test for a nutrient (protein or fat) will fulfil the requirements for Question 6.

7   Roughage must be included in the diet of a calf.

   (a) Suggest a reason for including roughage.

   (b) When is roughage introduced?

   (c) Name a suitable food that could be used as roughage.   *(HL 2012)*

Key-points!

- Bulky feeds are high in water or fibre.

- Fibre is important in the diet of ruminant animals, as it helps to develop the rumen of calves and lambs. It also ensures the correct functioning of the rumen in older animals.

- Concentrated rations are formulated to give the correct balance of protein, carbohydrates, minerals and vitamins. They are high in energy.

- Metabolisable energy is the energy from feed that an animal can convert into live weight gain (LWG), milk and wool and is measured as MU/kg.

- Food conversion ratio (food conversion efficiency) is a measure of an animal's efficiency at converting a mass of food into live weight gain. It is expressed as a ratio of the food consumed to live weight gained. Animals with a low food conversion ratio (FCR) are efficient converters of feed to LWG.

- Conformation: The shape of an animal and the distribution of fat and muscle around its body.

- Body condition scoring (BCS) is commonly referred to as the ratio of lean meat to fat on an animal's body. The fat reserves on the animal are assessed both visually and by feeling along the back of the animal.

- Colostrum is the first milk secreted by mammals after giving birth. It is high in nutrients and antibodies and is essential for the survival of the newborn animal.

- The ability of the newborn animal to absorb the antibodies present in colostrum directly into its bloodstream is greatest in the first 24 hours. After this time period, the digestive system of the newborn will break down the antibodies.

30 Pig Production and Management

Key points of information for pigs

- **Length of the oestrus cycle:** 21 days.
- **Duration of oestrus (standing heat):** 2–3 days.
- **Length of gestation:** 115 days (3 months, 3 weeks and 3 days).
- **Average litter size:** 11.
- **Weight of bonhams at birth:** 1–1.5 kg.

> **Remember**
>
> Pig breeds and their characteristics are dealt with in Chapter 34 on animal identification.

Criss-cross breeding of pigs

- The ideal sow in pig production is a crossbred Landrace-Large White.
- Criss-cross breeding is employed in pig production to roughly maintain the best characteristics from both breeds in a cost-effective manner without any loss in hybrid vigour.
- Purebred Large White and Landrace boars are employed in this criss-cross breeding strategy.

- First generation crossbred gilts from two purebred pigs (Landrace × Large White) are used to start the breeding programme. These crossbred gilts have 50% of their genes from the Landrace and 50% from the Large White; thus they exhibit hybrid vigour.

Establishment of criss-cross breeding

- **First generation:** A crossbred gilt is mated with either a Large White (LW) or Landrace (LR) boar. In the example below, a Landrace boar is crossed with the crossbred gilts. The best females from this litter are kept as replacements for breeding purposes.
- **Second generation:** The replacements from the above cross are mated with a Large White. This maintains hybrid vigour.
- **Third generation:** The best gilts from the cross in the second generation are kept for breeding purposes and will be bred by a Landrace boar. This continuous switching of boars is maintained with every successive generation. However, there is some hybrid vigour lost along the way. Under this system the boars must be changed every two years to prevent inbreeding. Many pig production units in Ireland use AI (artificial insemination) but still have to maintain a boar.

Table 30.1 Criss-cross breeding in pigs

Sire	Crossed with	Dam	Progeny/offspring
LR	×	LW-LR	LR-LW-LR
LW	×	LR-LW-LR	LW-LR-LW-LR
LR	×	LR-LW-LR-LW	LR-LW-LR-LW-LR

Bacon production

The majority of pig production in Ireland takes place in integrated pig production units. Here the pigs are born and reared for slaughter. This reduces the movement of pigs between farms and decreases the risk of diseases entering the farm. The rearing of pigs on these farms primarily takes place indoors. For Leaving Cert purposes, all of the following sections deal specifically with pigs raised in an integrated pig production unit.

Overview of a sow's production year

A sow can ideally produce 2.39 litters a year, but in reality this value is closer to 2.3.

Fig 30.1 *Sow production year*

Dry sow house

- Sows and gilts are housed in the dry sow house.
- The boars are also housed in the dry sow house. The boars must be in sight and smell of the sows, as pheromones released by the boar encourage both the gilts and the sows to come into oestrus (heat).
- A sow that has previously had a litter and has been moved to the dry sow house after this litter was weaned will come back into heat 5–7 days later.
- The boars will detect a sow or gilt that is in heat.
- When a boar detects a sow or gilt in heat, that sow is double served within 24 hours, using either the boar or AI. Double serving helps to increase the litter size. If a sow comes back into oestrus repeatedly, she is culled from the herd.
- Pregnant sows and gilts are kept in the dry sow house until one week before farrowing. They are fed 2.5 kg of dry sow ration per day. In the final 3–4 weeks prior to farrowing, the sows are fed 0.5 kg extra ration per day. Steaming up the sows at this stage ensures that the sows have good milk production and produce healthy bonhams. Dry sow ration contains 17.5% crude protein, 4% fibre and 1% lysine.

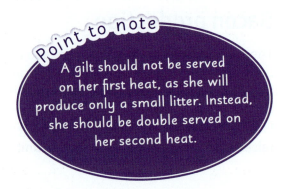

Point to note

A gilt should not be served on her first heat, as she will produce only a small litter. Instead, she should be double served on her second heat.

Farrowing house

- Before the pregnant sows and gilts are moved into the farrowing house, they are washed and disinfected. They are deloused and dosed for endoparasites (roundworms and tapeworms). The sows should also be vaccinated.

- The farrowing house should be cleaned and disinfected and maintained at a temperature of 20°C. The pregnant sow or gilt is placed into a farrowing crate.

> **Point to note**
>
> The farrowing crate prevents the sow from crushing the bonhams. The farrowing crate allows movement of the sow and also allows the bonhams access to the sow for suckling.

- The farrowing unit has a creep area with an infrared lamp.
  The temperature of this area is approximately 30°C. This creep area keeps the bonhams warm, as their small bodies lose heat easily. In addition, the infrared lamp attracts the bonhams away from the sow when they are not suckling, preventing them from being crushed. Bonhams are provided with additional feed (creep feed) in this area.

Birth, suckling and weaning

- Bonhams have their teeth and tails clipped and will be given an injection of iron (to prevent anaemia).

- Potential replacement gilts will have their ears notched.

- The sow will suckle the bonhams for 4–5 weeks.

> **Remember**
>
> The management of a newborn animal has been dealt with in Chapter 29 (pp.119–220). The particular requirements of bonhams have also been dealt with in that section.

- Sows are fed 1.8 kg of suckling ration daily with 0.5 kg of ration per bonham.

- After one week, creep feed containing 21% protein and 1.5% lysine is introduced to bonhams.

- Bonhams are weaned by removing them from the sow after 4–5 weeks.

- The sow is returned to the dry sow house.

Factors that contribute to mortality in bonhams

- Not vaccinating the sow
- Not giving an iron injection to the bonhams
- Having the farrowing house at the incorrect temperature

- Not using a farrowing crate
- Incorrect feeding of the sow
- Feed not containing lysine (an essential amino acid required by pigs).

Weaner management and feeding

- Weaners are normally 9 kg upon entering the weaner house. They are mixed and grouped according to size and weight.
- They are fed a link ration containing 21% protein and 1.45% lysine *ad lib* for the first two weeks.
- They are then moved onto a weaner ration that contains 18–20% protein and 1.3% lysine.

> **Point to note**
>
> The farrowing house and the weaner house are collectively known as the breeding unit in pig production. In a breeding unit, pigs are bred and reared from birth until they are 12 weeks old and weigh 32 kg.

- The temperature in the weaner house is maintained at 24°C.
- When weaners reach 32 kg they are moved to the fattener house.

Fattener management and feeding

- Fatteners are grouped together according to size and weight.
- They are fed a fattener ration of 14–16% protein and 1.1% lysine.
- The temperature of the fattener house is 22°C.
- Fatteners remain in the fattener house for approximately three months, until they reach a slaughter weight of 80–82 kg.

> **Point to note**
>
> The fattener house in the pig production unit is also known as a finishing unit.

- Females that are selected for breeding purposes (replacement gilts) are housed for a further 4–6 weeks, until they reach a weight of 100–140 kg. They are then moved to the dry sow house.

Factors that affect food conversion ratio in pigs

> **Remember**
>
> Food conversion ratio (FCR), its meaning and the factors that affect it in general have been dealt with in Chapter 29.

Food conversion ratio (FCR) in pigs is affected by:

- **Diet:** In pig production, the rations are specially formulated for the various stages of the pig's growth (creep feed, weaner ration, fattener ration, dry sow, etc.). These feeds contain the correct protein, vitamins, minerals, etc. for the pig at its various growth stages.

Top Tip!

Know the correct FCR values for weaners (1.75:1) and fatteners (3.25:1). Remember: a low FCR means that the animal is very efficient at converting feed into live weight gain (LWG).

- **Breed:** Large White confers good FCR on its offspring. As a result, the offspring reach slaughter weight much faster and cost less to feed compared to a breed with a higher FCR.

- **Health:** Healthy, disease-free animals will have a low FCR. Pigs are regularly vaccinated against common diseases and dosed for parasites. The farrowing house, weaner and fattener houses are regularly cleaned and disinfected. All houses are well ventilated to minimise airborne diseases. The movement of pigs is in one direction. Fatteners are never moved back to the weaner house. This one-way movement reduces the risk of disease.

- **Housing:** In pig production, the various houses used are well insulated, with low roofs. This is to maintain the temperature of the house. Pigs will use energy from feed to generate heat to keep warm, thus increasing their FCR if they are cold.

Top Tip!

Memorise the correct temperature for each of the houses used in an integrated pig production unit.

- **Management:** A farmer who maintains an efficient feeding regime and proper disease control will have a healthy herd with a good FCR.

Table 30.2 Housing temperatures for pig production

House	Temperature
Creep area	30°C
Dry sow house	20°C
Farrowing house	20°C
Weaner house	24°C
Fattener house	22°C

Carcass grading in pigs

- Pigs are graded according to estimated lean meat percentage content.
- They are classified according to the scale in Table 30.3.
- The thickness of the back fat and muscle depth are measured and used to estimate the lean meat percentage.
- Carcass quality is influenced by breed and diet.

Table 30.3 Carcass grading of pigs	
Lean meat as percentage of carcass weight	**Letter grade**
60 or more	S
55 or more but less than 60	E
50 or more but less than 55	U
45 or more but less than 50	R
40 or more but less than 45	O
Less than 40	P

Diseases in pigs

Table 30.4 Diseases in pigs				
Disease	**Cause**	**Symptoms**	**Treatment**	**Prevention**
Anaemia in bonhams	Lack of the mineral iron	Pale skin, weakness and scour and poor growth in first 2–3 weeks of life	An iron injection	An iron injection is given when bonhams are 2–3 days old
SMEDI	Enteroviruses Gut-borne viruses	Stillborn bonhams, mummification of embryos and infertility	No treatment	Routine vaccination of sows

Disease	Cause	Symptoms	Treatment	Prevention
Internal parasites	Roundworms and tapeworms	Coughing, vomiting, diarrhoea and loss of condition	Dose pigs	Dosing every 6 months
Porcine reproductive and respiratory syndrome (PRRS)	Caused by a virus	Respiratory problems, loss of appetite, early farrowing, stillbirths and weak bonhams	No treatment	Maintain biosecurity (avoid buying in stock) and vaccinate all animals
Coliform scour	*E. Coli* bacteria Lack of hygiene in housing units	Scour, dehydration and weight loss in weaners	Antibiotics and rehydrate with fluid replacement solutions	Maintain high standards of hygiene and avoid sudden changes in diet

Questions

1   (a) For the disease SMEDI, give the cause and symptoms of the disease.
    (b) What preventative measure can a farmer take to prevent the entry of diseases like SMEDI onto the farm?

2   (a) Outline the criss-cross breeding system employed in pig production.
    (b) What are the advantages of using this type of breeding programme?

3   Give an explanation for **each** of the following practices in pig production:
    (a) Ear notching
    (b) Tail clipping
    (c) Creep feeding
    (d) Dosing
    (e) Disinfecting farrowing crate.

4   Outline the feeding programme and management of a weaner to slaughter.

1 (a) Give the recommended temperature for **each** of the following in relation to pig housing: **(i)** creep area **(ii)** weaner house and **(iii)** fattener house.
   (b) Why do bonhams have their teeth clipped soon after birth?
   (c) Give the approximate weight at which pigs are finished for slaughter.
   (OL 2012)

2 Describe the husbandry practices involved in preparing a sow at the end of gestation for transfer from the dry sow house to the farrowing house. *(HL 2011)*

3 Give a scientific explanation for the fact that the creep area for bonhams is kept at a higher temperature than the rest of the farrowing house. *(HL 2011)*

4 (a) Indicate the average litter size **and** the target number of bonhams weaned per annum for a sow.
   (b) Suggest **two** ways by which bonhams weaned per annum could be increased. *(HL 2012)*

5 Highlight the main difference between a breeding unit and a finishing unit. *(HL 2012)*

6 Give a scientific explanation for the locating of boars in dry sow houses. *(HL 2012)*

7 Describe the management of bonhams (piglets) from birth to weaning. *(HL 2014)*

Key-points!

- Length of the oestrus cycle: 21 days; duration of oestrus (standing heat): 2–3 days; length of gestation: 115 days (3 months, 3 weeks and 3 days); litter size: 11; weight of bonhams at birth: 1–1.5 kg.

- Criss-cross breeding is employed in pig production to roughly maintain the best characteristics from both breeds in a cost-effective manner without any loss in hybrid vigour.

- The boars are housed in the dry sow house. The boars must be in sight and smell of the sows, which encourages the sows to come into oestrus (heat).

- When a boar detects a sow or gilt in heat, that sow is double served within 24 hours, using either the boar or AI. Double serving helps to increase the litter size.

- A sow is moved from the dry sow house to the farrowing house one week prior to farrowing. She is washed, disinfected, dosed, vaccinated and placed into a clean and disinfected farrowing crate. The farrowing house is maintained at a temperature of 20°C.

- When the bonhams are born, they have their teeth and tails clipped. They are given an injection of iron to prevent anaemia. They have a creep area with an infrared lamp and are provided with creep feed in this area.

- The bonhams are weaned at 4–5 weeks old when they are removed from the sow. The sow is returned to the dry sow house, where she will come back into heat 5–7 days later and will be served with the boar or with AI.

- Weaners are normally 9 kg upon entering the weaner house. They are mixed and grouped according to size and weight. The temperature of the weaner house is 24°C. They are fed a weaner ration containing 21% protein. Once the weaners reach 32 kg, they are moved to the fattener house.

- Fatteners are grouped together according to size and weight. They are fed a fattener ration of 14–16% protein and 1.1% lysine. The temperature of the fattener house is 22°C. Fatteners remain in the fattener house for approximately three months, until they reach a slaughter weight of 80–82 kg.

31 Sheep and Lamb Production and Management

Key points of information for sheep

Top Tip!
Exam papers frequently ask for the length of gestation in days.

Remember
Common sheep breeds and their characteristics will be dealt with in Chapter 34 on animal identification.

- **Time of year when sheep breed:** Sheep are short-day breeders and they come into heat during autumn, when day length starts to decrease. Sheep are **polyoestrus**, meaning they have several oestrus cycles during this time of year.
- **Length of the oestrus cycle:** 17 days.
- **Duration of oestrus (standing heat):** 36 hours.

- **Length of gestation:** 147 days (roughly five months).
- **Litter size:** Can vary (singles, twins, triplets, etc.).
- **Weight of lambs at birth:** 3–5 kg.

Sheep production in Ireland

Sheep production is divided into two categories: mountain/hill sheep and lowland sheep.

Table 31.1 Comparison of mountain/hill and lowland sheep enterprises

Mountain and hill	Lowland
Extensive farming	Intensive
Low production targets	High production targets
Rough grazing	Rotational grazing
Ewe and lamb mortality rates can be high	Lambing indoors reduces ewe and lamb mortality
Ewes generally only have one lamb	More ewes give birth to twins and triplets
Sheep breeds suited to exposed conditions	Larger, muscular sheep used to produce meat
Blackface Mountain, Wicklow Cheviot	Suffolk, Texel, Galway, Charollais

Breeding strategy for sheep production in Ireland

- In mountain and hill farming, purebred mountain ewes (Blackface Mountain or Wicklow Cheviot) are always crossed with a purebred mountain ram.
- Mountain ewes usually only produce one lamb (due to harsh conditions and poorer feed quality).
- Lambs are either kept for replacements or sold as meat.
- Mountain ewes are sold to lowland farmers as cast ewes and are renowned for their good mothering abilities.

> **Point to note**
>
> A **cast** or **draft ewe** is a ewe whose fertility has declined due to the harsh conditions of its mountainous environment. It is bought by a lowland farmer and once it is placed on an improved plane of nutrition, it will continue to produce lambs for many years.

- The mountain ewe is then crossed with a prolific breed to increase litter size (Belclare, Border Leicester or a Bluefaced Leicester).
- The crossbred ewes produced from this cross demonstrate **hybrid vigour**. They have hardiness, good mothering ability and good milk production from their mother and prolificacy from the ram.
- The cross-breed ewes are then crossed with a terminal sire (purebred Suffolk or a Texel ram) to produce lambs for slaughter.
- The lambs produced from this cross are sold as early lamb (for the Easter market) or mid-season lamb.

> ## Key definition
> **Terminal sire:** A ram that is used to produce offspring with high growth rates, good conformation and good carcass quality for slaughter.

Criteria for ram selection

Rams of superior genetic quality (with a lamb plus euro star rating) are used for breeding purposes. A common saying in sheep production is 'the ram is half the flock'. The reason for this is that the ram will spread his genes over a greater proportion of the offspring than a ewe. In addition, the ram breeds look after the quality of the offspring (growth rates, carcass quality and conformation), while the ewe delivers on quantity (litter size).

> ## Top Tip!
> Be familiar with the different terminal sires used in lamb production as well as the characteristics of those ram breeds.

Ram selection is a vital part of the breeding programme in sheep production. The **breed of the ram** must match the type of production. On mountain or hill farms, the mountain ewes are always crossed with mountain rams, as they are a hardier breed.

In lowland sheep production, ram selection depends on whether the farmer is aiming for the Easter market or the mid-season lamb market. If a farmer is aiming for the Easter market, a Suffolk ram is used, as it has the fastest growth rates – the lambs will reach slaughter weight in time and get a higher price than mid-season lamb. For mid-season lamb, a Texel ram is used. His progeny do not mature as quickly as the Suffolk ram's, but have a higher carcass quality and a greater kill out percentage. A Charollais ram is often used on first-time ewes, as this produces a smaller lamb and decreases the chances of lambing difficulties.

Other factors that should be considered when choosing a ram include:

- Purebred
- Age

- Pedigree and performance tested
- Good conformation
- Body condition score of 3.5 to 4.0.: rams have a higher BCS than ewes at mating, as they lose condition during mating
- Sound feet and legs
- Teeth and mouth: no undershot jaw.

Point to note

The criteria for the selection of replacement ewes for breeding has been discussed in Chapter 29, p.222.

Breeding for meat production

Farmers aiming to produce lamb for the Easter market must start planning for this in July.

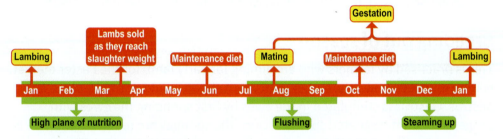

Fig 31.1 *Easter lamb production calendar*

Flushing

This involves placing the ewes on an improved plane of nutrition prior to mating.

Key definition

Flushing: The process by which the ewes are moved from a low plane of nutrition to a high plane of nutrition prior to mating.

This can also be achieved by placing the ewes on pasture at a high stocking rate and then three weeks before mating, starting to reduce the stocking rate.

Advantages of flushing

- It increases ovulation rate, leading to more eggs being released at ovulation.
- It increases conception rates.
- It ensures better implantation of the embryo to the uterine wall.
- It ensures more regular oestrus cycles.

Top Tip!

Know the advantages of flushing.

Flushing continues for four weeks after mating to ensure the embryos develop properly. After this the ewes are placed back on a maintenance diet.

Synchronised breeding

- **Ram effect:** The sudden introduction of a ram to a flock of ewes can encourage the ewes to come into oestrus and start cycling. Rams produce **pheromones** that stimulate oestrus in ewes. This method of synchronised breeding is only successful if the rams and the ewes have been separated for at least six weeks prior to mating.
- **Sponging:** To prevent a prolonged lambing season, farmers often encourage all the ewes to come into oestrus together by sponging the ewes. **Progesterone-impregnated sponges** are placed in the vagina of the ewes. They are removed 12 days later and the ewes come into heat after two days. If sponging is used, then the ram to ewe ratio must be reduced from 1:40 to 1:10.

Breeding out of season

This is practised by farmers who are aiming for early lamb for the Easter market. Mating must occur in July, earlier than when sheep would normally come into oestrus. Oestrus is stimulated in the ewes by first sponging the ewes with progesterone-impregnated sponges. Once the sponges are removed, the ewe is given an injection of PMSG (pregnant mare serum gonadotrophin). The ewe comes into heat 48 hours later. The ram to ewe ratio is 1:10.

Heat detection

Farmers need to be able to calculate lambing dates as well as identify repeats (ewes coming back into oestrus who are not in lamb). The most common device used for this is a **raddle** with a **coloured crayon**. The raddle leaves a mark on each ewe as they are mated by the ram. The colour of the crayon is changed every 17 days (length of the oestrus cycle in ewes) to check for ewes repeating. If large numbers of ewes are repeating, then the ram's fertility should be questioned.

Steaming up

In the last six weeks of gestation, the ewes are placed on an improving plane of nutrition, known as steaming up.

> ### Key definition
>
> **Steaming up:** The practice of increasing the amount of concentrates being fed to sheep in late gestation in order to prevent twin lamb disease, ensure a healthy lamb and promote good milk production.

In the last six weeks, 75% of foetal growth occurs. Poor nutrition at this stage can cause twin lamb disease or pregnancy toxaemia, which can be fatal for both lamb and ewe. Ewes are each fed 100 g of concentrates, which is gradually increased to 500 g for ewes carrying singles and 750 g for ewes carrying twins.

Top Tip!

Know the difference between flushing and steaming up and know the order in which they occur, with flushing before mating and steaming up prior to lambing. To help you remember, think **first for flushing** and **second for steaming up**. These are commonly asked on exam papers.

Scanning

- Scanning takes place 80 days after the ram was joined with the flock (after mating).
- It identifies barren ewes (ewes that are not in lamb), which can be culled.
- It is used to determine the number of lambs a ewe is carrying (single, twins, etc.).
- Ewes can then be separated into groups according to the number of lambs they are carrying so that they can be given the correct feed requirement.

Lambing

- Vaccinate ewes against clostridial diseases four weeks before lambing.
- Treat ewes for footrot to ensure ewes are able to graze properly.
- Lambing should take place indoors.
- Revive chilled lambs using an infrared lamp.
- If chill is severe, lambs should be given an injection of glucose.
- Lambs should remain with ewes to allow for bonding.

Remember

The care and management of a newborn animal and factors that contribute to mortality have been previously described in Chapter 29, pp.219–221.

Fostering

A lamb from a multiple birth can be fostered onto a ewe with a single lamb. This can be done by covering a foster lamb with the birth fluids from a ewe with a single lamb. The foster lamb's feet are temporary tied so that it cannot stand up and it is placed in front of the ewe so that she can lick the foster lamb clean.

A fostering crate can also be used. This prevents the ewe from hurting the foster lamb. It allows the foster lamb access to the ewe's udder and after a few days the ewe will have accepted the foster lamb.

Post-lambing

- Ewes are kept on a high plane of nutrition to ensure good milk production.
- Ewes should be provided with a mineral lick to prevent milk fever and grass tetany.
- The typical diet of a lamb from birth to slaughter would include colostrum, milk (provided by the ewe), hay (introduced in the first week to develop the rumen), concentrates and grass.
- Ewes and lambs should be rotationally grazed on good pasture.
- Creep gates and creep feeders are used to provide concentrates to the lambs, but not for the ewes. Creep feeding ensures lambs reach slaughter weight in time for the Easter market.
- Lambs are sold off as they reach slaughter weight (34–40 kg).
- Weaning takes place between the months of June and July. Ewes are put onto bare pasture and dried off in preparation for flushing.

General husbandry

- **Castration:** Castration of ram lambs should occur in the first few days. An elastrator or a burdizzo can be used. They are both bloodless forms of castration and can also be used for tail docking.
- **Dipping:** All sheep are dipped in summer to prevent flystrike and in winter to prevent mange mite (which causes sheep scab).
- **Dosing:** Sheep are dosed for stomach worms, liver fluke and other internal parasites.
- **Docking:** Docking is the removal of a lamb's tail using an elastrator. This is to prevent faeces building up around the tail and attracting bluebottle flies, causing flystrike.
- **Dagging:** Dagging involves the removal of wool around the tail and is a measure taken to prevent flystrike.
- **Foot bath:** To prevent footrot, animals are walked through a bath that contains copper sulfate or formalin.
- **Foot trimming and paring:** Foot trimming and paring is necessary when the outer surface of the foot grows beyond the soft sole of the foot. If the foot is not trimmed, the animal can become lame.
- **Shearing:** This is normally carried out in June. It prevents the sheep from overheating in warm weather and aids in the prevention of flystrike.

Diseases of lambs and sheep

Table 31.2 Diseases of lambs and sheep

Disease	Cause	Symptoms	Treatment	Prevention
Twin lamb disease	• Breakdown of fat reserves in the ewe's body leads to liver failure	• Separates from flock • Staggers, tremors • Collapse and death	• Fatal disease unless caught early • Administer energy solution (glucose)	• Steaming up with concentrates as rumen's size is restricted • Growing foetus limits the intake of hay and silage
Orf (zoonose)	• Virus	• Small spots on udder, ewes' teats, lips, gums, nose of young lambs and genitals of rams • Secondary infection of lesions can occur	• No treatment for virus • Treat sores with antibiotic cream	• Vaccinate ewes before lambing • Vaccinate lambs at a few weeks old
Milk fever (hypocalcaemia)	• Low levels of calcium occurs in late pregnancy or early lactation	• Similar to twin lamb disease • Listlessness, unable to stand, unconsciousness, death	• Injection of calcium borogluconate	• Dust ewes' feed with Calmag or provide mineral lick

Disease	Cause	Symptoms	Treatment	Prevention
Grass tetany (hypomagnesaemia)	• Occurs when ewes and lambs are turned out onto lush grass low in magnesium	• Twitching, muscle spasm • Coma, death	• Injection of soluble magnesium	• Dust ewes' feed with Calmag or provide mineral lick
Nematodirus	• Roundworm lays eggs in the lamb's gut, pass out of gut onto grass; overwinter as eggs; hatch in spring after cold spell • Large numbers can hatch together; young lambs most at risk as they lack resistance	• Many lambs showing scour • Lambs stop eating, become dehydrated and die	• Dose for worms at regular intervals	• Put lambs on clean pasture that has not been grazed by lambs the previous year
Coccidiosis	• Protozoa, parasite found in faeces, affects young lambs 4–8 weeks old • Parasite invades the lining of the intestines	• Lambs fail to thrive • Bloody scour • Dehydrated • In worst cases, death	• Lambs have initial immunity while suckling (ewe immune) • Oral dose lambs	• A medicated creep feed gives protection
Clostridial diseases	• Variety of bacteria that cause pulpy kidney, blackleg, lamb dysentery and tetanus	• Varied, most lead to sudden death	• Treatment is difficult	• Vaccine available • Vaccinate a '7 in 1' and an '8 in 1' • Vaccinate lambs • Give ewes an annual booster

Disease	Cause	Symptoms	Treatment	Prevention
Flystrike	• Green and blue bottle flies lay their eggs in fleeces soiled with faeces • Maggots eat into the sheep's flesh	• Maggots irritate sheep; tail wags constantly followed by dark stain on wool • Sheep lying on its own	• Spray on an insecticide • Treat flesh eaten by maggots with antiseptic cream to prevent infection	• Dip sheep • Dose sheep for worms to prevent diarrhoea • Use insecticidal sprays
Sheep scab (notifiable disease)	• Mange mite feeds on skin and flesh	• Extremely contagious • Sheep irritated by mites rub against fences and gates, causing wool loss • Yellow scabs visible on skin	• Notify district veterinary office immediately • Dipping and injections administered by vet	• Winter dip sheep

Wool

- Wool is a protein fibre that grows from follicles on the sheep's skin.
- Sheep have both hair and wool fibres.
- The ratio of hair to wool fibres varies between the breeds.
- Merino sheep produce the finest wool, with a ratio of wool to hair of 25:1.
- Most Irish breeds have a ratio of 8:1.

Questions

1 Give the meaning of the term *polyoestrus*.

2 Give the length of **each** of the following in days for sheep: **(a)** oestrus cycle and **(b)** gestation.

3 **(a)** What is meant by the term *cast ewe*?
  (b) Explain why cast ewes are in demand by lowland sheep farmers.

4 The phrase *The ram is half the flock* is commonly used in sheep production. Explain the meaning of this phrase and outline why ram selection is a vital part of sheep production.

5 Discuss the advantages of flushing prior to mating.

6 Outline the steps involved in breeding out of season.

Exam questions

1 **(a)** Discuss the role of scanning in sheep production.
  (b) **(i)** Explain the term *terminal sire* as it applies to sheep breeding.
      (ii) Suggest two breeds that could be used as terminal sires.
      (iii) Give a reason for each of your choices in part (ii).
  (c) Compare flushing with steaming up as feeding strategies in sheep production. *(HL 2012)*

2 Write a note on **each** of the following practices carried out in sheep production:
  (a) Tail docking
  (b) Shearing
  (c) Raddling a ram
  (d) Dipping
  (e) Walking the flock through a footbath. *(OL 2011)*

3   Several pieces of equipment are used to ensure good farm management.
    Explain the use of **each** of the following on farms involved in livestock
    production:
    (a) Isolation pen
    (b) Infrared lamp
    (c) Creep feeder.   (OL 2011)

4   (a) (i) Name **three** common sheep breeds.
        (ii) Name **two** parasites of sheep.
    (b) State **three** advantages of housing sheep at lambing time.
    (c) (i) Describe the diet of lambs from birth to slaughter.
        (ii) What is the normal weight in kilograms at which lambs are
             slaughtered?   (OL 2012)

5   Give a scientific explanation for the flushing of lowland ewes prior to
    mating.   (HL 2014)

6   (a) List the bodily characteristics to be considered in the selection of
        breeding ewes in a lowland sheep enterprise.
    (b) Explain the following practices commonly used in sheep breeding:
        (i) Flushing
        (ii) Sponging.
    (c) Describe the changes in the diet of lambs from birth to slaughter.
                                                                        (OL 2014)

Key-points!

- Length of the oestrus cycle: 17 days.
- Duration of oestrus (standing heat): 36 hours.
- Length of gestation: 147 days (roughly five months).
- Litter size: Can vary (singles, twins, triplets, etc.).
- Weight of lambs at birth: 3–5 kg.
- A cast or draft ewe is a ewe whose fertility has declined due to the harsh
  conditions of its mountainous environment.
- A mountain ewe is crossed with a prolific breed to increase litter size (Belclare,
  Border Leicester or Bluefaced Leicester) in lowland sheep production to produce
  crossbred ewes.
- These crossbred ewes are mated with a terminal sire (Suffolk or Texel) to
  produce lambs for slaughter.

- Terminal sire: A ram that is used to produce offspring with high growth rates, good conformation and good carcass quality for slaughter.

- Flushing: The process by which the ewes are moved from a low plane of nutrition to a high plane of nutrition prior to mating.

- Ram effect: The sudden introduction of a ram to a flock of ewes can encourage the ewes to come into oestrus and start cycling.

- Sponging: Compacts lambing season. Progesterone-impregnated sponges are placed in the vagina of the ewes. They are removed 12 days later and the ewes come into heat after two days.

- Breeding out of season: To produce lambs for the Easter market, mating must occur in July, earlier than when ewes would normally come into oestrus. Oestrus is stimulated in the ewes by first sponging the ewes with progesterone-impregnated sponges. Once the sponges are removed, the ewes are given an injection of PMSG (pregnant mare serum gonadotrophin). The ewes come into heat 48 hours later. The ram to ewe ratio is 1:10.

- Rams are raddled at mating time. The raddle leaves a mark on each ewe as they are mated by the ram.

- Steaming up: The practice of increasing the amount of concentrates being fed to sheep in late gestation in order to prevent twin lamb disease, ensure a healthy lamb and promote good milk production.

- In the last six weeks, 75% of foetal growth occurs. Poor nutrition can cause twin lamb disease or pregnancy toxaemia, which can be fatal for both lamb and ewe. Ewes are each fed 100 g of concentrates, which is gradually increased to 500 g for ewes carrying singles and 750 g for ewes carrying twins.

- Scanning takes place 80 days after the ram was joined with the flock (after mating). It identifies barren ewes (ewes that are not in lamb), which can be culled. It is used to determine the number of lambs a ewe is carrying (single, twins, etc.).

- Post-lambing: Ewes are kept on a high plane of nutrition to ensure good milk production. Ewes should be provided with a mineral lick to prevent milk fever and grass tetany. The typical diet of a lamb from birth to slaughter would include colostrum, milk, hay, concentrates and grass. Ewes and lambs should be rotationally grazed on good pasture. Creep gates and creep feeders are used to provide concentrates to the lambs but not the ewes. Creep feeding ensures lambs reach slaughter weight in time for the Easter market. Lambs are sold off as they reach slaughter weight (34–40 kg).

Dairy Production and Management

32

Key points of information for dairy cows

- **Length of the oestrus cycle:** 21 days.
- **Duration of oestrus (standing heat):** 18 hours.
- **Length of gestation:** 283 days (roughly 9.5 months).
- **Litter size:** Single, but twins and triplets can occasionally occur.
- **Average lactation period (produces milk):** 305 days.
- **Peak milk yield:** Roughly 37 days after lactation starts.
- **Dried off:** 60 days.

Calendar year for a spring calving dairy herd

The dairy industry in Ireland is divided into two systems: **liquid milk production** and **creamery milk production**.

Farmers who supply the liquid milk market operate both spring and autumn calving herds, which allows them to supply milk all year round. Farmers are paid in relation to the quantity of milk they produce.

Farmers who provide milk for creamery milk production usually operate a spring calving system. This system allows them to take advantage of grass growth over spring and summer to meet their feed requirements. In addition, farmers supplying milk to creameries to produce commodities (butter, cheese and yoghurt) are normally paid in relation to the percentage of protein and fat in their milk.

Figure 32.1 outlines the calving year for a spring calving herd.

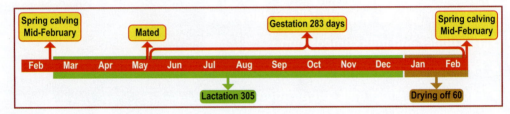

Fig 32.1 *Spring calving year*

The udder and milk composition

The udder

- The udder is divided into four independent quarters, each with its own teat.
- The right half of the udder is divided from the left half by the medial suspensory ligament.
- The rear quarters are separated from the front quarters by a fine membrane.
- The milk-producing tissue of the udder is called alveolus.
- Milk produced by this tissue travels down through ducts into the gland cistern.
- The gland cistern can store approximately 500 cm³ of milk.
- The gland cistern is connected to the teat cistern.
- Milk exits the teat through the streak canal.

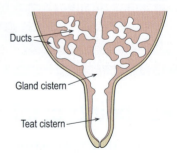

Fig 32.2 *Cow's udder with ducts and gland cistern*

Milk let-down

Milk let-down in cows is controlled by the hormone **oxytocin**. When a calf suckles a cow or when a farmer washes the udder prior to milking, nerve receptors on the surface of the udder send a signal to the brain that triggers the pituitary gland to secrete oxytocin. The hormone travels in the bloodstream to the alveoli tissue in the udder and causes these cells to produce milk.

Disruptions should be avoided during the milking routine. Loud noises, rough treatment and pain can cause the cow to release the hormone **adrenaline** from the adrenal glands. This hormone blocks the release of oxytocin from the pituitary gland and prevents it from reaching the udder.

Milk composition

The composition of cow's milk is represented in Table 32.1.

Table 32.1 The composition of milk	
Component	**Percentage**
Water	87.8%
Butterfat	3.5%
Protein	3.2%
Lactose	4.7%
Minerals (calcium, magnesium, phosphates, etc.)	0.8%

The percentage of lactose, protein and minerals found in milk is commonly referred to as solids non-fat (SNF).

 Experiment

To determine the butterfat content of milk

1. Using a strip cup, remove a sample of milk from the **start of milking** and one from the **end of milking**.
2. Heat samples until they reach **20°C**.
3. Add **sulfuric acid** to two **butyrometers**.
4. **Add the milk samples gently down the sides of the butyrometers.**
5. Add **amyl alcohol**.
6. **Stopper**, **invert** and place in a **centrifuge**.
7. **Remove samples** and **place in a water bath at 65°C.**
8. Read the **percentage fat**.

Result

The percentage fat is between 3% and 5%. The butterfat content of milk is lowest at the start of milking and highest at the end of milking.

Factors that affect milk composition

Milk composition varies depending on a number of factors.

- **Breed:** Milk yield and milk composition vary between breeds. A Jersey cow will produce a smaller milk yield but with a higher protein and butterfat content than a Holstein-Friesian.

Table 32.2 Comparison of milk yield and milk composition of dairy breeds

Breed	Milk yield (kg)	Fat (%)	Protein (%)
Holstein-Friesian	5,651	4.12	3.49
Jersey	4,220	5.32	4.03
Jersey × Holstein-Friesian	5,272	4.77	3.88

- **Animal feed/diet:** Good grassland will increase milk butterfat and protein. Feeds high in fibre will increase the butterfat content of the milk.
- **Stage in lactation:** The percentages of fat and protein are high immediately after calving (in colostrum). They then decrease for 10–12 weeks and rise again towards the end of lactation.
- **Age:** The percentage of fat and protein in the milk decreases with the age of the cow.
- **Disease:** Mastitis causes a decrease in the percentage of fat, protein and lactose, and the concentration of somatic cells (white blood cells) and antibodies increases.

Point to note

Mastitis is a bacterial infection of the udder. It is extremely contagious and can be spread during milking through the operator's hands and the milking machine. The different types of mastitis that can occur in a dairy herd are dealt with at the end of this chapter.

Lactation cycle of the dairy cow

- The average lactation period for a dairy cow is 305 days.

- The cow will produce milk soon after the calf is born.

- The cow produces colostrum (also known as beastings) for the first four days after she has given birth. Colostrum is not accepted by the creameries.

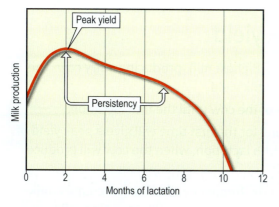

Fig 32.3 *Lactation curve*

- A lactation curve plots the milk production of a dairy cow over the course of her lactation.

- Milk production increases from the start until a **peak yield** is reached (roughly 5–6 weeks after calving).

- A high peak yield normally results in a higher total yield.

- A cow must be on a high plane of nutrition (production diet) in order for her to reach her potential peak yield.

Points to note

A cow's peak yield will depend on the lactation number of the cow. A heifer calving for the first time will give a peak yield of 75% of a mature cow's peak yield. A cow will produce her maximum peak yield on her fifth lactation.

- After a cow reaches her peak yield, her milk yield will start to decline.

- The rate at which a cow's milk yield declines is known as **persistence**.

- The cow is dried off for 60 days prior to the birth of her next calf.

Benefits of drying off a dairy cow

- It allows time for the udder to repair itself.
- It maximises milk yields in the following lactation.
- A dry cow treatment can be administered to each teat. This contains a long-lasting antibiotic that will treat and prevent any bacterial infection, such as mastitis in the udder.
- It allows the cow to regain body condition.
- It allows the cow to complete the development of her next calf in her uterus. Most of the calf's growth occurs during this time.

Factors that affect milk yield

- **Breed:** The Holstein-Friesian is the highest milk-producing dairy cow. The Jersey has a significantly smaller milk yield.
- **Age:** Milk yield rises with the age of the cow until the fifth lactation.
- **Lactation number:** A heifer calving for the first time will give a peak yield of 75%. This will increase until the fifth lactation, when the cow will produce her maximum peak yield.
- **Frequency of milking:** Increasing the frequency of milking increases milk yield. Frequently milking the cow encourages the milk-secreting cells (alveoli) to work to their full capacity. Decreasing the frequency of milking also leads to a decrease in milk yield.
- **Drying off:** Drying off for 60 days maximises milk yields in the following lactations. Lactation yields can be reduced by 20% to 40% if the drying off period is less than 40–60 days.
- **Body condition score (BCS):** Pre-calving, the body condition score of a dairy cow should be between 3.0 and 3.25. A low BCS before calving decreases the lactation yield of the cow.

Milk hygiene

Milk tests

Milk undergoes a number of tests in the creamery. Milk can contain contaminants such as bacteria, somatic cells (white blood cells), antibiotics or sediments (soil, hair, dung, etc.). Penalties can apply if these contaminants are outside parameters set by the creamery.

- **Total bacterial count (TBC):** Indication of the hygiene on a farm. High bacterial counts can be due to mastitis, a dirty milking machine, not changing milk filters or failing to properly cool milk to below 4°C.

- **Somatic cell counts (SCC):** Somatic cells are white blood cells that occur naturally in milk. The number of somatic cells increases if the udder has mastitis. High SCC affects the processing of milk.
- **Temperature:** If milk is stored incorrectly, bacteria (such as *Lactobacillus*) grow and convert lactose (milk sugar) into lactic acid, souring the milk. Penalties apply if the temperature of milk at the collection point exceeds 6°C.
- **Antibiotics:** Antibiotics must be absent from milk at all times, as antibiotics present in milk contribute to **antibiotic resistance** developing in bacteria. Antibiotics in milk interfere with the processing of milk in the production of yoghurts and cheese. Cows must undergo a withdrawal period if treated with antibiotics and their milk must be kept separate from the milk in the bulk tank.
- **Thermoduric test:** These are bacteria that are resistant to high temperatures and can survive pasteurisation.
- **Sediment:** Sediment can include dirt, soil and hair from the cow's udder. Milk must be free from sediment. To ensure this, farmers must clean the udder and teat prior to milking and change the milk filters (which trap sediments) regularly.

Husbandry and management in maintaining high hygiene standards in milking

- Maintain clean housing and cubicle beds. Applying a small amount of lime on cubicle beds can help to reduce bacterial numbers. The dairy parlour and holding yard must be washed down after use.
- Wash cow's udder and teat prior to milking.
- Use a strip cut to check for signs of mastitis (check for lumps, clots or other abnormalities: these are all signs of mastitis).
- Treat infected cows with antibiotics and use a dry cow treatment when drying off.
- Cull cows that have chronic mastitis.
- Teat dip after milking.
- Have proper fly control (prevent summer mastitis).
- Filter milk.
- Wash the bulk tank and milk lines regularly.
- Ensure proper cooling of milk before it enters the bulk tank.
- Refrigerate milk at < 4°C.

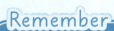
Remember

The experiment to determine the hygiene quality of milk has already been described in Chapter 6.

Mastitis

Mastitis can be divided into three groups: clinical mastitis, sub-clinical mastitis and summer mastitis.

Mastitis in dairy cows

Table 32.3 Mastitis in dairy cows

Disease	Cause	Symptoms	Treatment	Prevention
Clinical mastitis	• Variety of bacteria	• Inflammation of the udder, affecting one or more quarters • Visible changes in milk, clots • Milk may be more watery	• Antibiotics • Milk from the cow is withheld from the bulk tank	• Use a dry cow treatment during drying off • Ensure milking machine works correctly, as faulty machines damage teats • Change milk liners regularly • Use teat disinfectant after milking; dirt on udder or teat increases infection; strip teat regularly to check for mastitis • Ensure clean and dry bedding in winter housing calving shed • Cull chronically infected cows
Sub-clinical mastitis	• Variety of bacteria	• No obvious change in milk, may be some inflammation of the udder • Only clear indication is a high somatic cell count	• Treat cows with sub-clinical mastitis with a long-lasting dry cow treatment that helps to regenerate tissue and prevent new infection • Treatment during drying off ensures no milk loss during the lactation period	• Same as above

Disease	Cause	Symptoms	Treatment	Prevention
Summer mastitis	• Variety of bacteria, spread by flies	• Seen in dry cows and heifers in July to September • Udder swells • Foul-smelling discharge from affected udder • Severely affected cows may abort	• Early detection vital; look for flies constantly around a single teat • Irrigation of infected quarter • Administer antibiotics	• Treat sores and wounds on animal • Control flies with pour-on or spot-on • Use long-lasting dry cow treatment • Apply Stockholm tar as a physical barrier

Calving

Care of calves from birth to weaning

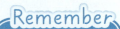

Remember

The care of a newborn animal is dealt with in Chapter 29, pp.219–220.

- On a dairy farm, the calf is removed from the cow and is grouped with other calves of similar age.
- The calves are fed colostrum as long as it is available.
- They are then fed **milk** or **milk replacer** either once or twice a day.
- The calves are given access to **hay** (to develop the rumen) and **concentrates** from the first week of their life.
- Calves should be housed in well-ventilated, draught-free houses. **Poor ventilation can lead to pneumonia in calves**.
- **Good hygiene is essential to prevent scour**. Feeders and troughs should be kept clean.
- Calves are weaned off milk or milk replacer and onto grass and concentrates from six weeks old. Concentrates are fed continuously to calves until they adjust to their new diet of grass.
- Calves are grazed in the **leader-follower system** ahead of older animals. This system of grazing results in a greater live weight gain (LWG) for the calves, and the calves are exposed to fewer parasites (worms and flukes).
- The weanlings are housed for winter at around nine months old.

> **Top Tip!**
>
> Remember that the typical diet of a dairy calf from birth to housing would include colostrum, milk/milk replacer, hay (to develop the rumen), concentrates, grass and silage (when housed for winter).

Management of cows during lactation

Management of cows in early lactation

- A cow loses weight after giving birth, as her feed intake does not meet her energy output. The cow uses her own energy reserves to make up for this deficit. The phrase 'milking off her back' refers to this process.

- The dairy cow should be on a high plane of nutrition in early lactation. Her diet should include good-quality silage (if not out on grass) and concentrates. This ensures she reaches her lactation peak.
- The cow's diet should also include a mineral lick or Cal-Mag (dusted onto the silage) to prevent milk fever and grass tetany.
- Out on grass, the dairy cow should be rotationally grazed on good-quality pasture.

Management of cows in mid- and late lactation

- The diet of the dairy cow does not change significantly in mid-lactation. The dairy cow is rotationally grazed on good-quality pasture.
- When the dairy cow is dried off (60 days before she is due to calve again), she should be placed on a high plane of nutrition so that she can regain a BCS of 3.25 before she calves. The diet should include good-quality silage (DMD 75%) and concentrates.

Heat detection

During mid-lactation, the dairy cow should come back into her oestrus cycle. When a cow is in standing heat (oestrus), she will stand and allow other cows to mount her. Heat detection aids are vital in identifying cows in standing heat.

- **Tail painting:** The top of the cow's tail is painted with a bright colour. If a cow is in heat, other cows will mount her and rub the paint off.
- **Kamar device:** This is a pressure-sensitive chamber containing a dye that is attached to the top of the tail. When a cow is mounted, the chamber bursts and the dye changes colour.
- **Activity meter:** Activity meters measure the activity of a cow and compare it to her activity over the previous few days. The activity meter identifies cows with increased activity as being in heat.
- **Vasectomised bull:** A vasectomised bull cannot inseminate a cow in heat. He is fitted with a chin ball that contains a dye and he will mount and mark any cow in heat. Vasectomised bulls are often used to identify heifers in heat.

Replacement heifers

- The optimum replacement rate for a dairy herd is 17%. If a higher replacement rate is used, milk production will drop significantly.
- Farmers are encouraged to raise their own replacement heifers, as this maintains a closed herd and prevents the entrance of disease into a herd.

- Rearing replacement heifers requires good management, with the aim of breeding the replacement heifer at 15 months so that she can calve down for the first time at two years old.

Target weights for replacement heifers

Target weights vary greatly depending on the breed of dairy cow.

There is a number of **key target weights** that must be reached if a replacement heifer is going to calve at two years old.

- A replacement heifer must be at least **200 kg** at winter housing in her first year (nine months old).
- The bulling target (target weight at mating) must be at least **300 kg** at 15 months old. The BCS of a first-time heifer must be 3.25 to ensure that the heifer is cycling (coming into oestrus).
- At winter housing in her second year, she should be **450 kg**.
- Prior to calving she should be between **525 kg** and **550 kg**.
- In order to reach these target weights, the replacement heifers must be kept on a high plane of nutrition, which should include good-quality pasture during the summer months and high-quality silage (DMD 75%) while in winter housing.

Point to note

An easy calving bull (such as an Aberdeen Angus) should be used on a first-time heifer to produce a small calf and reduce calving difficulties.

Diseases of dairy cows and calves

Table 32.4 Diseases of calves

Disease	Cause	Symptoms	Treatment	Prevention
Nutritional scour	• Fed too much milk • Irregular feeding times • Milk ball develops in calf's stomach, can develop into infectious scour	• Diarrhoea • Dehydration, weak • Not life-threatening unless it develops into infectious scour	• Take off milk immediately • Feed calf water with glucose and electrolytes • Feed weak calves with a stomach tube • Feed fluid for 3–5 days and gradually put calf back on milk or milk replacer	• Good feeding routine • Make gradual changes to the calf's diet
Infectious scour	• Bacteria • Viruses • Protozoa	• High temperature • Foul-smelling diarrhoea • Dehydration • Listlessness • Hypothermia • Shock followed by death	• Take off milk, feed fluid replacement • Identify causative agent, treat with antibiotics if bacterial • Consult vet • If calf's temperature drops below 37°C place it under infrared lamp • Isolate infected animal	• Calf houses, buckets and bedding must be clean and disinfected • Maintain good hygiene • Ensure calf gets adequate colostrum at birth

Disease	Cause	Symptoms	Treatment	Prevention
Navel/ joint ill	• Bacteria; initial infection starts in the navel and then spreads to the joints • Usually affects calves less than one week old	• Navel ill: Navel is swollen and painful; thick pus may ooze • High temperature • Joint ill: Swollen, stiff, painful joints • Death in severe cases	• Treat with antibiotics and painkillers • Vet is required to remove abscesses if they develop	• Dip navel in iodine after birth • Calve in a clean environment • Ensure calf receives adequate intake of colostrum
Viral pneumonia	• Initial infection is by a virus followed by a secondary infection by bacteria due to weakened immune system caused by the first infection	• Rise in temperature • Discharge from the nose and eyes, rapid breathing, coughing • Calf lies down a lot • Weight loss, loss of appetite • Death in severe cases	• Isolate calf • Vet required • Treat bacterial infection with antibiotics	• Well-ventilated, warm, dry and draught-free housing essential • Avoid over-crowding • Ensure calf receives adequate intake of colostrum • Vaccine available
Ringworm	• Fungal infection (zoonose)	• Circular patches of hair loss develop into grey, crusty scabs on the animal's head, neck and flank	• Apply a topical medicine to infected skin • Animals recover in a few weeks	• Clean and disinfect housing, as spores survive on walls of buildings • Vaccine available

Table 32.5 Diseases of cattle

Disease	Cause	Symptoms	Treatment	Prevention
Contagious abortion	• Bacteria: *Brucella abortus* (zoonose) • Notifiable disease; Ireland declared brucellosis-free in July 2009	• Causes abortion or premature calving between the 5th and 8th months of gestation	• Cull infected cow • Foetus and placenta sent to district vet office • Disinfect all areas	• Maintain a closed herd • Rear own replacement heifers • Vaccinate heifers • Purchase cattle from reliable sources • Quarantine all bought-in stock
Lameness	• Numerous causes, including bacterial infection of the hoof, overgrown hoof • Swollen joints	• Cow constantly rests sore leg, limps • Not feeding • Failure to thrive	• Pare the hoof • Treat with antibiotics for bacterial infection • Dip hooves in disinfectant	• Routine hoof care • Maintain good hygiene
Liver fluke	• Flatworm, endoparasite	• Failure to thrive • Reduced milk production in dairy cattle, lower FCR in beef cattle • Diagnosed by faecal examination for fluke eggs	• Dose cattle	• Dose animals regularly • Drain land, fence off wet areas • Keep vulnerable stock like calves away from wet areas • Treat dairy cows when drying off

Disease	Cause	Symptoms	Treatment	Prevention
Hoose	• Nematode *Dictyocaulus*	• Young calves are susceptible to hoose • Causes coughing and failure to thrive in calves	• Dose calves	• Good grassland management • Graze dairy calves in leader-follower system
Stomach worms	• Nematode *Ostertagia* • Cooperia	• Young calves are susceptible to stomach worms • Causes scouring and failure to thrive	• Dose calves	• Good grassland management • Graze dairy calves in the leader-follower system

Top Tip!

Be familiar with causes, symptoms, treatments and prevention for a number of diseases related to calves and cows.

Remember

Grass tetany and milk fever have been dealt with in Chapter 31 in sheep production.

Questions

1. **(a)** Draw a lactation curve for a dairy cow. On the curve, label **(i)** peak yield and **(ii)** persistence.
   (b) How many days after the birth of a calf does a dairy cow produce her peak yield?

2. Discuss **four** factors that affect milk yield.

3. State the target weights that a replacement heifer must reach in order to calf down at two years.

4. Describe a diet suitable for a replacement heifer to reach those target weights.

5. Write a brief note on each of the following heat detection aids:
   (a) Tail painting
   (b) Activity meter
   (c) Vasectomised bull.

6. Outline the benefits of drying off a dairy cow prior to calving.

Exam questions

1. **(a)** Using a table or a pie chart, show the composition of cows' milk.
   (b) **(i)** List **four** factors that can cause changes in milk composition.
      (ii) Fully explain any **two** of the factors referred to above.
   (c) Contamination of milk is a problem in milk processing.
      (i) List **three** contaminants of milk.
      (ii) Describe an experiment to test the hygiene quality of milk.   *(HL 2012)*

2. **(a)** Suggest a suitable mastitis prevention programme in a spring calving dairy herd.
   (b) Outline the role of any one hormone in milk production in a lactating cow.   *(HL 2012)*

3. **(a)** Give the name of **two** breeds of cattle commonly used in **milk** production.
   (b) Read the following paragraph on dairy farming and, in your answer book, fill in the blanks from the list below.
      37 days; 21 days; 60 days; 282 days; 4 days; 305 days.
      Cows are in heat or 'bulling' every _____ days. The cow is pregnant or 'in-calf' for _____ days. After calving the cow produces a special type of milk called colostrum for about _____ days. The cow produces milk for an average of _____ days in the year. The cow reaches her peak milk yield about _____ days after calving. The cow should be 'dried-off' about _____ days before the birth of the next calf.

(c) Calving is a very important event on a dairy farm. List four steps to help ensure successful calf rearing or successful replacement heifer rearing.

(d) Describe any two ways to ensure good hygiene during milking and milk storage. *(OL 2012)*

4 Describe four visible features a dairy farmer would look for when selecting a replacement heifer for a dairy herd. *(HL 2014)*

5 Describe the target weights, nutrition and housing of a replacement heifer in a spring-calving dairy herd at each of the following stages:
(a) Newborn calf stage
(b) Weanling stage
(c) Yearling stage
(d) Mating stage. *(HL 2014)*

Key-points!

- Length of the oestrus cycle: 21 days; duration of oestrus (standing heat): 18 hours; length of gestation: 283 days (roughly 9.5 months); litter size: single, but twins and triplets can occasionally occur; average lactation period (produces milk): 305 days; peak milk yield: roughly 37 days after lactation starts; dried off: 60 days.

- The udder is divided into four independent quarters, each with its own teat. The milk-producing tissue of the udder is called alveolus. Milk produced by this tissue travels down through ducts into the gland cistern. Milk let-down in cows is controlled by the hormone oxytocin. When a calf suckles a cow or when a farmer washes the udder prior to milking, nerve receptors on the surface of the udder send a signal to the brain that triggers the pituitary gland to secrete oxytocin. Oxytocin targets the milk-secreting cells (alveoli) to produce milk.

- The average composition of milk is 87.8% water, 3.5% butterfat, 3.2% protein, 4.7% lactose and 0.8% minerals (calcium, magnesium, etc.). The percentage of lactose, protein and minerals found in milk is commonly referred to as solids non-fat (SNF).

- Milk composition varies depending on a number of factors, including breed, animal feed, stage of lactation, age and disease.

- Mastitis is a bacterial infection of the udder. It is extremely contagious and can be spread during milking through the operator's hands and the milking machine. It is treated with antibiotics. Cows receiving antibiotics for mastitis must have their milk withheld from the bulk tank.

- A lactation curve plots the milk production of a dairy cow over the course of her lactation. Milk production increases from the start until a peak yield is reached (roughly five to six weeks after calving). A high peak yield normally results in a higher total yield. A cow must be on a high plane of nutrition (production diet) in order for her to reach her potential peak yield.

- Benefits of drying off a dairy cow: Allows time for the udder to repair itself. Maximises milk yields in the following lactation. A dry cow treatment can be administered to each teat. Allows the cow to regain body condition. Allows the cow to complete the development of her next calf in her uterus.

- Factors that affect milk yield include breed, age, lactation number, frequency of milking, drying off and body condition score.

- Milk undergoes a number of hygiene tests in the creamery: total bacterial count, somatic cell count, temperature, antibiotic test, thermoduric test and a test for sediments.

- The typical diet for a calf from birth to winter housing in its first year is colostrum, milk or milk replacer, hay, concentrates, grass (rotationally grazed in the leader-follower system) and good-quality silage at housing.

- Calves should be housed in well-ventilated, draught-free houses. Poor ventilation can lead to pneumonia in calves. Good hygiene is essential to prevent scour. Feeders and troughs should be kept clean.

- There are various methods available for heat detection in a dairy herd: tail painting, kamar device, activity meter and a vasectomised bull.

- Target weights for replacement heifers are 200 kg at first winter housing; 300 kg at mating and a BCS of 3.25; 450 kg at second winter housing; and 525–550 kg at calving.

- An easy calving bull (Aberdeen Angus) should be used on a first-time heifer to reduce the chances of calving difficulties.

33 Beef Production and Management

Learning objectives

In this chapter you will learn about:

1 Growth, maturity and slaughter weights of beef animals

2 Beef production systems in Ireland

3 Summer grazing and winter fattening system for finishing beef animals

4 EU Beef Carcase Classification Scheme

5 General husbandry for cattle

> ### Remember
>
> Key points of information, such as length of oestrus, gestation, etc., have already been covered in Chapter 32. Common beef breeds and their characteristics are dealt with in Chapter 34.

Growth, maturity and slaughter weights of beef animals

The minimum time required to get a beef animal from birth to slaughter on a grass-based system in Ireland is two years.

Figure 33.1 shows the deposition of fat and muscle from the birth of an animal until it is four years old.

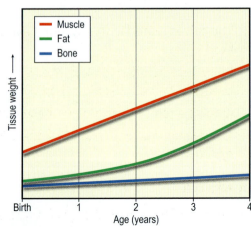

Fig 33.1 *Tissue growth relative to age*

- A young animal puts on fat slowly at the start.
- The rate of muscle deposition decreases as the animal reaches maturity.
- The amount of fat that is deposited increases from the age of two years.
- Fat is trimmed from the animal's carcass when slaughtered.
- The weight at which fat deposition increases depends on the breed of the animal.
- British beef breeds are early-maturing beef breeds and start fat deposition at lower live weights. Continental breeds are later maturing, with high growth rates, and finish at higher live weights before fat deposition occurs.

Table 33.1 Finishing weights of British and Continental beef breeds

Beef breed	Finishing weights for steers
British breeds	
Hereford	530 kg
Aberdeen Angus	500 kg
Continental breeds	
Belgian Blue	700 kg
Charolais	700 kg
Simmental	680 kg
Limousin	650 kg

Beef production systems in Ireland

Calf to beef in two years

- The calves reared in this system have predominantly come from a dairy herd.
- Dairy farmers often use a beef bull on some of their herd to improve the conformation of the calves.
- In this system, calves are purchased every year by beef farmers.
- The disadvantage of this is that there is a risk of buying in disease in this system.

Buying a calf

- Check calf for any discharges from its eyes, mouth and nose. Check for signs of scour and check the animal's navel.

- Calf should be bright, alert and have a shiny coat.
- Breed of calf: Buy a beef-crossed calf rather than a pure dairy calf. (Beef-crossed calves will have better conformation.)
- Sex of the calf: A male calf will have a better growth rate than a female calf.

Target weights for calf to beef production

Table 33.2 shows the recommended target weights that beef farmers should aim to meet in order to finish the calves in two years.

Table 33.2 Production target weights for Friesian and Continental × Friesian				
	Friesian		Charolais × Friesian	Time of year
Slaughter age (months)	24 months		25 months	Year 1
	Kg	ADG*	Kg	ADG	
Born: 0 months	40		50		Feb/March
Turn out to grass: 3 months	100	0.8	100	0.8	April
Winter housing: 9 months	220	0.5	230	0.5	November
					Year 2
Turn out: 13 months	300	0.9	310	1.0	March/April
Housed: 20 months	470	0.86	500	1.0	November
Slaughtered: 24/25 months	600		680		

ADG* = Average daily gain

Note the above target weights apply to Friesian and Friesian-Charolais crosses only; growth rates of other Continental breeds will vary.

Top Tip!

Target weights is a common question on past exam papers. These target weights apply to a Hereford × Friesian calf. The following target weights are slightly less than the Charolais cross because the Hereford is an early maturing British breed.

The target weights in Table 33.3 should be memorised.

Table 33.3 Target weights for a Hereford × Friesian beef animal	
Time	Target weight
Born (February)	40 kg
Out on grass 1st year (April)	90 kg
Winter housing (November)	200 kg
Out on grass 2nd year	280 kg
Winter housing 2nd year	460 kg
Slaughtered	550 kg

Growth curve for calf to beef in two-year production system

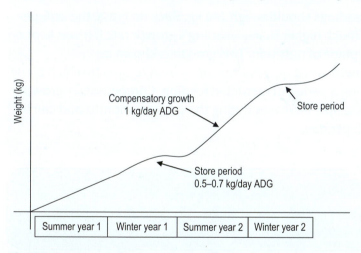

Fig 33.2 *Growth curve for the two-year calf to beef production*

- **Summer year 1:** Calves should be rotationally grazed on good pasture in the leader-follower system. This ensures a good growth rate in calves, as they get the leafy grass and it helps control the number of parasites the calves are exposed to. Calves are dosed for hoose (lungworm) and stomach worms.

Top Tip! Practise drawing and labelling this growth curve. Note: The growth rate of summer year 2 is much greater than in summer year 1 and is represented by a steeper line.

- **Winter housing year 1:** Turned into winter housing on 1 November.
Weanlings should weigh 200 kg. Cattle are housed for the winter to prevent poaching of the land. Winter housing for weanlings should have good

ventilation, adequate lighting, a fresh water source, adequate space (1.4 m^2 of floor space per animal in a slatted house) and space at the feeding trough. Weanlings are dosed for stomach worms and flukes. Weanlings should be fed good-quality silage (DMD 75%). Concentrates should also be fed if silage quality is poor. Weanlings enter a **store period**, as there is a decrease in their live weight gain (LWG) as they move from a high plane of nutrition (grass) to a lower plane of nutrition (silage). At this time, the animal's frame grows but it puts on very little muscle.

> ## Key definition
>
> **Store period:** A period of restricted feeding that occurs during winter housing when there is a change of feed from a high plane of nutrition to a low plane of nutrition. This results in a decrease in the live weight gain (LWG) of the animal.

- **Summer year 2:** Yearlings should weigh 280 kg. Back on grass, the LWG per day of yearlings is much higher than a yearling's growth rate if it was kept on a continuous high plane of nutrition. This growth is known as **compensatory growth** and it occurs when an animal returns to a high plane of nutrition following a period of restricted feeding. Compensatory growth occurs when grass supply increases during the summer months and can be as high as 1 kg ADG per day.

> ## Key definition
>
> **Compensatory growth:** The increase in growth rate that occurs following a period of restricted feed.

- **Winter housing year 2:** The yearlings should weigh 460 kg when turned into winter housing in year 2. Yearlings are dosed for worms and flukes. They should have between 2–2.3 m^2 of space in the slatted house. Yearlings should be fed high-quality silage (DMD 75%) and concentrates to ensure that the beef animals reach their finishing weight of 550 kg and maintain an ADG of 1 kg per day.

Suckler herd

This system relies on the suckler dam (female beef cow) producing and feeding a calf each year. Most suckler herds in Ireland are spring calving, allowing for maximum utilisation of summer grass and reduced feed costs compared to autumn calving suckler herds.

Suckler cow

The suckler cow is usually a cross between a dairy animal and a Continental beef animal, therefore possessing hybrid vigour. This has a number of advantages:

- Higher fertility
- Lower calf mortality
- Longer reproductive life
- Higher milk yields, which give higher growth rates in calves and result in heavier weaned calves
- Shorter calving interval
- Produces a hardier calf.

The use of a purebred dairy cow would be unsuitable for a suckler dam, as a purebred dairy cow would produce too much milk for one calf and this would result in scour in the calf. In addition, a purebred dairy cow has poor conformation and this would result in a poor carcase grade in her progeny.

Target weights for suckler calves

Calves from a suckler herd have higher growth rates than calves from the calf to beef in two years system. This is largely due to the calf's consumption of milk from the suckler dam.

Table 33.4 Growth rate of bull calf from suckler herd compared to calf to beef in two years

System	Birth weight	Weaning weight	ADG from birth to weaning
Suckler herd	45 kg	300 kg	1.2 kg/day
Calf to beef	40 kg	230 kg	0.8 kg/day

Management of suckler herds out on grass

- The suckler herd should graze good-quality pasture rotationally, using either paddock or strip grazing.
- Calves initially will depend on the suckler dam for milk.
- As the calves start to graze grass, they should be allowed to creep graze ahead of the herd.
- Calves should also be given access to concentrates using creep feeders.
- Heat detection aids should be used to identify suckler dams coming back into heat.

Winter housing and suckler herd

- Calves are normally separated from the dams when they go into winter housing.
- The feeding of suckler weanlings is the same as that for weanlings in the calf to beef in two years system.

Reproductive efficiency and calving interval for a suckler herd

Reproductive efficiency aims to produce one calf per cow per year. Having the suckler dam at a body condition score (BCS) of 2.5 at mating and using heat detection to determine when the suckler dam comes back into heat is vital to achieve this.

Key definition

The reproductive efficiency of a suckler herd is the number of calves weaned per 100 cows served.

- The calf's access to the dam is restricted once the calf is 30 days old. This encourages the dam to come back into heat quicker.
- Suckler cows with poor fertility should be culled.
- An Aberdeen Angus bull should be used on maiden heifers to prevent calving difficulty.
- The calving interval in a suckler herd should be kept to 365 to maintain an efficient suckler herd.

Key definition

Calving interval: The time that has elapsed between successive calvings.

Bull beef production

Uncastrated male beef breed animals are used for beef production.

Advantages of bull beef production

- Bulls have a better food conversion ratio (FCR).
- Bulls produce testosterone, which increases their weight gain compared to castrated males (steers).
- Bulls have a greater carcase weight at slaughter.
- Bulls have more lean meat on their carcase than steers and better conformation scores on grading.
- If managed correctly, bulls can be finished and ready for slaughter at 15–16 months old.

Disadvantages of bull beef production

- Bulls must be kept separate from heifers.
- Bulls must be handled with care due to their aggressive nature.
- Stress before slaughter can darken the colour of bull meat, making it difficult to market.

Heifer beef production

- This usually involves rearing beef-crossed heifers from the dairy herd for beef production.
- They are finished in 19–22 months and then slaughtered.
- Heifers have a much lower live weight gain (LWG) than steers or bulls and finish at lower slaughter weights.

Cull cow finishing

- Cows from the dairy herd that are being culled are fed to get them to the correct body condition score (BCS) of 3.5 before slaughter.
- The aim is to maximise the value of the carcase and attain a conformation score of P+ and a fat score of 3L or 4L.

Summer grazing and winter fattening system for finishing beef animals

Summer grazing as a finishing system for beef cattle

- Animals are purchased in spring and are finished on grass during the summer.
- Animals are sent for slaughter as they reach finishing weight (late summer to autumn).
- There is no conservation of grass, since silage or hay is not required; this system does not need winter feed.
- No housing is required, as all animals are sent for slaughter before winter.
- Concentrates are only fed if grass is scarce, so feed costs are low.
- Labour requirements are low.

Winter fattening as a finishing system for beef cattle

- More labour is involved, as grass must be conserved for winter feed (silage and hay).
- Animals are purchased in autumn, kept over winter and sold for slaughter in spring.

- Winter housing is required.
- Concentrates must be fed to ensure animals reach target weights for slaughter.
- Winter finishing of beef animals is more costly, as concentrate feeds must be purchased compared to finishing on grass.

EU Beef Carcase Classification Scheme

The EU classification scheme assesses the slaughtered carcase under the following criteria.

- **Conformation:** The shape and width of the carcase and its muscle development are visually assessed. Conformation is divided into five classes: E, U, R, O and P. The letter **E represents excellent** and **P represents the worst**. A category E animal would be a double-muscled beef animal with excellent carcase quality. A purebred dairy animal (Holstein-Friesian) would have the worst conformation.
- **Fat:** Visual assessment of the degree of fat cover. There are five fat classes, with 1 indicating the least and 5 indicating the most. Consumers demand lean meat, so the ideal fat class at slaughter is 3.
- **Sex:** Carcasses are classified by sex: A (young bull), B (stock bull), C (steer), D (cow) and E (heifer).

Table 33.5 Beef classification grid

Conformation	E	U	R	O	P+	P	P–
Fat score 1		①					
2							
3							
4L			②				
4H							
5							

① Only double-muscled purebred Continental animals are classified in this range.

② Most Irish beef animals score in this range after slaughter.

General husbandry for cattle

- **Castration:** Male animals not intended for breeding are castrated at 12 weeks old. The most popular method of castration is a bloodless castration using a burdizzo. Bull calves are normally castrated because it makes them easier to handle (bulls can be aggressive) and because uncastrated bulls will interfere with the breeding programme of the farmer by serving heifers and cows that are in heat.
- **Dehorning calves:** Dehorning is done to prevent injury to other animals and to anyone handling the calf. Dehorning is done in the first two weeks after the calf is born using a dehorning iron.
- **Tagging a calf:** This is a legal requirement to ensure stock traceability. Calves are usually tagged at birth and details are sent to the Calf Registration Agency.
- **Dosing:** Cattle are routinely dosed for stomach and intestinal worms and for liver fluke. In addition, calves are dosed for hoose (lungworm).
- **TB testing:** TB (bovine tuberculosis) is a notifiable disease and herds are regularly tested for this disease to eradicate it.

Questions

1. Explain each of the following terms in relation to beef production:
   (a) Store period
   (b) Compensatory growth
   (c) Reproductive efficiency
   (d) Calving interval.

2. Explain why the growth rate of a suckler calf is greater than the growth rate of a calf in the calf to beef in two years system.

3. Give reasons why a cow with 50% dairy genes and 50% beef genes makes an ideal suckler dam.

4. Discuss the advantages and disadvantages of producing beef from steers compared to beef production from bulls.

5. The majority of beef animals in the calf to beef in two years system are purebred dairy or dairy beef crosses. As a result, the conformation of these animals tends to be poorer and they tend to be slaughtered at lower live weights compared to beef animals from a suckler herd. Discuss the relevance of this statement.

6. More Irish beef farmers are choosing Continental beef animals over British beef breeds in their beef herds. Give reasons for this.

1 (a) Construct the typical growth curve graph for the two-year calf to beef
       production system.
   (b) On your graph, show clearly:
       (i) Target weights at first winter housing **and** second winter housing
       (ii) Where compensatory growth begins.
   (c) Suggest a suitable diet for beef cattle in the first **and** second winter.
                                                                              (HL 2012)

2 Identify **two** reasons why male animals are castrated on farms.   *(HL 2012)*

3 (a) Describe **three** features of good winter housing for weanlings.
   (b) Give the approximate live weight for cattle at the following stages of the
       two-year calf to beef system: **(i)** first winter housing and **(ii)** slaughter.
   (c) At slaughter, the beef carcass is graded for **conformation** and **fatness**.
       Explain **each** term.   *(OL 2012)*

Key-points!

- The minimum time required to get a beef animal from birth to slaughter on a
  grass-based system in Ireland is two years.

- As an animal grows, it puts on fat slowly at the start. The rate of muscle
  deposition decreases as the animal reaches maturity. The amount of fat that is
  deposited increases from the age of two years. Fat is trimmed from the animal's
  carcass when slaughtered. The weight at which fat deposition increases
  depends on the breed of the animal. British beef breeds are early maturing beef
  breeds and start fat deposition at lower live weights. Continental breeds are
  later maturing, with high growth rates, and finish at higher live weights before
  fat deposition occurs.

- Store period is a period of restricted feeding that occurs during winter housing
  when there is a change of feed from a high plane of nutrition to a low plane of
  nutrition. This results in a decrease in the live weight gain (LWG) of the animal.

- Compensatory growth: The increase in growth rate that occurs following a
  period of restricted feed.

- The suckler cow is usually a cross between a dairy animal and a Continental
  beef animal, therefore possessing hybrid vigour. Crossbred dams have a longer
  reproductive life, higher fertility, higher milk yield and produce a hardier calf.

- Calves from a suckler herd have higher growth rates than calves from the calf
  to beef in two years system. This is largely due to the calfs consumption of
  milk from the suckler dam.

- A suckler herd should graze good-quality pasture rotationally, using either paddock or strip grazing. As the calves start to graze grass, they should be allowed to creep graze ahead of the herd. Calves should also be given access to concentrates using creep feeders.

- The reproductive efficiency of a suckler herd is the number of calves weaned per 100 cows served.

- Calving interval: The time that has elapsed between successive calvings.

- Bull beef production: Bulls have a better food conversion ratio (FCR) and have a greater weight gain compared to castrated males (steers). Bulls have a greater carcase weight at slaughter. However, bulls are aggressive and difficult to handle.

- Heifer beef production: Heifers have a much lower LWG than steers or bulls and finish at lower slaughter weights.

- Cull cow finish: Cows from the dairy herd that are being culled are fed to get them to the correct body condition score (BCS) of 3.5 before slaughter.

- Summer finishing in beef production: Cattle are bought in spring and brought to slaughter weight on grass. Lower feed costs than winter fattening. Less labour, as no winter feed or housing are involved.

- Winter fattening: More costly system, as concentrates must be fed to animals. Housing and conservation of grass as hay or silage are also required. Animals are bought in the autumn under this system and finished during the winter months.

- EU Beef Carcase Classification Scheme: Grades slaughtered animals on conformation, fat and sex. Conformation is graded as EUROP. E represents excellent and P represents the worst. The fat cover is graded as 1 to 5, 1 being very lean and 5 having a lot of fat cover.

34 Plant and Animal Identification

Learning objectives

In this chapter you will learn about:

1 Plant identification

2 Food-producing animals: Breeds of cattle (dairy and beef), sheep and pigs

3 Animals related to agricultural science: Non-food-producing animals

4 Animal identification

5 Life cycles of non-food-producing animals

Plant identification

Top Tip!

In the practical exam for Agricultural Science, students are expected to **identify five plants** related to agriculture and **their plant family**. The plants used for exam purposes can be a mixture of agriculturally important plants (grasses, cereals and clovers) and weeds. Plants are often live examples and not pictures, so it is vital that you are able to identify these plants from their leaves and their flowers.

Family Gramineae

This family contains productive perennial ryegrasses and cereal crops (maize, wheat, barley and oats). All members of this family are monocots. The grass flower is composed of many florets (small flowers) contained on a structure called the spikelet. Many important agricultural species belong to this group, including perennial ryegrass, barley, wheat, maize and oats.

Fig 34.1 *Perennial ryegrass*

Fig 34.2 *Cocksfoot*

Fig 34.3 *Wild oats*

Fig 34.4 *Barley*

Family Compositae

The flower heads of these plants are composed of many individual flowers that all share the same receptacle. The individual flowers are so densely arranged that they resemble a single flower. Members of the Compositae family use wind to disperse their seeds. Plants in the Compositae family include ragwort, dandelion and daisy.

Fig 34.5 *Ragwort flowers*

Family Cruciferae

Members of this family produce a flower with four petals in the shape of a cross. This family includes a number of important agricultural crops, such as turnips, oilseed rape, kale and cabbage. Common weeds in this group include charlock (wild turnip), shepherd's purse and lady's smock.

Fig 34.6 *Charlock (wild turnip)*

Fig 34.7 *Kale variety Maris Kestral*

Family Leguminosae

Red clover and white clover are two agriculturally important plants. They have a symbiotic relationship with the bacteria *Rhizobium*, which lives in the root nodules of these plants. *Rhizobium* has the ability to fix nitrogen into nitrates for plant use.

Fig 34.8 *Red clover*

Fig 34.9 *White clover*

Family Polygonaceae

There are two main species of docks: the curled dock and the broadleaf dock.

Fig 34.10 *Broadleaf dock*

Family Ranunculaceae

Creeping buttercup, meadow buttercup and lesser celandine are all members of this family. They can be identified by their big yellow flowers and the different shapes of their leaves.

Fig 34.11 *Creeping buttercup*

Family Umbelliferae

The inflorescence of the members of this family consists of a number of short stalks with small white flowers that originate from the same point. Members of the Umbelliferae family include cow parsley, commonly found in hedgerows, and crops such as carrots, parsnips and parsley.

Fig 34.12 *Cow parsley*

Family Urticaceae

The common nettle is a member of this family. Male and female flowers are on separate plants.

Fig 34.13 *Common nettle*

Family Rosaceae

This family produces large flowers with five petals and sepals. Hawthorn, blackthorn and silver weed are all members of this family.

Fig 34.14 *Silver weed*

Family Plantaginaceae

Members of this family have leaves with parallel veins and produce small flowers on spikes. Plantain is a member of this family.

Top Tip!

Although the majority of plant and animal identification occurs in the practical exam, this section should not be ignored for the written exam, as questions relating to plant families and animal identification have occurred on past exam papers.

Fig 34.15 Plantain

Fig 34.16 Potato plant with flowers

Family Solanaceae

Members of this family include potatoes and tomatoes. The potato itself is a modified stem called a tuber.

Family Chenopodiaceae

Sugar beet, fodder beet and beetroot are all members of this family. These are biennial plants, storing food in a modified taproot in year 1 and producing flowers and seeds in year 2. Sugar beet is used to make sugar and a number of by-products, including molasses (used in silage making), beet tops (can be used as feed for sheep and cattle) and beet pulp (used in the production of livestock feed).

Fig 34.17 Sugar beet plant

Food-producing animals

Top Tip!

For the practical exam, students are expected to identify food-producing animals (for example, breeds of cattle, sheep and pigs) and describe some of the characteristics of those animals.

Breeds of cattle

Dairy breeds

Holstein-Friesian

Dairy breed, wedge-shaped and have black and white markings. Holstein-Friesians are the highest milk-producing breed, producing large milk yields but with a low milk solids content.

Fig 34.18 Holstein-Friesian

Ayrshire

A dairy breed that originates from Scotland with red and white markings. It is known for easy calving. It produces milk that has a moderate butterfat content and is high in protein.

Fig 34.19 Ayrshire

Jersey

This breed originates from the Channel Islands. It produces milk with a high butterfat and protein content, but a much lower milk yield compared to a Holstein-Friesian. The Jersey is a smaller breed of dairy cow and is known to be easy calving, has high fertility and is less prone to lameness compared to other dairy breeds.

Fig 34.20 Jersey cow

British beef breeds

Aberdeen Angus

This breed originates from Scotland. It has a black coat and is naturally polled (hornless). It is renowned for its easy calving and is often used as a sire on maiden heifers in both dairy and beef herds. It is an early maturing breed and finishes at a lower slaughter weight compared to Continental breeds.

Fig 34.21 Aberdeen Angus bull

Hereford

This breed originates from Herefordshire in England. It has a deep red coat, white face and underside, giving it the name 'whiteheads'. This breed has good conformation, is well muscled and has strong legs and feet. It is an early maturing breed and finishes at a lower slaughter weight compared to Continental breeds.

Fig 34.22 Hereford cows

Continental beef breeds

Belgian Blue

This breed usually has a whitish-blue coat but can sometimes have a black and white coat. It is a double-muscled breed with a high growth rate. Belgian Blues have a high kill out percentage and produce a high percentage of lean meat on the carcass. It is a late maturing breed and reaches a higher slaughter

Fig 34.23 *Belgian Blue bull*

weight than the British beef breeds. The major disadvantage of this breed is that the double muscle causes calving difficulties.

Charolais

The most popular beef breed in Ireland. It has a white or cream coat and is renowned for its fast growth rate, good conformation and lean carcass. There is a risk of calving difficulties with this breed due to the blocky conformation and high birth weight of the calf. It is a late maturing breed and finishes at a higher slaughter weight compared to the British beef breeds.

Fig 34.24 *Charolais suckler cow*

Limousin

A popular beef breed in Ireland. It is easily recognised by its reddish-brown coat and its long, slender body. It has a high muscle to bone ratio, good conformation, high fertility and easy calving. It has a lower growth rate compared to the Charolais.

Fig 34.25 *Limousin beef bull*

Simmental

This breed originates from the Simmen Valley in Switzerland. It has a red and white spotted coat, usually with a white face. There are two types of Simmental: a beef breed for beef production and a dual-purpose breed for milk and beef production. The dual-purpose breed is popular for suckler herds because of their beef and milk traits.

Breeds of sheep

Mountain and hill breeds

Blackface Mountain

The Blackface Mountain is also known as the Scottish Blackface. This is a small, extremely hardy breed with long wool, a black face and horns. Blackface Mountain ewes are known for their good mothering ability and good milk production. It is a popular mountain breed along the west coast of Ireland.

Fig 34.26 *Blackface Mountain sheep*

Wicklow Cheviot

This breed originates from Scotland. It is a hardy mountain breed with a white face and of medium size. The ewes are known for their good mothering ability.

Fig 34.27 *Wicklow Cheviot sheep*

Lowland sheep breeds: Prolific breeds

Border Leicester

This is a large breed, with long white wool, hornless (polled) and large, upright ears. This breed is known for its prolificacy (increasing litter size) and is used as a maternal sire when breeding crossbred ewes for replacements. When a Border Leicester ram is crossed with a Blackface Mountain sheep, the offspring ewes are known as Greyface.

Fig 34.28 Border Leicester sheep

Bluefaced Leicester

This is a popular prolific breed in Ireland and is commonly used as a maternal sire. When a Bluefaced Leicester ram is crossed with a Blackface Mountain sheep, the offspring ewes are known as Mules. The Bluefaced Leicester is a large breed, with a white head and a slight roman nose. It acquired the name Bluefaced because its skin appears dark blue through its white hair.

Fig 34.29 Bluefaced Leicester sheep

Lowland sheep breeds: Terminal sire breeds

The Suffolk

The Suffolk has a black head with long ears and black legs. It is a short and solid breed with excellent conformation and good carcase quality. It has a fast growth rate and is used as a terminal sire in the production of lambs for the Easter market. Suffolk crossed lambs are early maturing and reach slaughter weight in less than 14 weeks.

Fig 34.30 Suffolk sheep

Texel

This breed has a white wide face and short ears and it lacks wool on its head and legs. The breed has good conformation and carcase quality. It produces very lean muscle. The Texel has a slower growth rate than the Suffolk and is normally used as a terminal sire for mid-season lamb.

Fig 34.31 Texel sheep

Charollais

The Charollais is a French breed and is a medium-sized, heavy sheep with a long loin and muscular hindquarters. It is a popular terminal sire as it decreases lambing difficulties (produces small lambs), especially if ewe lambs are being bred. This breed produces lean and fast-growing lambs.

Irish sheep breeds

Galway

This is the only native Irish breed. It is a large, white, polled lowland breed with long wool. It has a good growth rate but prolificacy is poor (normally only producing a single lamb).

Fig 34.32 Galway sheep

Belclare Improver

Teagasc undertook research to improve the Galway breed by crossing Galway ewes with the Finnish Landrace (to improve prolificacy) and then crossing the offspring ewes with a Lleyn ram (to improve prolificacy and conformation). The resulting offspring were known as the Belclare Improver. The Belclare have high prolificacy (normally giving a litter of two lambs), little lambing difficulty and good mothering ability.

Fig 34.33 Belclare Improver sheep

Pig breeds

Landrace

The Landrace is a Danish breed identifiable by its long body and ears that point forward. It has good conformation, with small shoulders and large hams.

Fig 34.34 Landrace pig

Large White

This is a British breed. It has high prolificacy (large litter size), fast growth rate, good meat quality and good food conversion ratio.

Fig 34.35 Large White pig

Duroc

The Duroc is easily identified by its distinctive red coat. It is large in size and is often used as a terminal sire in pig production, as it is known for its fast growth rate.

Fig 34.36 Duroc pig

Pietrain

A medium-sized white pig with black spots. It produces large hams with a good ratio of lean meat to fat.

Fig 34.37 Pietrain pig

Animals related to agricultural science: non-food-producing animals

Students must be able to identify non-food-producing animals and explain the importance and relevance of the study of the organism in relation to agriculture. Some animals may be of benefit to agriculture and some may be considered pests.

> **Top Tip!**
>
> Students are often asked to name an animal, its defining characteristics or its phyla in the Higher Level paper. Ordinary Level candidates are often asked to identify pictures of animals and state their characteristics or importance.

Table 34.1 Animal phyla

Phylum name	Characteristics	Example and importance
Protozoa	• Unicellular • Classified by locomotion	• Babesia: Causes redwater disease in cattle
Platyhelminthes	• Bilaterally symmetrical, possessing a distinct front and rear end • Do not possess an internal body cavity (aceolomate structure) • Triploblastic – they possess three cell layers • Flattened dorsoventrally • Hermaphrodite	• Tapeworm: An endoparasite that lives in the intestine of the infected animal and absorbs nutrients from the animal • Liver fluke: Found in the liver and bile ducts of cattle, sheep, pigs and goats, causing liver damage
Nematoda	• Rounded in cross-section • Separate sexes – the male is usually smaller than the female and has a coiled tail with a spicule to attach himself to the female during copulation • A body cavity known as a pseudocoelome • Body covered in a cuticle	• Eelworms: Attack the stems and roots of crops such as potatoes, causing stunted growth and small tubers • Lungworm (hoose): Found in bronchial tubes in lungs, causing husky cough and breathing difficulties • Cooperia (roundworm): Found in the intestines of cattle, causing diarrhoea and poor weight gain

Phylum name	Characteristics	Example and importance
Annelida	• Segmented body • Rounded in cross-section • Has a *clitellum* (saddle) • Body cavity known as a coelome • Bristles known as setae or chaetae (characteristics of earthworm)	• Earthworm: Aerates soil, improves drainage, mixes soil layers, breaks down organic matter into humus and brings it down to deeper layers
Mollusca	• A muscular foot that secretes mucus to aid movement • A rasping tongue known as a radula • Dorsal concentration of internal organs	• Slugs: Eat foliage of crops • Snails: Eat and damage crop foliage • Mud snail (*Lymnaea*): Is a secondary host in the life cycle of the liver fluke
Arthropoda: Class Insecta	• Segmented bodies. 3 main segments: head, thorax and abdomen • Jointed limbs: 6 legs in 3 pairs • Exoskeleton • Adults normally have 2 pairs of wings	• Aphids (greenfly): Suck sap from plants and crops. Also transmit viruses to crops, e.g. leaf roll in potatoes • Leatherjacket: Larva of cranefly eats roots of grasses, cereals and vegetables • Wireworm: Larva of click beetle eats roots of grass and damages potato tubers sown after grass • Ladybird: Natural predator of aphids • Caterpillar: Larva of butterfly, eats leaves of plants, causing damage

Phylum name	Characteristics	Example and importance
Arthropoda: Class Arachnida	• Segmented bodies. 2 main body segments: a cephalothorax and abdomen • Jointed limbs: 8 legs in 4 pairs • Exoskeleton	• Red spider mite: A plant parasite that sucks the sap of many fruit and vegetable plants, e.g. strawberries • Tick: Sheep ticks are ectoparasites that transmit Babesia, which causes redwater disease • Mites: Mange is caused by the mange mite, which lives on the skin. The burrowing action of the mites causes itching in the animal
Chordata: Class Aves	• Wings • Have feathers • Have a beak with no teeth	• Chickens, ducks, turkeys: Produce meat and eggs for human consumption • Crows: Pests that attack crops
Chordata: Class Mammalia	• Produce milk in mammary glands to feed young • Have hair on their bodies • Have sweat glands	• Cattle, pigs, sheep: Food-producing animals that are used for breeding stock and producing meat and/or milk for human consumption

Animal identification

Table 34.2 Animals related to agriculture

Aphid (green fly)	Wireworm	Liver fluke
Sheep tick	Garden snail	Tapeworm

Life cycles of non-food-producing animals

The life cycle of Babesia

1 A tick sucks blood from an infected cow. The blood contains Babesia sporozoites.

2 They form gametes, which form a zygote (sexual reproduction).

3 Many spores are then formed in the tick by asexual reproduction.

4 When the tick next bites the cow to suck blood, it transmits the spores into the cow's bloodstream.

5 The spores form sporozoites, enter the cow's red blood cells and break them down. The haemoglobin that is released from the red blood cells is passed in the urine of the cow; hence the name redwater disease.

Symptoms of Babesiosis (redwater disease)

- Red urine due to the presence of haemoglobin produced by the rupture of the red blood cells
- Increased pulse rate
- Diarrhoea followed by constipation.

The life cycle of liver fluke

1 The adult fluke lays its eggs in the bile duct of the primary host (cow, sheep) and they make their way to the intestines, where they are excreted.

2 In temperatures greater than 10°C, the eggs hatch a larvae known as a miracidium. The miracidium must then find a mud snail within 24 hours to act as a host.

3 The miracidium burrows into the mud snail and undergoes a number of larval stages.

4 The miracidia produce a larval stage called a redia, which can produce even more rediae asexually.

5 The rediae develop into cercaria, which are tadpole-like in their physical structure.

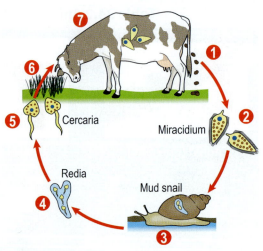

Fig 34.38 *The life cycle of the liver fluke*

6   At this point the cercaria leave the mud snail and form cysts on vegetation.

7   If the cyst is eaten by an animal, it releases the young fluke, which burrows its way to the bile ducts and matures.

Symptoms of liver fluke in animals

- Weight loss
- Reduced milk yields in dairy cattle
- Lowered weight gains
- Loss of condition.

Life cycles of insects

Incomplete metamorphosis

In this process of development, the immature insect undergoes a series of moults, shedding its exoskeleton at each stage to allow for growth and development. Immature insects undergoing incomplete metamorphosis are known as nymphs. They are similar in appearance to their adult counterparts, only smaller. Wings do not appear in these insects until they reach adulthood. Aphids, dragonflies and damselflies are examples of insects that undergo incomplete metamorphosis.

Life cycle of an insect that undergoes incomplete metamorphosis:

> Egg – Nymph – Adult

Complete metamorphosis

In this process of development, each stage of the life cycle is physically different from the previous stage.

Life cycle of an insect that undergoes complete metamorphosis:

> Egg – Larva – Pupa – Adult

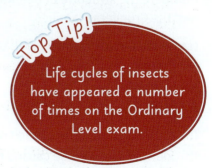

Top Tip!

Life cycles of insects have appeared a number of times on the Ordinary Level exam.

Questions

1. (a) Name the family oats belong to.
   (b) Which of the following plants is considered to be a weed: clover, thistle or sugar beet?
   (c) Name a by-product of the processing of sugar beet.

2. Identify **each** of the following food-producing animals and give a characteristic of each.

(a)  (b)  (c)

(d)  (e)  (f)

3. Complete the table below in relation to the leatherjacket and the earthworm.

	Leatherjacket	Earthworm
(a) Phylum to which animal belongs		
(b) One characteristic of a member of the phylum		
(c) Importance in agriculture		

Exam questions

1. Compare the structure of the flowers on **named** examples from the Rosaceae and the Cruciferae families. *(HL 2011)*

2. Name the family to which **each** of the following plants belong:
   (a) Clover
   (b) Ragwort
   (c) Kale. *(HL 2010)*

3. (a) Name **one** member of each of the phyla Platyhelminthes and Arthropoda.
   (b) Identify **one** disease caused by **each** member of the phyla you have mentioned. *(HL 2011)*

4 Highlight the main differences between the members of any **three** of the following pairs:
   (a) Lungworm and ringworm
   (b) Eelworm and wireworm
   (c) Flatworm and earthworm
   (d) Complete and incomplete metamorphosis.
      (Parts (a) and (b) are *HL 2010* and *2011*)

5 Choose **two** dairy breeds from the list of cattle breeds:
   Charolais   Friesian   Simmental   Jersey   Hereford   *(OL 2010)*

6 Liver fluke (Fasciola hepatica) is an endoparasite that occurs in the liver of some farm animals.
   (a) To what phylum does F. hepatica belong?
   (b) Give two characteristics of members of this phylum.
   (c) Draw a diagram of an adult fluke, labelling any three structures.
   (d) Describe in detail, with the aid of a labelled diagram, the life cycle of the liver fluke.   *(HL 2014)*

Key-points!

- In the practical exam, be able to identify the plants based on their leaves and flowers and identify the family the plant belongs to. You will be expected to identify five plants and their plant family in the examination.

- For the written exam, plant identification and family may be asked again. Know some of the characteristics of the major plant families.

- In the practical exam you will be asked to identify food-producing animals (for example, various breeds of cattle, sheep and pigs). You will be expected to describe some of the characteristics of the breed you have identified. For example: A Jersey is a dairy breed. It is wedge shaped and produces a small yield of milk compared to other dairy breeds, but its milk is high in butterfat and protein.

- In the written exam you may be asked again about characteristics of particular breeds of food-producing animals.

- For the practical exam you will be expected to identify other animals related to agriculture. These animals can be preserved specimens or pictures/photos. You will be expected to explain how these animals are related to agriculture.

Example 1: The picture below is of a liver fluke. It is an endoparasite that lives in the ducts of the liver of cattle and sheep, causing liver damage. Dosing is commonly carried out on farms to eliminate this parasite.

Example 2: The picture below is of an earthworm. It is a segmented worm that burrows through the soil, mixing the soil layers and improving aeration and drainage. It is often referred to as the 'farmer's friend' due to its beneficial activities.

- In the written exam you may be asked again to give examples or characteristics of animals related to agriculture. The question may be presented in a number of forms, such as identifying a picture and naming the phylum it belongs to, giving characteristics of a phylum and/or distinguishing between animals from different phyla.

Example: Distinguish between a flatworm and a roundworm. Answer: Flatworms are from the phylum platyhelminthes. They are dorsoventrally flattened (flat from head to toe) and are hermaphrodites. Examples from this phylum include liver fluke and tapeworms. Roundworms are from the phylum nematode. They are round in cross-section and the sexes are separate. Examples of roundworms include cooperia and nematodirus.

Scientific Explanations 35

Scientific explanations appear as a question (Q9) on the Higher Level paper every year. They also appear frequently on the Ordinary Level paper and can be in Section A or Section B of this paper.

A scientific explanation requires students to apply scientific principles to the statements provided to them in the question. It does not require students to give definitions of terms in the statement, a mistake that is commonly made. In the Higher Level paper, there are five statements provided. Students must give correct explanations for four of the statements to attain full marks in the question. Typically, a student must provide three or four correct pieces of information to attain full marks for each part. A student should aim to provide more if possible.

A number of scientific explanations from past papers along with their solutions have been provided below. Each one contains at least four points. At the end of the section there are a number of scientific explanations available for practice.

Scientific explanations

Give a scientific explanation for:

1   **Progeny testing of AI bulls**   *(HL 2011)*

  — Progeny testing involves testing the calves of the bull.
  — The calves' growth rates and food conversion ratios (FCR) are compared with progeny from other bulls kept under the same conditions.
  — Records of progeny testing are kept.
  — Progeny testing is more reliable than performance testing.

2   **The addition of soya bean meal to cereals in pig rations**   *(HL 2010)*

  — Soya bean meal is rich in protein, while cereals are low in protein.
  — High-protein feeds increase muscle growth in pigs.
  — Soya bean meal is high in lysine, an essential amino acid required by pigs and one that they themselves cannot manufacture in their bodies.

3 **Feeding bought-in calves only water and glucose for the first 24 hours on arrival on a farm** *(HL 2007)*

   − The stomachs of young calves are extremely sensitive and do not take well to stress or sudden changes in diet, especially after transport.

   − Water provides rehydration after transport.

   − Glucose provides energy for the young calf.

   − Feeding water and glucose after transportation helps to prevent scour.

   − Water and glucose allows the calf a gradual transition so it can be weaned onto milk replacer and concentrates.

4 **The practice of housing a boar near sows and the double serving of sows in a pig breeding enterprise** *(HL 2007)*

   − The sight and smell of a boar in a dry sow house brings on oestrus in sows, as boars produce pheromones.

   − Boars can be used to identify when a sow is in heat.

   − Double serving increases the conception rates.

   − Double serving increases the litter sizes.

5 **The feeding of colostrum to a calf in the hours immediately after birth** *(OL 2011)*

   − Colostrum is high in antibodies.

   − Antibodies give the calf resistance to disease.

   − Colostrum is high in digestible nutrients (high in protein, fat and minerals).

   − Colostrum has a laxative effect, which helps to clean out the calf's digestive system.

   − Colostrum warms up the calf.

6 **The benefits arising from shelter belts on exposed farms** *(HL 2012)*

   − The shelter belt provides protection for animals.

   − The shelter belt provides protection for crops.

   − Shelter belts increase soil and air temperatures.

   − Shelter belts reduce wind damage.

   − They are a habitat for wildlife and have an aesthetic purpose.

7 **Trace element deficiencies in crop production** *(HL 2011)*

   − Deficiencies are caused by the wrong soil type.

- There may be a deficiency in the soil or parent rock material, or leaching may have occurred.
- The pH may be too high or too low.
- Overcultivation and overliming may lead to deficiencies.
- An incorrect rotation may have been used or a farmer may be practising monoculture.

8 The increase in the number of fish kills in lakes and rivers in summer *(HL 2010)*

- Oxygen is more soluble in cold water.
- Water is warm in May, which leads to less oxygen.
- Water levels are lower in summer.
- Silage operations begin in summer. Silage effluent has a high BOD.
- Eutrophication may occur, leading to algal bloom, and oxygen may be used up by bacteria.

9 The use of plastic in maize cultivation *(HL 2009)*

- The plastic raises temperatures.
- Maize needs high temperatures to germinate (17°C).
- The plastic gives maize a longer growing season.
- Biodegradable plastic breaks down in sunlight.
- It does not have to be collected afterwards.
- Plastic conserves moisture and serves as a form of weed control.

10 The formation of an iron pan in a soil profile *(HL 2009)*

- There is higher rainfall.
- Acidic conditions lead to leaching.
- Iron is washed out of the A horizon.
- It accumulates in the B horizon.
- The iron solidifies as a thin layer.

Exam questions

Give a scientific explanation for:

1 The treatment of cereal seeds with fungicide before sowing. *(OL)*

2 The control of the mud snail (*Lymnaea truncatula*) on wet land. *(OL)*

3 The spread of vegetatively propagated weeds as a result of cultural operations. *(OL and HL)*

4 Root pressure in plants. *(OL)*

5 A change in the colour of blue litmus on being poured into the dissected stomach of an animal. *(OL)*

6 The abnormal extension of the stem in cereal plants growing adjacent to the hedgerow. *(HL)*

7 The application of a solution of proprionic acid to undried grain immediately after harvesting. *(HL)*

8 Failure of plants to produce starch in a nitrogen-filled atmosphere. *(HL)*

9 The practice of culling sows at 4–5 years old. *(HL)*

10 The failure of crop plants to respond normally to the application of a nitrogenous fertiliser during the winter months. *(HL)*

STUDY GUIDE

Date:				
Time:				
Section to be revised:				
Date:				
Time:				
Section to be revised:				
Date:				
Time:				
Section to be revised:				
Date:				
Time:				
Section to be revised:				
Date:				
Time:				
Section to be revised:				
Date:				
Time:				
Section to be revised:				

Night before exam:

Sections to be revised: